MANAGEMENT OF
POST-MORTEM PREGNANCY

In memory of my beloved Grandmother, Gizela Smilovici

Management of Post-Mortem Pregnancy

Legal and Philosophical Aspects

DANIEL SPERLING

Routledge
Taylor & Francis Group

LONDON AND NEW YORK

First published 2006 by Ashgate Publishing

Reissued 2018 by Routledge
2 Park Square, Milton Park, Abingdon, Oxon, OX14 4RN
711 Third Avenue, New York, NY 10017, USA

Routledge is an imprint of the Taylor & Francis Group, an informa business

Typeset by Saxon Graphics Ltd, Derby

ISBN 13: 978-0-815-39039-8 (hbk)
ISBN 13: 978-1-351-15336-2 (ebk)

2017 002 788

MIX
Paper from
responsible sources
FSC
www.fsc.org   FSC® C013985

Printed in the United Kingdom
by Henry Ling Limited

Contents

Preface

A pregnancy is generally understood to last 40 weeks. The further the fetus is *in uterus* in terms of gestational age the greater its chances of survival if the fetus is to be delivered before full term. When a pregnant woman is struck by brain-death, that is 'the irreversible loss of capacity for consciousness combined with the irreversible loss of all brainstem functions including the capacity to breathe' (Beaulieu *et al.*, 1999; Wijdicks, 2002),[1] the chances of fetal survival are seriously and immediately threatened. Until recently there were two choices in such a situation: letting the mother (and the fetus) naturally die without further medical intervention, or delivering the fetus through a cesarean section when the death of the fetus was a tragic but an expected result.

However, recent advances in medical technology have provided physicians with the control over the time, and manner of, death in ways that were never previously considered by their patients. A new option has thus become available: maintaining the brain-dead pregnant woman on 'life-support' by the successful delivery of the fetus. Despite this novelty, the length of the time a mother can be maintained, once brain-death occurs, for a successful delivery is a matter of some medical uncertainty. Reports in the literature show that medical experts have been capable of 'maintaining' a fetus alive inside a brain-dead woman for periods as long as 63 (Field *et al.*, 1988), 70 (Heikkinen *et al.*, 1985), 100 (Feldman *et al.*, 2000), and even up to 107 days (Bernstein *et al.*, 1989).

These long periods of time have, of course, been for a good reason. Fetal survival increases from 36 per cent at 24 weeks, to 38 per cent at 25 weeks, to 61 per cent at 26 weeks and 76 per cent at 27 weeks (Dillon *et al.*, 1982, p. 1091). In fact, in the medical literature it is even suggested that a pregnant brain-dead woman be maintained until 'utero-placental blood flow has ceased and placental function has become impaired' (Dillon *et al.*, 1982, p. 1089; Dillon *et al.*, 1981, p. 688). May be. But should we encourage this?

From ethical and legal perspectives we should distinguish between three different conditions from which the woman can suffer: 1) reversible loss of capacity caused from cerebral injury; 2) irreversible loss of capacity from cerebral injury or 3) brain-death. In the first two conditions, since the woman is considered 'alive' the general rule that applies is that decisions with regard to medical treatment are made by obtaining consent from the patient's surrogate decision-makers or her next-of-kin. When there are no explicit directives from the patient and when her wishes are hard to tell, treatment decisions are made for the patient's 'best interests'. Usually, in cases of maternal 'conflict' between the mother's interests and her 'fetus's' interests, the first outweigh the latter. Not only is brain-death a different medical condition than the first two conditions mentioned above, but it is primarily regarded as legal death. Hence, according to (what will be shown in this book) false assumption, mainly held by physicians and judges, a dead woman does not have interests that deserve significant legal protection. Apparently, what is left in these tragic situations is the fetus as an aggregate of cells on its way to becoming a human being and an abstract construct of the law called 'the interest of the fetus' whose bearer is usually another abstract, the state. Of course, the more the fetus is biologically developed the more proximate are its 'interests' to become real. The true dilemma occurs when the fetus is in its early stages of development. On the one hand, only by maintaining the brain-dead pregnant woman on life-support will the fetus be able to develop and eventually be delivered healthy. On the other hand, no ethical or legal justification seems to exist that can be applied to these early stages of being in the context of pregnancy.

Delivering a baby from a dead mother has some historical precedents (Loewy, 1987; Arthur, 1978, p. 176). It is believed that the Greek physician Asklepios was delivered after the death of his mother. Julius Caesar was born in a cesarean section performed on his dead mother, and traditionally, from a linguistic point of view the term 'Cesareans' followed this supposed incident and was originally referred to procedures performed on women who had died before delivering their fetuses.

Loss of capacity during pregnancy is not a hypothetical scenario nor is it a local phenomena. It has been already reported to happen in many states all over the world. In Germany, a young pregnant woman, Marion Ploch, died in a car accident on 5 October 1992. She was 13 weeks pregnant, so the decision to maintain her on life-support was for at least 12 weeks. Marion's parents feared that their daughter would be misused for an inappropriate experiment. They went to a reporter from the mass-circulation newspaper, the *Blid-Zeitung*, for help. Marion's doctor consulted other doctors, and almost six weeks after Marion's parents eventually agreed to maintain her on life-support, the efforts to save the fetus failed. A spontaneous abortion occurred, and the fetus was born dead (Anstotz, 1993). In a legal reported case at Georgia, a court ordered that life-support be maintained for a brain-dead pregnant woman. The order of the court was supported by the child's father, but was opposed by the mother's husband. The child was delivered at 22 weeks, but died two days later (*University Health Services, Inc. v. Piazzi*, 1986). A few years later, in California, on 24 April 1999, Maria Lopez was declared brain-dead. At that time, Lopez was pregnant with twins, leaving her family with the difficult decision whether to maintain her on life-support for the delivery of her twins, or not. Even though Lopez's family was advised to withdraw life-support measures, they did not. Subsequently, Lopez's two children were successfully delivered prematurely through cesarean section. In Canada, Sophia Park, a 25-year-old woman, lost consciousness on 17 November 1999, and was declared brain-dead ten days later. At that time, Park was 10 weeks pregnant. Park's husband and parents, a devoutly Christian family, asked their doctors at Toronto Western Hospital to keep her on life-support. The Park family went to the press and accused Sophia's doctors of trying to convince them to stop the life-support. The fetus died on 3 December, while Park was still on life-support (Gatehouse, 1999). In Ireland, a woman who was 14 weeks pregnant was struck by brain-death in May 2001. Due to uncertainty regarding the hospital's obligation to the fetus, the woman was maintained on life-sustaining treatment until further opinion was sought. The fetus nevertheless died *in uterus*, two weeks later.[2] In

Turkey, the Turkish Government ordered a Hospital in Istanbul not to turn off the life-support of Nina Typol, a 25-year-old pregnant German woman, who lay in a coma after being shot in the head by her fiancé on 5 February, 2003.[3] Finally, in Israel, two legal cases of maternal brain-death are reported. The husband of a 28 week pregnant woman who was in a permanent vegetative state asked for the declaration of the court that in the case of brain-death the hospital would be compelled to immediately deliver the fetus. The order was issued. In another case, the husband of an eight-month pregnant brain-dead woman sought an order to deliver the fetus. The court *refused* to issue such an order.[4]

No doubt, maintaining a brain-dead pregnant woman on life support is one of the advanced technologies that lead to a situation where the technical capacity develops before any moral consequences arise or any legal framework is devised, with which to decide whether we *should do* what we *can do*.[5]

In this book, the moral and legal aspects of maintaining a brain-dead woman on life-support will be discussed. The main question that will be present throughout this discussion is whether it is permissible to artificially maintain a dead woman solely for the sake of her fetus, and what is the motivation for doing so. More specifically, the book will inquire whether there is any justification for the proposed medical procedure, or does supporting it merely derive from a 'glorification' of high-tech rescue medicine along with an anxiety regarding the medical condition of the fetus and an effort to save the life of the fetus at all costs (Gallagher, 1989, p. 192).

The new medical solutions to maternal brain-death are available before any legal or ethical discussion has been made. It is therefore impossible to approach the issue of management of post-mortem pregnancy directly. An indirect way is necessary but also preferable. It seeks to establish a coherent approach that will depart from the existing legal and ethical rules, but that will also adjust itself to the new situation. Hence, the question as to whether a brain-dead pregnant woman should be maintained on life-support for the delivery of her fetus will be approached in this book from three different angles.

The first angle will attempt to look at the 'maternal' component on the one hand, and at the 'brain-death' element, on the other hand. The common feature of the analysis based on these two perspectives is that of casuistry. In other words, in both aspects of analysis a comparison of maternal brain-death to similar cases will be made, so that the application of the principles established under these other cases to maternal brain-death will be examined. The 'maternal' component analysis will consist of the legal frameworks related to pregnancy. These will include the legal and ethical aspects concerning the decision whether to abort a fetus or whether to force any other medical treatment on the pregnant woman that will involve some form of bodily intervention, for example accepting a blood transfusion against one's religious convictions or forcing a woman to have a surgical delivery, or another form of interference, *i.e.* in the woman's habitual behavior. Another group of legal interventions during pregnancy that will be analysed is the regulation of pregnancy clauses in the general law that governs the mode by which advance directives of former competent patients are valid in health related matters. The 'brain-death' element analysis will consist of the legal model for bodily interventions with brain-dead patient in general, mainly but not exclusively for organ donations.

The second angle will seek to look into the main *issues* that are directly identified in the case of maternal brain-death. Though the case of maternal brain-death has not been discussed as a whole in the literature, many concepts play an important part in it. The moral and legal status of the fetus, the moral and legal status of the dead mother, the practical obstacles to the proposed medical treatment, the general requirement of consent, the status of the next-of-kin and the physician-patient relationship in the obstetric context are some of the concepts which will be examined here.

The third angle will approach the case of maternal brain-death through the discussion of two disciplines other than the law. First, a relational feminist theory will be applied to the dilemma whether to maintain a brain-dead pregnant woman on life-support. The major ideas of this genuine theory will be conceptualized here. Second, ethics of care, ethics of relationships and ethics of families will all shed light on the moral duties the pregnant mother owes to her fetus and the unique bond the two have during pregnancy, and will examine the question whether these duties and bond survive the death of the mother.

Although the book is divided into eight separate chapters, each chapter is connected to another and should be read as part of a whole story or puzzle establishing the preferable course of action when maternal brain-death occurs. I begin with my first chapter on abortion law. Here, the general principles of abortion law will be discussed. A large part of this chapter will be devoted to the American leading decision, *Roe v. Wade*, which marked the establishment of the right of a woman to abort her fetus as part of her interest to privacy. A critique on the *Roe* decision as well as a description of the legal response to it will further be included. The chapter will also analyse Canada's abortion law, and examine it in light of the analysis of the *Roe* decision. The final section discusses whether the main features of abortion law can be applied to the case of a brain-dead pregnant woman.

The second chapter deals with situations in which pregnant women experience bodily interventions prescribed by law. The introduction of such phenomena is followed by a description of the special procedural structure of these legal interventions. Then, two specific legal rights involved in these cases: the right to self-determination and the right to refuse life-sustaining treatment will be elaborated. A separate part is devoted to discuss specific case law regarding decisions taken by pregnant women that could result in the death of their fetuses followed by a description of three sorts of legal interventions with pregnant women: interventions in the pregnant woman's life-style, interventions in the pregnant woman's physical state, and intervention through the release of pregnant women from tort liability. Having disputed legal interventions performed on pregnant women, the chapter concludes with a call to apply current thinking in this area to that of maternal brain-death.

The third chapter discusses the legal regime of advance directives in general and that of pregnancy clauses specifically. A short introduction on the purposes of advance directives is followed by description of their regulation with regard to pregnant incompetent women in the American, Canadian and English legal systems. A separate discussion on the constitutionality of pregnancy clauses in the American context is also included. Then, the chapter introduces the arguments for and against pregnancy clauses in living will legislation, that will result in practical recommendations regarding the proper approach to pregnancy clauses that should be applied to Canadian law given the American and English approaches. These recommendations will also reflect a moral and legal attitude that will be part of the proposed solution to the legal and ethical dilemmas occurring in post-mortem pregnancy.

The fourth chapter discusses 'post-mortem gift law', that is the legal mechanism to authorize the use of cadavers for different purposes, mainly for organ transplantation. After a description of the Canadian, American and English legal frameworks on this issue, some of the proposals in the literature to apply the organ donor model to the case of a brain-dead pregnant woman will be discussed. By rejecting these proposals, this chapter will show not only their weakness as such but it will also demonstrate how an opposing view is consistent with the previous analysis made in the first three chapters of this book. Hence, a coherent approach will be established between the 'maternal' component and the 'brain-death' element, so that the move to the second angle of my analysis will be made smoothly.

In the fifth chapter, which will mark the beginning of my second angle of analysis, the main issues raised by the situation of maternal brain-death will be discussed. These issues include the moral and legal status of the fetus and the interest or right of the fetus to be born. Other problems that will be discussed in this chapter are the relevance of the gestational age of the fetus to the dilemma raised by maternal brain-death; the pragmatic obstacles to maintaining a brain-dead pregnant woman on life-support; the legal requirement for consent to medical treatment; the rights of next-of-kin and friends of the deceased; and the physician-patient relationship in the obstetric context. A special emphasis will be put on the moral and legal status of the dead and the unique significance the dead have in the life of the living. The latter discussion will consist of our psychological inclinations toward the dead and the moral obligations to them, our religious convictions and linguistic habits while talking about the dead and our sense of personal identity as well as our perception of our life in a context of history formed as a narrative. By examining these issues, the chapter will sketch a broad picture of the basis for the legal and ethical policy that should be framed with regard to the dilemmas caused by maternal brain-death.

In the sixth chapter, which will establish my third angle of analysis, the major concepts that a relational feminist theory would raise with regard to the proposed medical procedure of maintaining a brain-dead pregnant woman on life support will be examined. These will include the redefinition of autonomy, the metaphor of field, the concept of boundary, the relational significance of the human body, the interest to privacy and the right to property. These concepts were, in part, inspired by Pedro Almodóvar's movie, *Talk to Her*. In this film, Benigno is a nurse who provides nearly 24 hour care for Alicia; he bathes her, gives her sensual massages, talks to her and tells her every minute detail of his day. Alica never interrupts him because she has been in a coma for four years after a car accident. Benigno gradually but madly falls in love with her. At one point, Alica becomes pregnant, and Benigno is arrested as the primary and only suspect. Almodóvar wants us to think that Benigno is misunderstood, that he and Alicia might really be in love, or at least that he might really love Alicia. This is the kind of love a fan of a certain actor or singer has with an artist. It is a form of obsession that he somehow knows her well enough to develop the feelings beyond lust or admiration that constitute 'standard' love. What is implied in the film, which sends Benigno to prison, affects the message of the movie. Almodóvar allows an incompetent person to completely dominate the feelings, thoughts and life of Benigno. Moreover, it is a man's use of superior force against a woman who is not in a position to either defend herself or make a choice that forms the tragedy of this film.

The idea of communicating with the brain-dead pregnant woman and her engagement with her surroundings is supported by the concepts brought in my fifth chapter. By discussing these concepts, this chapter brings a new and original way of thinking and talking about questions that occur in the situation of maternal brain-death.

My seventh chapter deals with the moral duties of a pregnant woman towards her fetus as derived from the special relationship between the two (or within the mother). This special relationship is analysed from four related ethical theories: ethics of relationships, responsibilities to society, ethics of families, and ethics of care. Finally, a religious perspective is introduced. This perspective supports my practical conclusion for the application of the maternal-fetal relationship analysed by the various ethical theories to the case of maternal brain-death.

Finally, in my last chapter of the book, the few legal reported cases which specifically discuss situations of maternal brain-death are presented, followed by the examination of their application to the Canadian legal system. In order to establish a proper legal opinion regarding the treatment of brain-dead pregnant women, it will be asked whether an analogy from other situations of posthumous reproduction could and should be made. After discussing some of the direct proposals to the proposed medical procedure of maintaining the woman on life-support, the book will be finalized by framing the main conclusions of the analysis concerning maternal brain-death, accompanying them with some practical suggestions for present and future pregnant women, families, health-care providers, lawyers, and other policy makers.

The case of a brain-dead pregnant woman is perceived as, and indeed *is* a tragic one. Medical technologies enable us to 'use' the mother as an incubator for the successful delivery of her fetus. As will be shown in this book, such a 'use' is not only ethically disturbing, but it is also legally questionable. It raises many difficult questions and seems to go against basic elements formed in similar and even less complicated matters. Most of all, it should make us take one step back and reflect whether this is the right thing to do for the mother, for the fetus, and for their families. It is hoped that this book will establish the path for these ethical and legal complicated queries.

Daniel Sperling
Toronto, Canada, 2005

NOTES

1 For the development of the brain-death criterion see Shemie *et al.*, 2003. For a report of a pregnancy in which the fetus survived maternal persistent vegetative state see Ayorinde *et al.*, 2000.
2 See www.butterworthsireland.ie/newsdirect/archive/2001/june/foetus15, accessed on 17 March 2003.
3 See www.news.bbc.co.uk/1/hi/world/europe/2737015.stm, accessed on 20 March 2003.
4 For the discussion of these cases, see *infra* section 1 of chapter 8 to this book.
5 A more complex, yet real situation is where the vital organs of an irreversibly brain-damaged mother which are maintained to support a fetus are considered for organ donation. In the literature there has been a report of two such cases. See Feldman *et al.*, 2000.

Acknowledgments

I wish to thank Julia Hall, Kaye Joachim and David Dyzenhaus for giving me the opportunity to pursue my research in the excellent and enriching environment of the faculty of law at the University of Toronto. Many thanks to Ted Tjaden and Esme Saulig for finding the rare bibliographical sources needed for this book.

Special acknowledgements are given to Bernard Dickens and Trudo Lemmens who provided substance, method, and spirit to this project. Jennifer Nedelsky's seminar on *Feminist Theory: Challenges To Legal and Political Thought* held at the University of Toronto provoked many thoughts leading to chapter 6 of this book.

Finally, I would like to express my gratitude to my parents, to Aryeh and to the other close people in my life without whom this book would not have been what it is.

List of Abbreviations

AIH   Artificial Insemination by the Husband
DNR   Do Not Resuscitate
UDDA   Uniform Determination of Death Act

Chapter 1

Abortion Law

INTRODUCTION

Both abortion and the decision not to maintain a brain-dead pregnant woman on life-support result in fetal death. Both contexts expose the tension between a woman's freedom to choose and the state's interest in the preserving the life of the fetus. It is thus useful to begin the analysis of maternal brain-death by discussing the general principles of abortion law. From a first look, the application of these principles to the dilemma whether to maintain a brain-dead pregnant woman on life-support for the delivery of her fetus or not seems appealing. However, one may argue that the decision to forgo 'life-sustaining' treatment does not involve the morally condemnable intent to kill the fetus, even when the woman is competent and aware of her pregnancy. When the woman dies of natural causes, such as in brain-death, her fetus will do so too. While the termination of the fetus's potential life magnifies the human tragedy in such a situation, it can be claimed that the mother is no more morally responsible for the fetus's death than she is for the condition that has brought to her own death.

One can further argue that the theoretical distinction between intentionally aborting a fetus and letting a fetus die is no more appropriate with the natural death of the mother, as the availability of medical technology to sustain the life of the mother (and the fetus's consequently) creates the need for more practical solutions to the question of what we should do with the woman at the time the treatment dilemma arises (Lederman, 1994, p. 365). Therefore, abortion law analysis will be of an important value to better understand the legal and ethical problems that occur in our situation.

Although performing abortions on women goes back to as early as Aristotle,[1] two main theories on the moral status of abortion have been dominant for many years. The conservative theory of abortion holds that abortion is never acceptable or, at most is permissible only when it is necessary to bring about some great moral good such as saving the pregnant woman's life. This theory is influenced by the principle of 'double effect', which provides specific guidelines for determining when it is morally permissible to perform an action in pursuit of a good end in full knowledge that the action will also bring about bad results. Under this principle, in cases where the proposed action has both good effects and bad effects, the action is permissible only if it is not wrong in itself and if it does not require that one directly intends the evil result.[2] By applying the principle of 'double effect' to abortions the conservative theory of abortion allows to morally distinguish among cases where a pregnancy may need to be ended in order to preserve the life of the mother.

According to the liberal theory of abortion, abortion is always permissible, whatever the state of fetal development. This view emphasizes the freedom of choice of the mother and the right of a woman to make decisions that affect her body. An intermediate approach between the liberal and conservative approaches is that abortion is ethically permissible up to a specified stage of fetal development or for some moral reasons that are believed to be sufficient to justify the performance of abortions under special circumstances. Such a view was framed in the leading 1973 American case of *Roe v. Wade* and its companion from the same year, *Doe v. Bolton*.

ROE V. WADE

In the *Roe* case, a pregnant single woman brought a class action challenging the constitutionality of the Texas Criminal laws, which prohibited procuring or attempting an abortion except for the purpose of saving the mother's life.[3] The appellant argued she was unable to get a legal abortion in Texas, and could not afford to travel to another jurisdiction, where it was legal under safe conditions.

In *Roe v. Wade*, the Supreme Court recognized the right to have abortion under the Fourteenth Amendment to the American Constitution. The court ruled that only where state interests are compelling may the state promulgate regulations limiting the woman's fundamental right of privacy. The court found two compelling state interests as a woman approaches full term: preserving and protecting the health of a pregnant woman, and protecting the potentiality of human life. The whole process of pregnancy was divided into three trimesters, in the course of which the court explained how these interests come into effect with regard to the decision whether or not to terminate the course of pregnancy. The court held, that during the first trimester of pregnancy (from conception to the end of the 12th week), because an abortion may be less hazardous than giving birth, the woman and her physician are free to determine whether or not to terminate the course of pregnancy without regulation by the state. During the second trimester of the pregnancy (until around the 28th week), the compelling interest of the state in maternal health allows the state to adopt regulations seeking to promote safe abortions. Finally, when the fetus reaches the point of viability, usually during the third trimester, the state may prohibit abortions except when necessary to protect the health of the mother.[4]

Thus, the court made a balance between the pregnant woman's interests and the state compelling interests in each of the trimesters. In the first trimester, the woman's interests outweigh the state interest in preserving and protecting the health of a pregnant woman, and in protecting the potentiality of human life. In the second trimester, the state interest in preserving and protecting the health of a pregnant woman outweighs the other state compelling interest and the woman's interests. Finally, in the third trimester, the state interest in protecting the potentiality of human life outweighs the other compelling state interest and the woman's interests.

At the basis of this balance of interests lies the assumption that the answer to the abortion dilemma can be found in the moral status of the fetus. This moral status is derived from a biological development, which has been roughly determined as depending on the point of viability. The idea of a biological criterion for the permissibility of abortions is not new and has a historical background. It is seen in 'Animation' of Thomas Aquinas where he develops the notion of 'quickening', that is the beginning of the period in which a mother could feel the fetus move in the womb (Bourne, 2003, p. 250). While in ancient days only the mother could tell when the fetus was moving in her, and hence aborting the fetus was fully dependent on her subjective state, the viability criterion set in *Roe* provided an objective assessment for this critical biological point that had significant moral and legal implications.

But, the court in *Roe* did not discuss the relation between the moral status of a fetus and the point of viability. More specifically, the court did not explain what is the justification for such a relation. Nevertheless, connecting between the two is not an obvious thing, as the Supreme Court of Ireland stated in *AG v. X.*, 'One cannot make distinctions between individual phases of the unborn life before birth, or between unborn and born life' (Sheikh *et al.*, 2001, p. 79).

It is also not clear from the court's decision in *Roe* when exactly a fetus deserves moral protection and why the viability criterion is good enough to serve as an ethical judgment on the moral status of the fetus. Why not, for example, link other biological points during pregnancy to the fetus's moral status. Perhaps the fetus should enjoy moral protection much before the point of viability, for example, immediately after conception, or after 24 weeks where there is a 50 per cent chance of surviving? Or perhaps the fetus should be accorded a protectable legal and moral status after the point of viability, for instance, after showing expulsion or extraction from the mother and breathing, or after showing any other biological evidence of life such as beating of the heart, pulsation of the umbilical cord, or definite movement of voluntary muscles?

Although the moral and legal status of the fetus and the state interest in protecting it are used as an argument to counterbalance the protection of the women's interest, the court in *Roe* refused to hold that the fetus is a 'person' within the meaning of the Fourteenth Amendment to the American Constitution. Moreover, an exception to the state interest in regulating the prohibition of abortions was given in *Roe*, according to which abortions can be proscribed unless it is necessary to preserve the life or health of the mother. Indeed, this exception was later used in *Thornburgh v. American College of Obstetricians* (1986). In this case, the court examined the constitutionality of a Pennsylvania statute that allowed in *post-viability abortions* the physician to use a technique that most likely would result in the birth of a live child, unless the technique would present a significantly greater medical risk to the life or health of the pregnant woman. The court held that this provision is unconstitutional on the ground that the health of the woman is paramount, *even after viability*, and she cannot be forced to bear any greater risk to her health in order to save the viable fetus.

Some have argued that the *Roe* decision contained reference to another issue related to the freedom of choice of the pregnant woman, that of the birth of an unwanted child (Gelfand, 1987, p. 780).[5] More specifically, the question in *Roe* could be rephrased as the following: whether one can be forced to raise an unwanted child particularly when the family is unable (emotionally or otherwise) to care for the child. However, if it were correct that *Roe* decision had essentially been about family planning, then the court presumably would have left the decision up to the woman and her husband, based on the constitutional right of privacy as it has done in a similar situation (*Griswold v. Connecticut,* 1965[6]). Instead, not only did the court agree that the right to have an abortion is derived from the woman's constitutional right to privacy (that later extended to activities and intimate decisions regarding marriage, contraception, and family relationships), but it also held that health providers, in consultation with the pregnant woman, are free to determine, *without regulation by the state,* that in their medical judgment the patient's pregnancy should be terminated. It seems then that the emphasis in *Roe* is about a woman's control over her own body, and not about whether she wants her or her family to be burdened with an unwanted child (Mahoney, 1989, p. 228).[7] Any conclusions regarding family planning from the *Roe* decision that would serve as a justification for the court's ruling on abortion are difficult to draw.

DOE V. BOLTON

Soon after the Roe decision, the Supreme Court heard a similar case of abortion. In *Doe v. Bolton* (1973), an indigent, 22-year-old married pregnant woman, who desired but had been refused an abortion after eight weeks of pregnancy, 23 other individuals (nine physicians licensed in Georgia, seven nurses, five clergymen, and two social workers), and two nonprofit Georgia corporations that advocated abortion reform instituted an action, seeking a declaratory judgment that the Georgia abortion statutes were unconstitutional and requesting an injunction against the statutes' enforcement. The Georgia statutes limited legal abortions to specific situations requiring a showing that a continuation of the pregnancy would endanger the life or seriously and permanently injure the health of the pregnant woman, or that the fetus would very likely be born with a grave, permanent, and irremediable mental or physical defect, or that the pregnancy resulted from forcible or statutory rape.[8] In addition, the statutes required certain other procedural or evidentiary aspects of the approval and performance of abortions.[9]

Although Doe did not fit into the formal requirements of the Georgia statutes, she had special circumstances that later made the Supreme Court hold she would be unable to care for her new child. Doe had three living children. The two older ones had been placed in a foster home because of Doe's poverty and inability to care for them. The youngest had been placed for adoption. Her husband abandoned her and she was forced to live with her indigent parents and their eight children. Doe had been a mental patient at the State Hospital and she was advised that an abortion could be performed on her with less danger to her health than if she gave birth to the child she was carrying.

Relying on *Griswold v. Connecticut* (1965) and other related cases the District Court held that a Constitutional right to privacy has been established broadly enough to encompass the right of a woman to terminate an unwanted pregnancy through an abortion in her early stages of pregnancy. The court gave declaratory, but not injunctive, relief, invalidating as an infringement of the woman's right to privacy and personal liberty the limitation to the three situations specified in Georgia abortions Statutes. The appellants, claiming entitlement to broader relief, directly appealed to the Supreme Court.

On appeal, the Supreme Court modified and, as so modified, affirmed the judgment of the District Court. Following the rationale of the *Roe* decision, it was held that a pregnant woman has no absolute constitutional right to abort her fetus and that voluntary abortion at any time and place regardless of medical standards would impinge on a rightful concern of society. However, the Court did not mention the trimester framework established in *Roe* nor did it explain how to balance the interests involved. The court found Georgia abortion legislation to be overbroad in favor of the State and not closely correlated to the aim of preserving prenatal life. Hence, the Court ruled that endangering the life of the woman or seriously and permanently injuring her health are standards too narrow for the right of privacy that is at stake when a decision to abort is about to be made.

FOLLOWING *ROE V. WADE*

In addition to a mass public and political response to the *Roe* decision (Bourne, 2003, pp. 262–5), two kinds of judicial reactions followed the *Roe* decision. The first is the expansion of the state interest in protecting potential life even before viability and even outside the realm of abortions. The second is the abandonment of the trimester framework for a new standard, the 'undue burden' test.

The protection of a pre-viable fetus beyond abortion

In *Webster v. Reproductive Health Services* (1989), the court dealt with a Missouri abortion act. This act required physicians to perform tests in order to determine whether the fetus is viable prior to an abortion on a woman who is 20 or more weeks pregnant. The statute also prohibited the use of public employees and facilities to perform or assist abortions for non-therapeutic purposes. The first provision before the court contained findings by the Missouri state legislature that the life of each human being begins *at conception*, and that unborn children have protectable interests in life, health and well being. The court found this provision to be imposing no limitations on abortions, but rather conferring protections in tort and probate law on fetuses' permissible legislative actions under *Roe*. By doing so, the court appeared willing to recognize the existence of fetal protection at least *outside the context of abortions*.

But the court also expanded the protection of a fetus with regard to its biological development. The court ruled that under the Missouri statute, a physician would only be required to administer those tests that are necessary or useful to determine viability. The majority held that the state's interest in protecting potential human life should come into existence not only at the point of viability as ruled in *Roe*, but even *prior* to that (during the *second trimester*).

Thus, the court explicitly recognized that requiring physicians to perform viability-determining procedures on 20-week-old fetuses directly conflicts with *Roe* because inevitably the requirement would result in the performance of procedures on non-viable second trimester fetuses. In doing so, the court suggested that the compelling interests of the state may exist throughout the pregnancy and not, as ruled in *Roe*, only upon and after viability. In its decision, the court criticized the trimester framework of Roe and regarded it as 'unsound in principle and unworkable in practice' (*Webster v. Reproductive Health Services*, 1989, p. 3056[10]).

The *Webster* decision explicitly stated that it did not overrule *Roe*, but rather based its decision on a narrow interpretation of *Roe*, as a decision striking down a criminal statute of non-therapeutic abortions. According to the court, the *Roe* decision could not be applied to the *Webster* case, which dealt with a statute prohibiting public funding, and that expanded the procedural protections for fetuses. Whether this is a convincing argument or not, the outcome of the *Webster* decision is far beyond the *Roe* decision, thereby calling for a wide protection of the state's interest in potential life even when such a potential is very small.

Undermining the viability criterion

Viability is, as Thomas Murray claims, a slippery concept (Murray, 1987, p. 332). This is especially true, because it is based on biological development of the fetus dependent on scientific knowledge, which is dynamic and changing. The legal standard of viability framed in the *Roe* decision, did not last long. It was altered in *Planned Parenthood v. Casey* (1992). In *Casey*, the Supreme Court considered the constitutionality of amendments to the Pennsylvania abortion statute. The Court first reaffirmed the *Roe* decision, and stated that 'any later divergences from the factual premises of Roe have no bearing on the validity of its central holding, that viability marks the earliest point at which the state's interest in fetal life is constitutionally adequate to justify a legislative ban on non therapeutic abortions' (*Planned Parenthood v. Casey*, 1992, pp. 835–6). Nevertheless, the court overruled the rigid use of the trimester criterion and fetal viability as a standard by replacing it with an 'undue burden test'. According to this test, a consideration has to be made whether a law's purpose or effect is to place a substantial obstacle in the path of a woman seeking an abortion of a nonviable fetus. In *Casey*, a profound interest in potential life had been established. This interest, however, was not based on the trimester framework.

But despite the novelty of the Casey decision, there were other voices at the Court opposing to the 'undue burden test'. The Chief Justice joined by Justice White, Justice Scalia and Justice Thomas concluded that the undue burden test has no basis in constitutional law and will not result in a simple limitation that will be applied easily by courts. They emphasized that:

> To evaluate abortion regulations under that standard, judges will have to make the subjective, unguided determination whether the regulations place 'substantial obstacles' in the path of a woman seeking an abortion, undoubtedly engendering a

variety of conflicting views. The standard presents nothing more workable than the trimester framework the joint opinion discards, and will allow the Court, under the guise of the Constitution, to continue to impart its own preferences on the States in the form of a complex abortion code.[11]

Instead, they referred to the *Webster* decision concluding that a pregnant woman's interest in having an abortion is a form of liberty protected by the Due Process Clause, but that States may regulate abortion procedures in ways *rationally related* to a legitimate state interest (*Planned Parenthood v. Casey*, 1992, p. 840). Nevertheless, no explanation was given as to what this rational relation really means.

Another important issue held in *Casey* relates to the role of the husband in the decision-making whether to perform an abortion or not. In *Casey*, the court struck down Pennsylvania law asking a married woman who wishes to abort her fetus to sign a statement indicating that she has notified her husband on her decision. The court found this legal requirement an undue burden on the pregnant woman. The court emphasized that:

> It cannot be claimed that the father's interest in the fetus' welfare is equal to the mother's protected liberty, since it is an inapplicable biological fact that state regulation with respect to the fetus will have a far greater impact on the pregnant woman's bodily integrity than it will on the husband.[12]

In sum, although *Roe* is still the leading decision in American abortion law, it is not clear if its main components – the trimester framework and the viability criteria – are well established in the judgments following *Roe*. As I suggested, American courts deviated from the *Roe* decision in two different directions: further protecting the fetus and framing a more flexible test for state intervention in abortion. Moreover, the popularity of the *Roe* case is still questionable. As Richard Bourne argues, 'American society has retained the same moral ambivalence towards legalized abortion as they demonstrated towards criminal abortion in earlier times' (Bourne, 2003, p. 262). A recent poll in the US shows that 52 per cent of the Americans agreed and 37 per cent disagreed with the result of *Roe v. Wade*, while 50 per cent identified themselves as pro-choice and 42 per cent as pro-life (Jost, 2002, p. 644). With this level of division it is also difficult to credit the *Roe* decision as expressing values that are representative of American public opinion and accepted by the public at large.

ABORTION LAW IN CANADA

In Canada, the prohibition against attempting to procure an abortion was enacted in the 1869 Act Respecting Offences Against the Person. This prohibition made the abortion of a 'quick fetus' a crime punishable by life imprisonment. In 1892, the same prohibition was incorporated into the Criminal Code[13] (section 251), and survived there until 1969.

Under pressure from the medical community, section 251 was amended in 1969 to allow for a therapeutic exception to the abortion prohibition. According to the new section, an abortion can be performed by a licensed medical practitioner in an accredited or approved hospital on the written advice of a three-member therapeutic abortion committee to the effect that the continuation of the pregnancy is dangerous to the pregnant woman's life or health. Under this new law, whether a pregnant woman would undergo an abortion or not was wholly contingent upon the committee's assessment of the threat the pregnancy posed *to her health or life*. Nevertheless, the woman could not represent her case to the committee. It is reported in the literature that in practice, the criteria of endangering the woman's health were applied unevenly from province to province and from committee to committee, additional criteria such as consent of a spouse, gestational age of the fetus, residency restrictions etc. were also required. Many hospitals did not establish committees, while others had just formal committees without considering any applications for abortions.[14]

It is important to note that the 1969 amendments to the Criminal Code did not change the substantive law on abortions by liberalizing the legal grounds for terminating pregnancy. As Bernard Dickens argues, these amendments only addressed the *means* of ensuring the legality of an abortion before it is performed (Dickens, 1981, p. 18). Before 1969, a physician acting in good faith could be lawful by terminating pregnancy to save life, physical or mental health. The legality of the physician's action could be tested and confirmed only *ex post facto*. By the 1969 amendments, legality of terminating pregnancy could now be established *beforehand*, by certification of a therapeutic abortion committee. A substantive approach to Canadian abortion law was established, however, by legal cases.

In the *Morgentaler* case, the Supreme Court of Canada considered, for the first time, the constitutionality of the criminal offence of performing an abortion under section 251 of the Criminal Code (*R. v. Morgentaler*, 1988). Dr. Henry Morgentaler was charged with illegally performing an abortion by the Province of Ontario. Morgentaler argued that section 251 to the Criminal Code violated several provisions of the Canadian Charter of Rights and Freedoms, including: section 7, which protects the 'right to life, liberty and security of the person'; section 2(a), which guarantees 'freedom of conscience and religion'; section 12 prohibiting cruel and unusual treatment; and section 15(1), which prohibits discrimination on the basis of sex.

The majority of the court held that section 251 of the Criminal Code creates a profound interference with a woman's body and, thus, a violation of the woman's right to security of the person. Justice Wilson wrote:

> She is truly being treated as a means – a means to an end which she does not desire but over which she has no control. She is the passive recipient of a decision made by others as to whether her body will be used to nurture a new life. Can there be anything that comports less with human dignity and self-respect? How can a woman in this position have any sense of security with respect to her person?[15]

Though the court acknowledged that the developmental stage of the fetus is an important factor in the decision whether to impose reasonable limits on the woman's right to security of the person under section 1 of the Canadian Charter,[16] the viability criterion was not set for such a biological development. Justice Bertha Wilson, for example, addressed the importance of the developmental facts of pregnancy by ruling that abortion legislation, which adopts a permissive attitude toward early term abortions and a more restrictive attitude toward late-term abortions, would probably be constitutional.

The court continued to rule that the state has a legitimate interest in protecting the interest of the fetus's life, although it did not directly consider the question whether the fetus is a 'legal person'. More specifically, the court did not address the question whether the term 'everyone' in section 7 of the Canadian Charter of Rights and Freedoms also refers to the fetus. Contrary to the American Supreme Court in *Roe* v. *Wade*, the Canadian Supreme Court in the *Morgentaler* case neither declared that the right to abortion is a fundamental right, nor referred to the right of privacy in overturning section 251 to the Criminal Code. However, the *Morgentaler* decision invalidated the only abortion law in Canada – section 251 of the Criminal Code – and performing an abortion became a medical procedure regulated by provincial regulation of health-care providers, hospitals and access to health-care services. A legislative response to overturn the *Morgentaler* decision has been unsuccessful. Sanda Rodgers reports that Bill C-43 which asked to recriminalize abortions except where a woman's medical practitioner was of the opinion that her health or life would likely be threatened was defeated in the Senate by a vote of 44 to 43 in January 1991 (Rodgers, 2002, p. 337).

In addition to the significant contribution of the *Morgentaler* case, abortion law in Canada has also been influenced by other judicial decisions, in which injunctions were unsuccessfully sought to prevent women from performing an abortion based on the recognition of the fetus as an entity entitled to constitutional protection.

In *Tremblay v. Daigle* (1989), the appellant was 18 weeks pregnant at the time of her separation from the respondent, who was the fetus's father. She then decided to terminate her pregnancy. The respondent obtained an interlocutory injunction from the Superior Court preventing her from having the abortion. The trial judge found that a fetus is a 'human being' under the Quebec Charter of Human Rights and Freedoms and therefore enjoys a 'right to life' under s. 1. The trial judge also based his conclusion on the recognition of the fetus as a juridical person set forth in the Civil Code of Quebec. He then ruled that the respondent had the necessary 'interest' to request the injunction; and concluded, after considering the effect of the injunction on the appellant's rights under section 7 of the Canadian Charter of Rights and Freedoms and section 1 of the Quebec Charter, that the fetus's right to life should prevail. On appeal, the injunction was upheld by a majority of the Court of Appeal.[17]

A right to appeal to the Supreme Court of Canada was given and the appeal was allowed. The Supreme Court declared that the substantial rights alleged to support the injunction preventing the abortion do not exist. The court declared that the fetus does not enjoy the right to life conferred by section 1 of Quebec Charter, and held that there are good reasons for not finding any fetal rights in general under the Quebec Charter. No discussion was held in the context of the Canadian Charter of Rights and Freedoms, as the case at issue involved a civil action between two private parties. Additionally, the court held that the provisions of the Civil Code of Quebec providing for the appointment of a curator for an unborn child as well as the provisions granting patrimonial interests to such child do not implicitly recognize that a fetus is a juridical person. It was further ruled that in Anglo-Canadian law, a fetus must be born alive to enjoy rights. Finally, the Supreme Court found nothing in the Quebec legislation or case law to support the argument that the father's interest in a fetus he helped to create gives him the right to veto a woman's decisions with respect to the fetus she is carrying, even though the woman is already in the midst of her second trimester of pregnancy.

In *Diamond v. Hirsch* (1989), the respondent, a married woman, who had lived in a common-law relationship with the applicant for almost a year, was eight weeks into her pregnancy. The applicant and the respondent no longer resided with one another and the woman sought an abortion out of fear from her father's reaction to her pregnancy. The applicant asked for an order enjoining and restraining the respondent from having an abortion performed upon her.

In response to the applicant's argument on the unique moral status of the fetus, the court held that from a medical perspective it was not convinced that an eight-week old fetus is in fact a distinct human being. The court added that there is always the possibility of an involuntary miscarriage, or that the child or the fetus when developing into a child could be born dead, and that there are many possibilities of the fetus not surviving the full pregnancy. But the overwhelming consideration that the court found to exist in the case was the fact that the woman, as a human being, has an absolute right, subject to criminal sanctions, to the control of her body, and if she has made the choice to terminate the pregnancy, she is entitled to do so.

In conclusion, Canadian case law reflects the reluctance of the courts to regard the fetus as a 'person' under the existing statutes of all sorts of constitutional level (from provincial legislation to the federal constitutional norm as the Canadian Charter). Sanda Rodgers comes to the same conclusion after analysing Canadian case law. She argues that it would be unlikely that the reference to the term 'everyone' in section 7 of the Canadian Charter would include the fetus (Rodgers, 2002, p. 339). Moreover, the cases mentioned above seem to follow the reasoning of the *Morgentaler* decision, thereby conferring on a woman full freedom of choice with regard to abortion, at least in the early stages of pregnancy.

APPLYING ABORTION LAW TO POST-MORTEM PREGNANCY

How can abortion law contribute to our discussion of maintenance of a brain-dead pregnant woman on life support?

Roe's criterion on viability had a logical and biological basis. With respect to the state's important and legitimate interest in the health of the mother, the 'compelling' point is approximately the end of the first trimester, since until then mortality in abortion is less frequent than mortality in normal childbirth. From that point onward, the state can regulate the abortion procedure to the extent that it reasonably relates to the preservation and protection of maternal health. With respect to the state's interest in potential life, the 'compelling' point is at viability, since in that point the fetus presumably has the biological capacity to survive outside the mother's womb. Under these logical and biological rationales it seems reasonable that state regulation may proscribe abortion during the period after viability, except when necessary to preserve the life or health of the mother.

However, applying these rationales to the situation of the pregnant brain-dead woman creates difficulties. Following the reasoning set in the *Roe* decision, no state intervention in the pregnant woman other than for the sake of the mother's health, should be allowed during the first and second trimesters of pregnancy. However, proponents of maintaining a brain-dead pregnant woman on life-support would argue that if the woman is not being maintained on life-support, she would not reach the third trimester, where the state apparently has a recognized interest in protecting potential life. Although it is clearly true that without life-support the fetus would not reach the third trimester, the trimester framework does not seem to imply an obligation to continue life-support. Under this framework, the state interests, which can outweigh the mother's interests, are being examined *when the physical intervention is being considered, and not afterwards*. Maintaining a brain-dead pregnant woman on her first or second trimester is not what the court in Roe meant to create. It is separating between the act of intervention in the woman's pregnancy and the state's interest that justify it. It is taking advantage of the mother's situation and protecting, *de facto*, potential life, at a point where it is clearly not viable. Thus, it is a fierce deviation from the *Roe* decision.

Indeed, as I showed above, the viability criterion and the trimester framework are difficult to apply. This is part of the reason why American courts replaced them in another test ('undue burden test'), or expanded their effect when they dealt with public funding (the *Webster* case). Moreover, the decisions following *Roe* emphasize that there may be another way to protect the state interest in potential life without interference in the pregnant woman's body. Such a way was explicitly formed in *Planned Parenthood v. Casey* (1992), where the court, while rejecting the rigid trimester framework of *Roe*, ruled that the task to promote the state's profound interest in potential life throughout pregnancy can also be fulfilled if the state takes measures to ensure that the woman's choice is informed, and also takes measures designed to advance this interest by persuading her to choose childbirth over abortion. The court recognized that such measures must not be an undue burden on the right to choose.

I find this alternative an adequate constitutional compromise, given the profound interest of the mother, on the one hand, and the uncertainty about the fetus's moral and legal status, on the other hand. I would suggest also applying this reasoning to the situation of maternal brain-death. The solution to the ethical and legal dilemma whether to maintain the woman on life-support or not can be achieved *ex-ante* and not necessarily *ex-post facto*. In other words, the case should not indispensably be resolved by deciding to maintain the woman on life-support or to let her (with her fetus) die. The woman should leave an advance directive as to what she would want to happen to her after her death.

She can be advised that she can be maintained on life-support if she so wishes, but ultimately her directive must be followed, with her body being treated as she desires. I will elaborate on this latter point in my discussion on living wills in chapter 3. It is important to show that if such a solution was proposed by the court with regard to the decision whether or not to perform an abortion, there is no reason why this could not be applied to a perhaps lesser traumatic physical medical intervention than that of being maintained on life-support.

The reading of *Roe*, as concerned primarily with family planning, would be difficult to be applied to the case of a brain-dead mother, where such an issue apparently does not arise. Although the woman's survivors would face both distress over the woman's death and the financial and emotional problems of caring for a motherless child, the decision to maintain the woman on life-support reflects a desire to bring a wanted child to the surviving family. In contrast to the abortion context, the goal of the medical intervening action is not to prevent the situation of an unwanted child, but quite the opposite.

But perhaps the *Roe* decision and the trimester framework cannot apply at all to our case. One can justifiably argue that the trimester approach set in *Roe* addresses only the abortion context where the state must consider *both* an interest in maternal health and an interest in potential life (Dyke, 1990, p. 876). The interest in maternal health seems to be irrelevant in our case because the woman is beyond recovery. According to this argument, *Roe* does not apply to situations where one of the compelling interests of the state no longer exists. Thus, adopting the rationales of *Roe* to the dilemma of whether the woman should be kept on life-support or not could be improper.

Are the principles framed in Canadian abortion cases more helpful? It seems to me that two basic ideas can be identified from Canadian case law. First, the idea of freedom of choice as an (almost) absolute principle. It is the woman's right to fully control her body to such an extent that even the biological father of the fetus cannot interfere with this right. The Criminal Code does not appear to give a spouse the power to veto the woman's decision to have an abortion (Dickens, 1981, p. 22). Second, courts are reluctant to interpret the existing law in a way that would confer the fetus a legal substantial status prior to birth. It is further difficult to infer what the legal view would be in cases where the fetus is after the point of viability, since all the reported cases are dealing with pre-viable fetuses. Nevertheless, the courts' interpretation of the term 'fetus' under the Canadian legislation is not restricted to pre-viable fetuses.

Applying these two general ideas to our case would probably result in an outcome that would respect the woman's choice and regard her right to control her body even after her death. It also seems reasonable to argue that the tendency of Canadian law to protect the potential life of the fetus would be less stringent than the American approach. The trimester framework will also not count as a mandatory guideline in the Canadian context. It is sound to think that the more developed the fetus is, the lesser the inclination to terminate the pregnancy will be. Canadian courts may be expected to be more flexible in this context.

To sum up, the *Roe* decision of American abortion law cannot easily be applied to the case of a brain-dead pregnant woman. The circumstances that led to its reasoning are very different from the ones that occur in the case of maternal brain-death. Nevertheless, if the Roe decision applies at all, its main rationales do not support the maintenance of a dead woman on life support in her first and second trimester. One can arrive to the same conclusion by applying the main ideas of Canadian abortion law. These include the percepts concerning the freedom of choice of a pregnant woman which is regarded as almost absolute, and that the fetus is not a legal entity substantially protected while *in uterus*.

To realize differently means to 'compel women to be not merely minimally decent Samaritans, but good Samaritans to unborn persons inside of them' (Thomson, 1999, p. 209). This would be contrary to other areas in which the law, at least in the common law system, does not expect a person to make large sacrifices to sustain the life of another who has no right to demand them. Applying abortion law to the case of a brain-dead pregnant woman, as it is shaped by Canadian and American legal system, strengthens this conclusion. We might look at other legal spheres to broaden our perspective. A general observation on bodily interventions to the pregnant women followed in the next chapter could be of additional help.

NOTES

1   For an excellent historical background of the practice of abortions see Bourne, 2003, pp. 250–56.
2   Classical formulations of the principle of 'double effect' ask for four conditions in order that the action in question be morally permissible: the action contemplated is in itself either morally good or morally indifferent; the bad result not be directly intended; the good result not be a direct causal result of the bad result; and the good result is 'proportionate to' the bad result.
3   The first state criminal statute was enacted in Connecticut in 1821, followed shortly by several other states. It is believed that these early criminal prohibitions against abortions are primarily health code legislation aimed at protecting women from being poisoned by quackery rather than as social regulations aimed at preventing abortions as such. Opposing to abortions on moral grounds did not appear before the second half of the nineteenth century. See Bourne, 2003, p. 252.
4   To a large extent the issue of viability is symbolic, as 98 per cent of abortions occur in the first 14 weeks of pregnancy. See Robertson, 1989, p. 267. For a discussion on the anatomic and physiologic changes that occur during the three trimesters of pregnancies see Haycock, 1984.
5   Of course, the term 'reproductive choice' has a broader meaning than the right to choose abortion. It also includes the decision whether to bear a child, the timing of childbearing, the means of avoiding or promoting pregnancy, the decision to give birth in a safe and supportive environment, and the techniques for childbirth.
6   The *Griswold* case involved a law forbidding the use of contraceptives. Based on the right for privacy under the Bill of Rights, the Supreme Court held that such a law as applied to married people is unconstitutional.
7   A proof for such a claim can be found in *Planned Parenthood of Central Missouri v. Casey* (1992). In this case, the court struck down a Missouri statute that would have required a woman to obtain her husband's consent for an abortion.
8   Ga. Criminal Code § 26-1202 (a).
9   Ga. Criminal Code § 26-1202 (b).

10 The court quoted *Garcia v. San Antonio Metro. Transit Auth.*, 469 U.S. 528 at 546 (1985).
11 *Planned Parenthood v. Casey*, 1992, p. 840.
12 *Planned Parenthood v. Casey*, 1992, p. 838.
13 Now, R.S.C. 1985, c. C-46, s. 287. Interesting to note here that the woman herself was also subject to criminal penalty although a lesser one than for the abortion provider. Section 251 reads:
   '(1) Everyone who, with intent to procure the miscarriage of a female person, whether or not she is pregnant, uses any means for the purpose of carrying out his intention is guilty of an indictable offence and is liable for imprisonment for life. (2) Every female person who, being pregnant, with the intent to procure her own miscarriage, uses any means or permits any means to be used for the purpose of carrying out her intention is guilty of an indictable offence and is liable to imprisonment for two years.'
14 See Canada, Department of Justice, *Committee on the Operation of the Abortion Law, Report* (Ottawa: Minister of Supply and Services Canada, 1977).
15 *R. v. Morgentaler*, 1988, pp. 173–4.
16 Section 1 to the Charter reads: 'The Canadian Charter of Rights and Freedoms guarantees the rights and freedoms set out in it subject to reasonable limits prescribed by law as can be demonstrably justified in a free and democratic society.' *Canadian Charter of Rights and Freedoms*, 1982 , c. 11 s. 1.
17 *Tremblay v. Daigle*, [1989] R.J.Q. 1735.

Chapter 2

Bodily Interventions During Pregnancy

INTRODUCTION

The state's interest in the potential life of the fetus has shaped the scope of pregnant women's procreative liberty beyond the abortion arena. An increasing number of court decisions justified the imposition of medical treatment upon unwilling pregnant women based on the protection of the fetus. Courts have ordered pregnant patients to undergo medical treatment, blood transfusions or cesarean sections, in order to save the fetus's life. They have also forced pregnant women to refrain from doing certain things that might (also) harm the fetus, such as drinking alcohol, using drugs,[1] smoking, having poor nutrition, driving negligently, doing vigorous exercise, sniffing glue,[2] etc.[3]

According to a large study made in 1987, court-ordered obstetrical interventions for a wide variety of situations have become a well-established routine (Kolder *et al.*, 1987). The study revealed that court orders were issued in 86 per cent of the cases in which they were sought for procedures deemed necessary for the life of the fetus, including cesarean section. The wide application of this legal mechanism is even more distressing, since it is applied in many situations where the ethical guidelines of the medical profession seem more respectful of the personal autonomy and liberty of the pregnant woman patient. The American College of Obstetricians and Gynecologists, for example, provides that:

> Obstetricians should refrain from performing procedures that are unwanted by a pregnant woman. The use of judicial authority to implement treatment regimes in order to protect the fetus violates the pregnant woman's autonomy and should be avoided unless the four stringent criteria specified in this opinion are met (high probability of serious harm to the fetus in respecting the patient's decision; high probability that the recommended treatment will prevent or substantially reduce harm to the fetus; there are no comparably effective, less-intrusive options to prevent harm to the fetus; high probability that the recommended treatment also benefits the pregnant woman or that the risks to the pregnant woman are relatively small.[4]

The message that is delivered from these guidelines is very clear. Medical interventions with a pregnant woman's body should be performed only in rare cases. According to these guidelines, the threat of imposed intervention erodes the trusts necessary to allow pregnant women to access prenatal care and other services for their health (Rodgers, 2002, pp. 354–55).

While some courts warranted orders following *Roe*'s criterion of viability (*Roe v. Wade*, 1973) as a biological point that legitimizes the state's interest in the fetus, others have forced medical treatment upon pregnant patients prior to that point. Most of the cases involving a pregnant woman's refusal to treatment rely on the viability distinction in striking a balance between a woman's right to privacy and her freedom to choose and the fetus' interest to life. At times, courts base their interventions with the pregnant woman's body on the principle of beneficence, so that its practical application is not only in considering fetal welfare, but also in the state's interest to protect dependent third parties from loss of a parent.

Unsurprisingly the impact of fetal rights/interests claims and legal interventions with pregnant women's bodies have fallen most heavily upon the most vulnerable groups of women. Janet Gallagher quotes a survey, which reveals that 81 per cent of the pregnant women subjected to court-ordered interventions in the US were black, Asian, or Hispanic; 44 per cent of them were unmarried; 24 per cent did not speak English as their primary language; and none were private patients. In addition, religious minorities have been particularly affected, as in almost all cases of refusing cesarean section the women were members of some religious group or subculture (Gallagher, 1989, p. 203).

THE PROCEDURAL STRUCTURE OF COURT-ORDERED INTERVENTIONS

An influential survey from 1987 found that applications for legal interventions with pregnant women are usually successful. Kolder and colleagues report that only in 14 per cent of the cases in which cesarean sections were carried out against the wishes of the mother had the application for the order been refused (Kolder *et al.*, 1987). In a later study it was also shown that among court-ordered interventions only rare cases reach the appellate level (Board of Trustees, 1990, p. 2664). In addition, requests for such interventions are likely to be made on extremely short notice and require immediate judicial intervention. A study of court-ordered obstetrical interventions reported that, for example, in 70 per cent of cases in which orders were considered, hospital administrators and attorneys were aware of the situation only a day or less before seeking a court order. In the study 88 per cent of the orders were obtained in less than six hours, and in 19 per cent of cases in less than an hour (Board of Trustees, 1990, p. 2665).

Furthermore, court proceedings for such requests are characterized with the following attributes. The pregnant woman is usually under considerable psychological stress and may also be suffering from substantial physical pain. Her ability to express her interests may be seriously impaired, and due to the short notice and the immediacy of the medical intervention, it is usually unlikely that she can find adequate counsel. Even if the woman finds legal aid, her counsel would not have time to prepare properly for the hearing. Moreover, the fact that there is little or no time at all to obtain the full range of medical opinions or facts, along with the inability of the court to fully understand the medical evidence, leads to mistakes or misunderstandings with serious and irreversible consequences.[5]

THE RIGHT TO SELF-DETERMINATION

While dealing with court-ordered interventions during pregnancy, one has to distinguish between interference with the pregnant woman's life style such as drinking, using drugs, or other addictive substances, and intervening with the woman's physical state without violating her life style.[6] In *Winnipeg Child and Family Services v. D.F.G.* (1997), Justice McLachlin, as she then was, touched upon the danger inherent in the first category, emphasizing the difficulties when the lifestyle in question is that of a pregnant woman whose liberty is intimately and inescapably bound to her unborn child. Justice McLachin asked: 'Are children to be permitted to sue their parents for second-hand smoke inhaled around the family dinner table? Could any cohabitant bring such an action? Are children to be permitted to sue their parents for spanking, causing psychological trauma or poor grades due to alcoholism or a parent's undue fondness for the office or the golf course?' (*Winnipeg Child and Family Services v. D.F.G.*, 1997, p. 947). Nevertheless, both the first and the second categories raise the question of whether the woman has a right to determine what will happen to her and her body.

The right of individuals to self-determination in health care related matters is deeply rooted in the common law. It is founded on the fundamental right to be left alone. It is tied to the right to privacy,[7] and 'turns on the subjective wishes of the patient, rather than on public opinion, state or familial preferences, or any objective test' (*In re Guardianship of Browning*, 1989, p. 273). The prohibition of an unwarranted invasion of the right to bodily integrity formulated the requirement of consent for medical treatment, and the doctrine of informed consent which was developed accordingly. The doctrine of consent, as will be elaborated on in chapter 5, is regarded as a fundamental human right that can also enjoy a constitutional protection (Sheikh, 2001, p. 76).

Moreover, as will be discussed in the next chapter, wide living will legislation provides individuals with the right of self-determination of what will happen to them when incompetent. In effect, all of these ethical-legal structures assure the 'liberty interest'[8] of a patient not to consent to some forms of medical treatment, including life sustaining treatment, nutrition and hydration. Although courts tend not to characterize this interest as a fundamental right, and hence ask for a 'clear and convincing evidence of the incompetent patient's wishes before treatment was discontinued' (*Cruzan v. Director, Missouri Department of Health*, 1990, p. 280) – a requirement that *de facto* is difficult to provide – the right to refuse life-sustaining treatment is classified as a constitutionally protected liberty interest under the Fourteenth Amendment to the American Constitution.

Perhaps the most far-reaching recognition of the right to refuse medical treatment has been manifested with the legal empowerment of terminal patients with the right to make decisions about their care, based on the *Cruzan* case (*Cruzan v. Director, Missouri Department of Health*, 1990). These decisions, along with the enactment of Oregon's Death with Dignity Act (1998), which allows physicians to prescribe deadly medications to their patients, and the abolishment of the crime of suicide, have created a new era. Although the courts are careful enough not to authorize physicians or the patient's next-of-kin to end a patient's life by lethal injection, mercy killing or active euthanasia, and despite the fact that courts are cautious in making decisions regarding assisted suicide, the law has recognized in a significant and meaningful way the right of individuals to make personal decisions including about their own death. I will turn to discuss these specific decisions now.

THE RIGHT TO REFUSE LIFE-SUSTAINING TREATMENT

The right to refuse life-sustaining treatment has been thoroughly developed in Canadian law. In *Malette v. Shulman* (1990), the Ontario Court of Appeal upheld a finding of battery against a physician who had ordered blood transfusions for an incompetent patient with life-threatening condition. Although the physician was aware that the patient had signed a Jehovah's Witness medical alert card, refusing blood under *any* circumstances, he ignored the directive in order to save her life. In 1992, the *Nancy B.* case explicitly recognized the right of a mentally competent patient to refuse artificial life-support and thereby hasten death (*Nancy B. v. Hotel-Dieu de Quebec et al.*, 1992). Nancy was totally and permanently paralyzed and unable to breathe on her own due to a neurological disease she suffered from. Nancy's request to disconnect the ventilator was acknowledged by the court although it was clear that such an action would inevitably lead to her death. The court justified its decision by holding that if Nancy died after the respiratory is disconnected it would not be an act of suicide, but rather, nature taking its course.

Originally, the right to refuse life-sustaining treatment was applied to patients in a permanent vegetative state, but it has subsequently been extended to patients in less extreme conditions, such as incompetent and terminally ill patients, competent and terminally ill patients, and even those who could be cured or have their lives significantly extended by treatment (Jordan, 1988, p. 1145).

Along with the recognition of the right for self-determination in the context of end-of-life issues is the legal opinion that 'insistence on heroic, but useless measures, is no more justified for the incompetent patient than it is for the competent'.[9] More generally, the focus should be on the efficacy of the treatment *to the patient* treated and not whether the patient is competent or not.[10] In fact, two Canadian cases support the view that futile treatment, which does not benefit the patient, should not be sought, even if ending the treatment results in the death of the patient (*Couture-Jacquet v. Montreol Children's Hospital*, 1986[11] and *Child and Family Services of Manitoba v. L. and H.*, 1997[12]). When focusing on the patient, maintaining a brain-dead pregnant woman for the delivery of her fetus is a futile treatment. When focusing on the fetus, letting the fetus die with its mother is not an act of assisted suicide. As Kristin Mulholland correctly argues 'unlike suicide, the discontinuance of treatment is not irrational self-destruction. It is an acceptance of death, not a desire for it that motivates the terminal patient' (Mulholland, 1987, p. 865).

Unlike the act of 'assisted suicide', the re-establishment and legalizing the distinction between 'passive' euthanasia and 'active' euthanasia is firmly rooted in medical law mainly through decision-making (Lemmens and Dickens, 2001) but also through public committees such as the the Royal Commission on Euthanasia and Assisted Suicide.[13] In the case of *Rodriguez v. British Columbia (Attorney General)* (1993), the Supreme Court of Canada upheld the constitutionality of the criminal offence of aiding anyone to commit suicide, set in section 241(b) of the Criminal Code. By this, the court rejected the claims of Sue Rodriguez, a 42-year-old woman who suffered from a devastating neurological disease, that the prohibition at the Criminal Code should be struck down. Although Rodriguez lost the trial and committed suicide by herself four months later, the court was sharply divided in its ruling (five to four).

The same legal opinion has been formed in the American context. In the case of *Washington v. Glucksberg* (1997), the court acknowledged that there was no fundamental right or liberty interest in physician-assisted suicide upon the Fourteenth Amendment of Due Process. In another case from the same year, the *Quill* case, the court ruled that the criminal prohibition of the State of New York against assisted suicide does not violate the Fourteenth Amendment of Due Process, thereby rejecting the argument that the law discriminated a person who is not on life-support over a patient who is on life-support, as the latter can ask for the cessation of his or her treatment (*Vacco v. Quill*, 1997).

It is thus clear that there is a difference between actively killing the fetus, as in abortion, and letting the fetus (passively) die along with the natural death of its mother. Deciding on the latter appears not to be in accordance with the common law principles on end-of-life issues.

PERSONAL DECISIONS AT PREGNANCY CONCERNING THE DEATH OF FETUSES

It seems that despite of these important changes, the law has remained conservative when personal decisions affect or result in the death of the fetus. In the case of *Re T*, for example, the English court of appeal considered such a decision as an exception to the general principle of free choice regarding medical treatment (*In re T*, 1992). Lord Donaldson stated in an *obiter dictum*:

> An adult patient who, like Miss T., suffers from no mental incapacity, has an absolute right to choose whether to consent to medical treatment, to refuse it or to choose one rather than another of the treatments being offered. The only possible qualification is a case in which the choice may lead to the death of a viable foetus.[14]

In *Re S.*, a competent pregnant woman refused to undergo cesarean section on religious grounds (*In re S.*, 1992). The woman's decision was supported by her husband. Nevertheless, she was forced to undergo the procedure on the evidence that the only means to save the woman, and the life of the fetus, was to carry out the cesarean section. The English court held that a cesarean section and any necessary consequential treatment aimed for the patient could be lawfully performed even with the patient's refusal, if it is vital for the patient's interests and those of her unborn child.

In a later case of *Re M.B.*, a cesarean section was recommended on a 40-weeks pregnant patient (*Re M.B.*, 1997). The mother had no objection, but she suffered from needle-phobia. The trial judge ordered to carry out the cesarean section with anesthesia. However, the English Court of Appeal delivered a reversed opinion in which it stated that:

> If the competent mother refuses to have the medical intervention, the doctors may not lawfully do more than attempt to persuade her. If that persuasion is unsuccessful, there are no further steps towards medical intervention to be taken. We recognize that the effect of these conclusions is that there will be situations in which the child may die or may be seriously handicapped because the mother said no and the obstetrician was not able to take the necessary steps to avoid the death or handicap. The mother may indeed later regret the outcome, but the alternative would be an unwanted invasion of the right of the woman to make the decision ... .[15]

Not only did the Court of Appeal rule against previous decisions, but it also relied on the *Re A.C.* case, which will be discussed below that held, under similar facts, an opposite result with a completely different justification (*In re A.C.*, 1990).

Indeed, the latter English case of *Re M.B.* was criticized for its wrong decision. Still, the cases described above represent the uncertainty that exists when the life of the fetus is at stake. Courts feel a need to protect the mother's interest to fully control her body and to determine what would happen to it, but they also appear to have a sense of responsibility to the fetus, regardless of the opinion of its competent mother about it. I would argue that the latter approach is no more than a paternalistic course of action that the courts undertake. It is a pedagogical role by which the courts see themselves better judges in all areas of life, including childbearing and family planning. No doubt, these matters lie at the 'very heart' of an individual's right to be free from any interventions when it comes to making important personal decisions. If the law truly wishes to protect this sanctified and nuclear right of a human being, it should let the competent woman make the decision by herself and be responsible for it, instead of patronizing over her.

The case of danger to the life of the fetus is, in my view, test-case for the protection of the woman's right to self-determination in the eyes of law. Just as one cannot be claimed to have freedom of speech when restrained from saying irritating and annoying things, a woman cannot be claimed to hold a right to self-determination if her most important decisions in life are dominated by a group of judges. Yet, this is a mere aspiration and may not necessarily represent the current legal view. If one wants to stick to the latter without the ambition to change it, I would suggest that the law, *as of today*, tends to regard the situation of danger to the life of a fetus as an exception to the woman's right to self-determination. Maintaining a woman on life-support for the sake of saving the life of her fetus, when it is in real and immediate danger could probably enjoy a legal support based on this analysis.

But the competing view may be sound as well. I will turn now to describe the special ways by which the law seeks to protect pregnant women's interests in cases of bodily interventions. I will identify three different means of legal protection: 1) Preventing attempts to restrict pregnant women in their life-styles; 2) denying physicians' actions for court orders which directly relate to the pregnant women's physical conditions; and 3) exempting pregnant mothers from tort liability over damage that allegedly originated during pregnancy.

Life-style legal interventions

As mentioned above, some of the legal interventions with the woman's pregnancy are in the form of interference with the pregnant woman's life style. By life style, I mean drinking habits, using drugs or other addictive substances, etc. Although they are distinguishable, life-style interventions are not necessarily more bearable than interventions directly related to the woman's physical condition. In this form of interventions, not only do courts use general principles with regard to a woman's right to self-determination, bodily integrity, and privacy, but they also address specific legislation from which they draw their authority to restrain the pregnant woman from acting in an allegedly dangerous way. Specifically, courts use child protection laws such as the Child and Family Services Act (1984) and the Mental Health Act (1980) to protect fetuses from the dangerous activities of their mother while pregnant. Although this legislation refers to a child as actually or apparently less than 16 years of age, courts tend to construe the legislative text so that it is also applied to a child while *in uterus* (*Re Children's Aid Society for the District of Kenora and L.J.*, 1981; *M. (J.) v. Superintendent of Family and Child Services*, 1982; *Re Children's Aid Society of City of Belleville and T.*, 1978). One of the arguments that support legal interventions during pregnancy is that just as the law prohibits parents from refusing to provide necessary medical treatment for their children and more generally to neglect them, it also should prohibit a woman from refusing treatment necessary to protect her fetus's health (Nelson, 1988, p. 1062). It is, nevertheless questionable whether such a comparison is in place.

The *D.F.G.* case serves as a good example of how the law can interfere with the liberty of pregnant women, mainly through restricting their habitual behaviors (*Winnipeg Child and Family Services v. D.F.G.*, 1996–7). Ms. G was the mother of three children, none of whom were living with her. She was five months pregnant and addicted to sniffing glue. Before the first order in case was issued, she had agreed to take treatment for her addiction. However, when arriving to escort her to the treatment centre, the social services agency worker found her intoxicated. On that occasion, the agency applied to have a mandatory detention order issued.

At the outset, the court relied on the language of the Mental Health Act to protect the fetus, which was found to be 'in need' for such a protection. The court ignored the evidence of an expert supporting the view that Ms. G. was competent and not suffering from any mental disorder. The court considered that the case in front of it required the execution of its inherit *parens patriae* jurisdiction over Ms. G., thereby extending this jurisdiction, which had formerly applied only to children, to also include fetuses. It ruled that Ms. G. would be detained in the custody of the Director of Child and Family Services until the birth of her child.

The Manitoba Court of Appeal struck down the detention order, finding no evidence to support the conclusion that Ms. G. was incompetent under the Mental Health Act, and holding that the trial judge was wrong in relying on the doctrine of *parens patriae*. In practice, Ms. G. voluntary remained at the Health Sciences Center until she delivered a healthy child who remained in her custody.

The Child and Family Services Agency was granted leave to appeal to the Supreme Court of Canada. The majority of the court held that neither statute, liability of the pregnant woman in tort law, nor the doctrine of *parens patriae* could support an order of detention and force treatment on the woman. The court emphasized that the fetus has *no legal rights until it is born*, and held that the Agency was not authorized to act on behalf of a legal person in seeking a detention order. Since changing the existing legal view would have far reaching implications on the lives of women in general, the court emphasized that such a change, if at all, should be made by the legislator.

Justice Major, who wrote the dissent opinion, held that it would be permissible to interfere with a woman's pregnancy only when four accumulative pre-conditions are met: the woman has to decide to carry the pregnancy to term; there is a proof, on a balance of probabilities, that the abusive activity which allegedly endangers the fetus, will cause serious and irreparable harm to the fetus; the remedy proposed is the least intrusive option possible; and the process of intervention is procedurally fair.[16]

Of course, the fact that a woman decides to continue pregnancy to term is not conclusive. A pregnant woman may continue her pregnancy not as a result of deliberate choice but because of lack of access to therapeutic abortion, or cultural, social, familial or other personal constraints. Thus, it seems that the 'heart' of the *D.F.G.* test lies in the last three elements of it. Applying these elements to the case of a pregnant brain-dead woman does not necessarily lead to a definitive conclusion. On the one hand, letting the woman die will inevitably result in the fetus's death. This is, of course, a serious and irreparable harm to the fetus. On the other hand, in contrast to forcing a woman to avoid a dangerous activity – a focused legal intervention that saves the fetus from a specific physical harm – keeping the mother 'alive' does not guarantee a successful outcome for the fetus. In many cases, the fetus dies *in uterus* or shortly after its delivery. Moreover, one can argue that maintaining the dead woman on life-support is not the least intrusive option possible, as there are no other options available to save the fetus. The *D.F.G.* test is designed to examine a proposed medical intervention in light of *other possible interventions*. It cannot be applied to a case where there is only one possible option of intervention in the woman's pregnancy.

Interventions with the pregnant woman's physical state

In addition to legal interventions with the woman's behavior or life style, another form of legal intervention is one that directly relates to the pregnant woman's physical condition. It includes forcing pregnant women to undergo certain medical treatments, have blood transfusions, or go through a cesarean section. Although there is a significant difference between the levels at which these various legal interventions violate the woman's liberty, courts tend to regard them in the same way. In most cases, courts use the same method of balancing the women's interest and the interest of the state in protecting potential life, and they also apply the same principles in nearly all of them. I will turn now to present some actual cases, which will reflect the way these interventions take place.

Blood transfusions

Usually, forcing a pregnant woman to have blood transfusions occurs when her religious views prevent her from consenting to this treatment. The legal intervention takes place when physicians want to save the life of the mother, her fetus, or both despite the pregnant woman's refusal. Although from an objective point of view, giving blood transfusions to a non-consenting pregnant woman is not as bodily invasive as a performing a cesarean section, it is a physical action that without a legal authorization would be considered a battery.

In *Raleigh Fitkin-Paul Morgan Memorial Hospital v. Anderson* (1964), a woman in her 32nd week of pregnancy was ordered to have blood transfusions if these were necessary to save her and/or her unborn child's lives. The legal background for the decision was not brought by the court. Rather, the court held that the welfare of the mother and child were so intertwined and inseparable, that it would be unreasonably difficult to distinguish between them. An interesting move by the court in this case was to legally compare a fetus to a child, and hence to ignore the legal significance of the common-law distinction between a child and a fetus. The rationale for such a move is that a child could be given transfusions over the parent's objections, and could even sue his or her parents for injuries inflicted prior to birth. By comparing the fetus to a child, the court also provided the fetus with a legal protection, hence forcing the pregnant mother to have blood transfusions.

Sometimes, the legal intervention with the pregnant woman's body goes against her explicit advance directive. In the English case of *In re T.*, for instance, the woman was required to have an urgent blood transfusion after she had given birth to a stillborn baby. Although the woman was a member of the Jehovah's Witnesses and had indicated earlier that she did not wish to have a blood transfusion, the English court ignored her express wishes. The court found that woman had not considered in her advance directive the possibility that she might die if she did not receive a blood transfusion. Consequently, the court held that her directive could not apply to the circumstances of that case (*In re T.*, 1992).

Cesarean sections

At times, pregnant women are forced to undergo more invasive and dangerous medical treatments than interference with their habitual actions or the forcing them to accept blood transfusions against their will. One example of such a medical treatment involves forced cesarean section. Due to its medical complications and to its advanced degree of intrusion on a woman's right of self-determination, bodily integrity and privacy, I will turn now elaborate on this specific legal intervention.

Cesarean section carries a very high risk of maternal death. Reports in the literature suggest that the maternal mortality rate is three to 30 times more than that associated with vaginal delivery (Gallagher, 1989, p. 207). Also 10–65 per cent of women who deliver by cesarean section, experience post-surgical infections – a rate five to ten times more than the risk following vaginal delivery.[17] Cesarean section can also cause complications for babies. The most serious risk is that of respiratory distress, a breathing difficulty caused by lung immaturity in newborns delivered too early. In addition, cesarean section can adversely affect the woman's future reproductive life, increasing the likelihood of rupture of her uterus in future pregnancies and of repeat cesarean section for each future delivery (Gallagher, 1989).

Besides these physical complications, surgical delivery may also have a negative impact on a woman's ability and motivation to care for and establish a relationship with her newborn. It is reported that women after cesarean section experience more pain, weakness and difficulty in caring for their newborns. Some of them report feelings of isolation, humiliation, anger, self-blame, and deep disappointment after undergoing cesarean section (Gallagher, 1989, p. 208).

There is also a deterrent effect of forced cesarean on pregnant women. Women fearful of forced cesareans may also avoid prenatal care altogether. They can consequently decide not to return to any hospital and give vaginal birth safely at home.

The physical circumstances of a pregnant woman, who has to make a decision whether to consent to cesarean section or not, can be very difficult. While usually under active labor, a pregnant woman has to balance the possible bad consequences that may derive from cesarean section with an estimation regarding the fetus's potential future life. This is a very stressful situation. As Alan Fleischman explains:

> The woman is lying in bed, in at least intermittent pain and probably constant discomfort; she is attached to several devices, including an intravenous infusion and a fetal monitor; and she may have received medication for pain relief that can affect her ability to analyse alternatives. This may result in the woman not being able to make a clear, rational and informed choice. Most frequently, she respects the advice of her physician and concurs with the proposed plan presented as the best course for her baby. The atypical woman, who questions the certainty of the recommendation, voices concern about her own well-being, or raises a question about the motivation of the physician concerning future malpractice protection is viewed by the physician and other caregivers as a difficult, non-compliant patient who wishes to hurt her baby.[18]

In addition to these physical obstacles, there is an inherent impediment based on the process of assessing the need for the proposed medical treatment and advocating for it. Deciding on a cesarean section involves medical judgment rather than certainty. This is an evaluative process. Not surprisingly, in many instances this judgment has proved to be wrong. Study has shown, for example, that in 1986 about half of the 906,000 cesareans performed were unnecessary.[19] It is also believed that one of the key factors leading to doctors' over-reliance upon cesarean sections is their enormous fear of malpractice suits if a child is born with a condition that could arguably have been prevented by surgical delivery. This fear has some evidence base. As Janet Gallagher mentions, obstetricians are subject to more frequent malpractice lawsuits than most other specialists, and damages in obstetrical cases, especially the 'brain-damaged baby' cases, can be spectacularly high (Gallagher, 1989, p. 210; Fleischman, 1989, p. 252).

Notwithstanding the danger to the women's physical and mental health and the potential complications to newborns in surgical deliveries, court orders for cesarean sections are often sought by doctors. In some cases, orders are issued regardless of the elemental difficulties in the maternal bodily circumstances and the risks that are built in the medical assessment for such surgeries. However, in most cases, courts protect women from bodily intervention without their consent, even when refraining to do so could seriously endanger the women and/or their fetuses.

In *Jefferson v. Griffin Spalding County Hospital* (1981), the respondent petitioned the Superior Court of Butts County for an order authorizing it to perform a cesarean section and any necessary blood transfusions upon the defendant who was an out-patient resident of Butts County in the event she presented herself to the hospital for delivery of her unborn child, which was due four days after the petition.

The woman was in the 39th week of pregnancy. A few weeks before the petition, she had presented herself to the respondent for pre-natal care. She was found to have a complete placenta previa, and the doctors assessed that it was a 99 per cent certainty that the child could not survive if it was delivered by vaginal delivery. On the basis of religious beliefs, the woman advised the Hospital that she did not wish surgical removal of the child and would not submit to it. Further, she refused to take any transfusion of blood. Although the defendant *did not appear* to the superior court, the hospital was authorized to administer to the defendant all medical procedures deemed necessary. The authorization was set to be effective only if the defendant voluntarily sought admission to either of the respondent's hospitals for the emergency delivery of her child.

In a following procedure, initiated by the State of Georgia Department of Human Resources and the Butts County Department of Family and Children Services, temporary custody of the unborn child was granted to the petitioners. The Superior Court ruled that the Department had to have full authority to make all decisions, including giving consent to the surgical delivery appertaining to the birth of the child. Although the parents explained their religious resistance to the medical interventions, they were taken out of the picture. The court stated that the state has an interest in the life of the unborn, which is regarded as a living human being. The court also found that the intrusion involved into the life of the parents is outweighed by the duty of the state to protect a living, unborn human being from meeting his or her death before being given the opportunity to live. Nevertheless, the court did not discuss how this potential life is going to be, and ignored parents' view regarding such potential.

On appeal [by the parents], the court justified the infringement upon the woman's right to religious freedom and bodily integrity by stating that the life of the viable fetus was intertwined with the mother's. The court found it necessary to give the child an opportunity to live. Thus, contrary to the woman's view, which was also supported by the father of the unborn, the court denied appellant's motion.

The most striking case concerning forced cesarean section is that of *A.C.* (*In re A.C.*, 1987–90). Angie C., a pregnant woman in her 25th week, was diagnosed as having a tumor mass on her lung and admitted to hospital. She deteriorated within days, and was heavily sedated so that she could continue to breathe. The hospital sought a trial court order to obtain permission to proceed a cesarean operation at 26 weeks.

As reflected in Angie's physician's testimony, Angie apparently had agreed to have a cesarean section preformed at 28-weeks gestation, when the fetus would have a reasonable chance of survival, but she had been unable to discuss an earlier date for the operation before she was sedated. Angie's physician, Dr Hamner, testified that:

> We had talked about the possibility at 28 weeks, if she had to be intubated, if this was a terminal event, would we intervene, and the expression was yes, that we would, because we felt at 28 weeks we had much more to offer as far as taking care of the child.[20]

Another evidence which was presented to court was that of Dr. Lawrence Lessin, an oncologist and another of Angie's treating physicians. Dr. Lessin testified that in meetings with Angie, he had heard nothing to indicate that, if faced with the decision, she would have refused permission for a cesarean section. Contrary to these opinions, Dr. Weingold, an obstetrician who was one of Angie's treating physicians, opposed the operation because he believed Angie had not seriously considered that she might not survive the birth of her baby. Dr. Weingold testified that at some point, Angie had said 'I don't want it done'. Thus, there was, in fact, considerable dispute as to whether Angie would have consented to an immediate cesarean delivery at the time the hearing was held.

Despite the contradictory evidence, and regardless of the fact that there had been some testimony that the operation may very well hasten the death of Angie, the trial court determined that the operation should proceed. The trial court based its decision on the state interest in protecting the life of the fetus after viability established in *Roe v. Wade* (1973). The right to privacy was declared to also include a right to bodily integrity, and the latter was also held to consist of the freedom to refuse medical treatment. However, the trial court added that the state has an interest in preserving life overriding the patient's choice to refuse medical treatment where the life of an innocent *third party* is at stake. The court took into consideration the fact that such an intervention will not make so much harm to Angie since she 'had, at best, two days left of sedated life; the complications arising from the surgery would not significantly alter that prognosis' (*In re A.C.*, 1987, p. 617).

An attempt was made to secure a stay from the court of appeals, but the motion was denied. The operation was performed and the baby died immediately. Angie died two days later. A few months later, the court ordered the case heard *en banc* and vacated the opinion of the motions division (*In re A.C.*, 1988). Although the case was moot in the sense that the surgery, which was ordered by the trial court, had been already performed, the court felt it was important to discuss the legal consequences of this case.

The court of appeal emphasized that from the available evidence, one could not tell whether Angie would have consented to the surgery or not. The court re-acknowledged the right of every competent person to make an informed choice to accept or forego medical treatment. The court also held that in some cases, especially those involving life-or-death situations or incompetent patients, there are four countervailing interests that may involve the state as *parens patriae*: preserving life, preventing suicide, maintaining the ethical integrity of the medical profession, and protecting third parties. Since only the state's interest in preserving life was at stake in the case of *A.C.*, the court emphasized that such an interest must be *truly compelling* to justify overriding a competent person's right to refuse medical treatment. The same is true for incompetent patients, who have just as much right as competent patients to have their decisions they made while competent respected, even in a substituted judgment framework.

More importantly to our case, the court went on to rule that the right of bodily integrity belongs equally to persons who are competent and to persons who are not, and that such a right is not extinguished 'simply because someone is ill, or *even at death's door* [my emphasis]' (*In re A.C.*, 1990, p. 1247). Finally, the court concluded that without a competent refusal from Angie to undergo the surgery, and without a finding through substituted judgment that Angie would not have consented to the surgery, the court of appeal held that it was an error for the trial court to proceed to a balancing analysis, weighing the rights of Angie against the interests of the state.

Belson Judge, who wrote the dissenting opinion, stated that in the rare instances in which the viable unborn child's interest in living and the state's parallel interest in protecting human life come into conflict with the mother's decision to forego a procedure such as a cesarean section, a balance should be struck in which the unborn child's and the state's interests are entitled to substantial weight (*In re A.C.*, 1990, p. 1254). He further added that when the unborn child reaches the state of viability, the child becomes *a party* whose interests must be considered, and declared that a viable unborn child is a *person* at common law, who has legal rights that are entitled to the protection of the courts (*In re A.C.*, 1990, p. 1255).

The *A.C.* case is a tragic one, not only because of the sorrowful fact that both Angie and her child died soon after the cesarean section, but especially given the serious dispute over the evidence regarding Angie's consent to the surgery. Still, it reflects a solid legal approach that recognizes the woman's right to self-determination and bodily integrity even with the cost of the death of her *viable* fetus. By vacating the legal opinion of the trial court, the court of appeal not only emphasized the importance of obtaining the competent woman's consent to bodily interventions over her body, but it also made even the requirement of consent from a competent patient to that from an incompetent patient, including one, who is 'at death's door'.

In the *Baby Doe* case an action was brought to compel a pregnant woman to undergo a cesarean section (*In re Baby Boy Doe*, 1994). The fetus was 36 and a half weeks, and the mother refused to have a cesarean section due to her religious beliefs. The Circuit Court denied relief, and appeal was taken.

On appeal, both the state and the Public Guardian argued that the circuit court should have balanced the woman's rights with the rights of the unborn viable fetus, which was nearly at full term and which, according to expert testimony, would have been born dead or severely disabled if Doe delivered vaginally.

The Appellate Court of the state of Illinois held that courts should not engage in such a balancing, and that a competent woman's choice to refuse cesarean section during pregnancy must be honored, *even in circumstances where the choice may be harmful to her fetus*. The court also held that a forced cesarean section, undertaken for the benefit of the fetus, cannot pass constitutional muster. The court stated:

> A woman's right to refuse invasive medical treatment, derived from her rights to privacy, bodily integrity, and religious liberty, is not diminished during pregnancy. The woman retains the same right to refuse invasive treatment, even of lifesaving or other beneficial nature, that she can exercise when she is not pregnant. *The potential impact upon the fetus is not legally relevant* [my emphasis].[21]

Finally, in the British case of *M.B.* (1997), a cesarean section under anesthesia was ordered to a pregnant woman who suffered from a needle-phobia but did not oppose the intervention. Despite the court's intervention a wide protection was given to the pregnant woman, one that outweighed the interest in protecting the potential life of the fetus as a recognized interest of the state in the American Jurisprudence. The English court declared that a woman has an *absolute* right to refuse to consent to medical treatment for *any reason*, rational or irrational, or *for no reason at all*, even when the decision may lead to her death. Moreover, the court ignored the viability criterion regarding that interest. Butler-Sloss L.J. stated that:

> ... The foetus *up to the moment of birth* does not have any separate interests capable of being taken into account when a court has to consider an application for a declaration in respect of a caesarean section operation. The court does not have the jurisdiction to declare that such medical intervention is lawful to protect the interests of the unborn child *even at the point of birth*.[22]

As discussed above, a great number of cases have involved direct legal attempts to intervene with the pregnant woman's physical condition, mostly without her approval. Although the severity of the interference in the woman's right to self-determination and bodily integrity varies from case to case, in most cases courts try to balance the woman's interests with the state interest in protecting the life of the unborn, and often viable fetus. While all these cases depart from the same point – the *Roe v. Wade* decision – they reach different destinies. Some are way too far from *Roe*, pronouncing an absolute right to refuse treatment, and consider the potential impact of the mother's decision upon the fetus as irrelevant. Others are more moderate in their holdings, thereby balancing the woman's interests with the state interest in potential life, and giving the latter more weight when the fetus is viable. It seems to me that all these cases reflect is a tendency of the courts to protect the woman's right to refuse treatment to a higher degree than the ones in the abortion context set in *Roe*. These cases also reflect an inclination to ask for a more serious harm to the fetus, if at all, in order to allow any interference with the pregnant woman's liberties.

Applying this reasoning to the case of a brain-dead pregnant woman by equalizing the requirement of consent from a competent woman to that from an incompetent woman can raise the necessity of the requirement to seek the woman's view on the proposed medical intervention. Whether through an advance directive or other methods used to infer the woman's opinion about the intended medical procedure, obtaining the woman's consent seems to be a precondition for any potential intervention with her body. Moreover, in contrast to the abortion context analysed in chapter 1, suggested in these cases is that the death of a fetus is not necessarily considered to be an unbearable result by the law, especially if the bodily intervention during pregnancy that aiming to save the life of the fetus is made without the woman's approval. Finally, as demonstrated by these cases, the debate over whether to intervene with the pregnant woman's body is one in which the mother and the state that purports to protect potential life, are the only participants. It seems that even at point of viability, the biological father of the fetus is out of this legal picture. If this is true, then asking for the view of the biological father of the fetus on the question of whether to maintain the dead woman on life-support or not, is irrelevant in the eyes of law. It is relevant only if and in as much as the biological father sheds light *on the woman's view*, but not otherwise.

Legal interventions through releasing pregnant women from tort liability

Another way in which courts chose to protect pregnant women from being bodily interfered with is through denying actions of impaired children for tort liability based on alleged harm caused by maternal conduct during pregnancy. In the *Dobson* case, the defendant was 27 weeks pregnant when had a car accident. Her son, who brought the action, was born with mental and physical impairments allegedly resulting from the accident (*Dobson (Litigation Guardian of) v. Dobson*, 1999).

The Supreme Court of Canada held that an action for alleged negligence during pregnancy would not lie against the mother. The court distinguished between obligations that would be imposed on a third party tort-feasor and those imposed on pregnant women themselves. From a public policy perspective, the court ruled that imposing a duty of care on pregnant women with regard to the fetus would interfere with the privacy and autonomy rights of women and engage the court in the difficult task of applying a judicial standard of conduct to the way pregnant women behave. In the court's view, imposing a duty of care upon the mother would not only constitute an extensive and unacceptable intrusion into her bodily integrity, privacy and autonomy, but would also constitute a 'severe intrusion into the lives of pregnant women, with attendant and potentially damaging effects on the family unit' (*Dobson (Litigation Guardian of) v. Dobson*, 1999, p. 775).

To sum up, the law protects the pregnant woman's right to self-determination and bodily integrity, whether competent or not, in three different ways: 1) preventing attempts to restrict pregnant women in their life-styles; 2) impeding physicians' actions for court-orders which were directly related to the pregnant women's physical conditions; and 3) releasing the pregnant mother from tort liability over damage that allegedly originated in pregnancy. In addition to their physical and emotional immediate outcomes, it appears that legal interventions with the pregnant woman's body are also wrong for indirect reasons. I will end this chapter by discussing a few of them.

DUTY TO RESCUE

One of the criticisms against judicial decisions imposing treatment upon pregnant women is that these decisions contradict the common-law rule to deny a duty to rescue (Lederman, 1994, p. 358). In contrast to civil law, common law courts do not compel one person to go through a significant intrusion upon his or her bodily integrity merely for the benefit of another person's health (*In re A.C.*, 1990, pp. 1243–4), even in cases where avoiding doing so would result in *the death* of the endangered person. This rule was established in the famous case of *Shimp v. McFall* (1978), where the court refused to order Shimp to donate bone marrow which was necessary to save the life of his cousin, McFall.

This rule against a duty to rescue was also specifically incorporated to the fetal-maternal relationship when the court ruled that the mother does not owe a duty to rescue the fetus, as the latter cannot have rights in this respect superior to those of a person who has already been born (*In re A.C.*, 1990, p. 1244). When taken strictly, this argument might not fully apply to the situation of a brain-dead pregnant woman who is being legally dead and hence without legal rights. As will be shown in chapter 5, the idea that the dead do not retain some of their rights or interests after death has many difficulties. But besides these difficulties, the absorption of this view into the maternal-fetal relationship reflects the perception that the law does not see this relationship as an exception to the non-obligatory nature of the duty to rescue under common law. This is especially true considering the dubious moral and legal status of the fetus.

IMPLICATIONS FOR PHYSICIANS

Legal interventions are unfavorable not only because of how they interfere with the pregnant woman's right of self-determination but also for their implications on physicians. The request for a court order in these cases demonstrates the physician's willingness to use physical force against a competent adult. This seems to me an unethical behavior and a violation of the physicians' fiduciary obligations to their patients. The tendency to resort to judicial intervention in cases of refusal to treatment may create an obligation for the physician to obtain a court order in any situation in which a pregnant woman's preference does not accord with the physician's evaluation of the fetus's needs. Sometimes, this conflict is wrongly resolved by transferring the treatment of the woman to another physician. Dr. Robert Goodlin, for example, reports on a court order for cesarean section on a dying pregnant woman against her refusal and the refusal of her obstetrician. After an appeal to the judge, another obstetrician on court order, nevertheless, performed the surgery, and the nonviable fetus died two hours later (Goodlin, 1989).

Moreover, developing a routine of legal intervention with pregnant women's body could create a legal obligation for physicians to seek court orders. Physicians may then be found negligent for not seeking a court order in situations where a pregnant woman's decision resulted in fetal impairment. Likewise, physicians would most likely be required to participate in the practical aspects of enforcing an overriding of a pregnant woman's treatment decision. The new role of physicians as legal enforcers will create adversarial relationships between physicians and their pregnant patients, and would damage the treatment relationship characterized with faith and trust between physicians and patients.

GENERAL EFFECT ON WOMEN

Legal interventions during pregnancies, undoubtedly, affect the woman involved, but also have broad implications on all women. They shape a negative image of the refusing pregnant woman. This image could be broadened to a larger picture of women in general. As Laura Purdy observes, 'Peeping out from under such judgments would be the assumption that women in general are self-centred, thoughtless individuals who cannot be expected to behave morally' (Purdy, 1990, p. 288).

In an indirect way, legal interventions with the body of a pregnant woman increase the domination of women by men and their subordination to court orders and reviews by 'an objective' opinion, where mostly men are in positions of power and decision making. In her criticism on the *D.F.G.* case, Sanda Rodgers argues that neither the majority nor the minority explicitly considered the proposed state interference in the reproductive lives of women *in a manner fully compatible with women's equality and participation in Canadian life* (Rodgers, 2002, p. 353). Rodgers adds that the court also failed to consider that state interference would be imposed on women disproportionately to men. In this regard, in addition to being discriminated on the basis of their pregnancy – a base which has already been recognized as impermissible sex-based discrimination[23] – pregnant women will be devalued and their needs will be ignored except to the degree that they serve the fetus within their reproduction capacity.

CONCLUSION

While the fetus is within the body of a pregnant woman, the power and responsibility to choose medical treatment must rest *with her*. The questions of legal interventions with the pregnant woman's body should not be questions that focus on the fetus, its status, whether he or she is a person, and whether he or she has a right to life. Rather, these are questions on the woman's rights to carry and bear children with dignity. As Janet Gallagher writes:

> Women have been driven into hiding, tied down to operating tables, and cut open against their will. They have been frightened away from hospital and prenatal care.

Legal enforcement of the primacy of the 'fetus as patient' threatens to create a climate in which pregnancy and birth are laced with intimidation, coercion, and raw physical violence.[24]

The ongoing call for protection of the life of the fetus troubles me. It seems that there can be no stopping point or 'bright line' to the fetal rights demands. John Robertson, for example, argues that, under *Roe v. Wade*, it would be legally permissible to order the forced feeding of a pregnant anorexic teenager (Robertson, 1984, p. 356). In another place, he claims that it is not unreasonable to require a woman, who had not yet had her pregnancy confirmed, to have a pregnancy test or to refrain from activities that would be hazardous to the fetus if she were pregnant (Robertson, 1984, p. 447). More generally, Robertson argues that it is reasonable to regard mothers as having a moral duty to the babies they choose to deliver. He emphasizes that mothers (and fathers) have moral obligation to refrain from harming their children *before* they are born just as they owe them the same obligation *after* they are born. In his view, if it is wrong to neglect or abuse a child *ex-utero*, then it is wrong to neglect or abuse a child *in utero* (Robertson, 1989). How far *in utero* is enough? How much can we expect pregnant women to bear?

Pregnant women, like other women and like other men, enjoy a right to self-determination and to bodily integrity. As long as they appreciate it, they deserve the right to say 'no'. They should not be discriminated against on the basis of their pregnancy. Hence, no duty to rescue the fetus shall be owed by them, even when the fetus is about to die. Like other moral beings, women are responsible for their acts. There is no meaning to talk about protecting potential life when the mother of such a potential being, who fully dominates its evolution, and whose consent to continue the pregnancy is a precondition for it to become real, chooses to risk herself with the fetus. The potential life does not exist in a void. The state's interest in potential life is, thus, dependent on the mother's willingness to have *within her body* such a potential.

Forcing medical treatment on pregnant women is wrong from beginning to end. It starts with inherent procedural obstacles that are accompanied by an unstable physical situation of the pregnant mother, who is at stake. On an immediate level, it ends with the possible imposing of physical and emotional danger to the mother and her fetus. In an indirect level, it puts physicians in an adversarial role and damages their relationship with pregnant patients. It also increases the subordination of women and devalues them as a group.

Therefore, forcing medical treatment on pregnant women should be justified only in very exceptional cases. The strongest case for forcing treatment should be a one-time intervention of minimal risk to the mother, such as administering a drug, blood, or surgery, when it follows from the circumstances, that the mother does not appreciate her condition, and therefore cannot give consent.

Approaching legal interventions with pregnant women's bodies the way I suggest can illuminate on the case of a brain-dead pregnant woman, whose maintenance on life support is being considered. As I have showed above, applying the *D.F.G.* test to medical interventions here does not necessarily lead to a definitive conclusion. No doubt, letting the woman die will inevitably result in a serious and irreparable harm to the fetus. On the other hand, keeping the mother 'alive' does not guarantee, like other medical interventions, a successful outcome for the fetus. Moreover, it cannot be said to be the least intrusive option possible, as there are no other options available to save the fetus.

Nevertheless, a better lesson can be taught from the cases, which deal with legal interventions directly related to the pregnant woman's physical condition. It follows that there is a great necessity to examine the woman's view on the proposed medical intervention. Obtaining the woman's consent seems to be a precondition to any possible intervention with her body, including maintenance on life-support. These cases can also support the conclusion that the death of a fetus could not necessarily be considered a non-bearable result by the law, when the proposed bodily intervention – maintaining the dead mother on life support – is done without her approval. Finally, as demonstrated by these cases, asking for the view of the biological father of the fetus on whether to maintain the dead woman on life-support or not, is irrelevant in the eyes of law. It can be relevant only if the biological father sheds light *on the woman's view*, but not otherwise. Focusing on the woman's prior wishes would naturally bring us to the next chapter on advance directives and pregnancy clauses.

NOTES

1 But see the recent decision of the American Supreme Court in *Ferguson v. City of Charleston* (2001). The court held that the practice of a state hospital to routinely examine the urine of pregnant patients for drugs and refer women, whose tests were positive, to the police for criminal prosecutions, violates the constitutional prohibition against unreasonable searches.
2 See Janet Gallagher, who discusses some extreme suggestions brought in the literature to intervene in pregnant women's lives: Gallagher, 1989. pp. 200–3.
3 As reported in the media, the following examples reflect the personal implications of such legal interventions. A woman was charged with child abuse after giving birth to her second cocaine-addicted baby; her child was placed in foster care. In another case, a woman was jailed for a week after she gave birth to a brain-damaged baby; she was accused, among other things, of drug abuse. In a third case, a woman arrested for cheque forgery was found to be using cocaine; a judge sent her to jail for four months to protect her fetus. See *Time*, 22 May 1989, p. 45.
4 The American College of Obstetricians and Gynecologists, *Patient Choice and the Maternal-Fetal Relationship: Committee opinion 214* (April 1999) 61 at 63. See also American College of Obstetricians and Gynecologists, *Patient Choice: Maternal-Fetal Conflict. Washington*, DC, Committee on Ethics, 1987.
5 For more discussion about the procedure of court-order hearings see Purdy, 1990, pp. 280–2 and Annas, 1987.
6 For a different distinction see Johnson, 1992. Johnson distinguishes between two models of social goals in supporting healthy pregnancies and birth outcomes. The first is the adversarial model, in which the state through its actors, mostly physicians, attempts to use the law to control and regulate pregnant women's behavior in the name of protecting fetal rights. The second is the 'facilitative model', which is premised on the view that pregnant women and fetuses are theoretically, legally and physically inseparable and that an extended set of services provided by the state and

available to all pregnant women will most effectively facilitate the goal of promoting the birth of healthy babies.

7 The right to privacy extends also to allow *a patient's surrogate* the right to refuse medical treatment for the patient. See *In re Quinlan*, 1976. It has been suggested that the privacy interest in bodily integrity is even more fundamental than the privacy interest in terminating pregnancy: MacAvoy-Smitzer, 1987, p. 1290.

8 Recognized basically under the 'due process clause', in the US. See *Cruzan v. Director, Missouri Department of Health*, 1990.

9 Law Reform Commission of Canada (1982), *Working Paper No. 28: Euthanasia, Aiding Suicide and Cessation of Treatment*, Ottawa, Canada: Minister of Supply and Services Canada, p. 57.

10 In its report, Law Reform Commission of Canada (1983), *Report 20: Euthanasia, Aiding Suicide and Cessation of Treatment*, Ottawa, Canada: Minister of Supply and Services Canada, p. 24, the Commission recommended that physicians would not be legally bound to continue administering or undertaking medical treatment, *when such a treatment has become therapeutically useless and is not in the best interest of the person for whom it is intended*.

11 In this case, a mother and grandmother of a three-year-old patient refused to have a fourth series of chemotherapy where the chance of striking down the child's cancer was estimated at 10–20 per cent. The court ruled in favor of the appellants and noted that the odds were heavily weighted against a successful outcome.

12 In this case, the patient, a three-month-old child, suffered from 'shaken baby syndrome', and was in a permanent vegetative state. The Child and Family Services of Manitoba joined the recommendation of the child's physician that a Do Not Resuscitate order be entered on the patient's chart. The patient's parents refused this recommendation and the agency went to court to seek an approval for the order. The order was granted and on appeal, the High Court of Justice concluded at p. 138 that 'there is no legal obligation on a medical doctor to take heroic measures to maintain the life of a patient in an irreversible vegetative state'.

13 Report of the Special Senate Committee on Euthanasia and Assisted Suicide (1995), *Of Life and Death*, Ottawa, Canada: Minister of Supply and Services, p. 51.

14 *In re T*, 1992, pp. 652–3.

15 *Re M.B.*, 1997, p. 224.

16 For a critique on that test see Rodgers, 2002, pp. 351–2.

17 Common infections include intrauterine, cystitis, peritonitis, abscess, gangrene, sepsis, urinary infections, and respiratory infections (Gallagher, 1989, p. 207).

18 Fleischman, 1989, pp. 252–3.

19 Janet Gallagher mentions at least six cases, in which doctors have declared cesareans necessary and asked judges to order surgery, and the women proceeded to give vaginal birth to healthy children. See Gallagher, 1989, pp. 205–7.

20 *In re A.C.*, 1990, pp. 1239–40.

21 *In re Baby Boy Doe*, 1994, p. 401.

22 *Re M.B.*, 1997, p. 227.

23 *Brooks v. Canada Safeway Ltd.*, 1989; *Symes v. R.*, 1993.

24 Gallagher, 1989, pp. 215–16.

Chapter 3

Pregnancy Clauses in Advance Directive Legislation

In the previous chapter, I discussed the importance of respecting the pregnant woman's wishes regarding the proposed medical treatment. In this chapter I will discuss the use of advance directives (specifically, living wills) – a common way to ensure such respect in circumstances when a woman is no longer capable of expressing her wishes directly herself.

Living wills are documents that give instructions to health-care providers about particular kinds of medical care that an individual would or would not want to have if rendered incompetent. Under the American legal system, pregnant women are not allowed, in most cases, to express their will at all, merely due to the fact that they are pregnant. In other cases, their will is much weaker than those of other women, not to mention other men. In Canada, however, the law is silent on this matter: in contrast to the American legal system, no special provision relates to the state of pregnancy. From this silence one can infer two possible conclusions. First, that Canada has a gap in its living will legislation concerning pregnant women. This gap could be attributed to the legislator who was not fully aware of the possibility that incompetency may also occur during pregnancy. Second, that Canada considered the American model and decided to reject it due to legal and cultural differences between the two nations. Of course, choosing one interpretation over the other has far-reaching practical implications. But what is it that we have to choose?

In order to answer the question suggested above, this chapter will examine the role of living wills at pregnancy. After a short introduction on advance directives – a broader group of living wills – I will describe the regulation of advance directives as they apply to pregnant incompetent women. I will include in this description the American, Canadian and English legal systems. Then, I will analyse the arguments that are invoked in the context of pregnancy limitations under living will legislation. Finally, I will make recommendations for what I see the most appropriate legal regime for Canada. My recommendations will consider the Canadian legal approach to living will legislation, in general, and to pregnant women, in particular. These recommendations will be linked also to my previous discussions on abortions and bodily interventions during pregnancy.

INTRODUCTION

Definitions

An advance directive is a legally binding document consisting of a living will, a durable power of attorney or both. A living will is 'the individual's written directive specifying that if the individual becomes terminally ill or goes into irreversible vegetative state, the individual's care givers should not use artificial life support procedures' (Benton, 1990, p. 1822).

Durable power of attorney, often referred to as a proxy directive, permits individuals to appoint another person to make health related decisions for themselves when they are incapable to do so. The significant advantage that a proxy directive has over a living will is that it provides a means for decision-making, even when the situation that actually arises *is not one that the patient might have contemplated*, and to which a living will might be inapplicable, or might lead to results that the patient would not have wanted.

Both a living will and a proxy directive are mechanisms by which competent individuals plan for medical decision-making, at some future time, when they might no longer possess decision-making capacity.[1] This stands in contrast to the ordinary medical decision-making process for competent patients, which is contemporaneous.

Purposes of advance directives

In his book, *The Right to Die*, Alan Meisel identifies three general and interconnected purposes for advance directives (Meisel, 1995, 6). The first, which he finds the most important from the perspective of those who issue the directives, is to provide a means of exercising some degree of control over medical care. As the core concept behind living wills lie in the right to privacy and autonomy in medical decision making, the primary purpose of a living will is to ensure that the individual's wishes are respected.[2] Living people are comforted with knowing that that their bodies will be treated with dignity and that their wishes will be followed, after they die. Under this purpose, advance directives effectuate the patient's own choice, thereby honoring the patient's right to self-determination even when she no longer possesses the capacity for it.

The second purpose of advance directives, according to Meisel, is to avoid some of the more serious procedural problems associated with making decisions for patients who lack the capacity for it, primarily by forestalling recourse to the judicial process. In this regard, advance directives motivate the health care professionals to avoid a judicial resolution to end-of-life decision-making for incompetent patients. Advance directives, thus, anticipate the need for either the clinical designation of a surrogate or the judicial appointment of a guardian.[3]

The third purpose of advance directives, which Meisel sees as the most important from the perspective of health-care providers, is to provide this group of people with immunity from civil or criminal liability. Since most litigated right-to-die cases wind up in court out of the fear from liability, the statutory immunity provisions that is provided by advance directives legislation facilitate decision-making by providing another reason for keeping cases in the clinical setting.

In addition to these general purposes, advance directives have an economic incentive. It is believed that the widespread use of advance directives helps to lower the costs of providing medical treatment to those who are not likely to benefit significantly from it. Two suggestions based on this rationale have been made in current literature: individuals having advance directives would be charged lower premiums for health insurance, and the issuance of health insurance should be contingent upon the execution of an advance directive – both of which overlook the fact that advance directives may either request treatment or request to forego treatment (Meisel, 1989).[4]

Finally, but not least importantly, living wills have a significant psychological role, as they also reduce the anxiety and stress on families and caregivers. With an advance directive, the family and health care team can be confident that they are giving the patient the treatment she would have wanted. Advance directives also educate patients about the treatment choices available to them, thereby changing the patient-physician relationship from one where decisions are made *for* the patient to one where decisions are made *with* the patient.

REGULATION OF ADVANCE DIRECTIVES

Advance directives are usually regulated by legislation. Advance directive statutes allow individuals to make decisions about the kind of care they want, if they are unable to make decisions on their own, and to appoint another person to make those decisions for them. They provide a mechanism that advances the ethical principles of individual autonomy, self-determination, and bodily integrity.[5] The legislation provides the form of the document, the procedure to create it and the scope of its effect. Living will legislation actually reflects the recognition by the state that the incompetent adult has the right, if the expression of intent is made, to have medical treatment discontinued, and, thus, that courts should uphold the individual's living will.

In the American legal system, a living will ceases to be effective, when the incompetent woman, who made the living will while competent, is pregnant. In Canada and the UK, no such exception exists. I will turn now to discuss these legal systems.

Canada

In Canada, advance directive legislation exists almost all over the country.[6] This legislation covers provinces of Alberta (Personal Directives Act, 2000), British Columbia (Representation Agreement Act, 1996), Manitoba (Health Care Directives Act, 1998), New Brunswick (Infirm Persons Act, 2000), Newfoundland (Advance Health Care Directives Act, 1999), Nova Scotia (Medical Consent Act, 1989), Ontario (Substitute Decisions Act, 1992), Quebec (Civil Code,

1991), Saskatchewan (Health Care Directive and Substitute Health Care Decisions Makers Act, 1997), Prince Edward Island (Consent to Treatment and Health Care Directives Act, 2000), and Yukon Territory (Enduring Power of Attorney Act, 2002). Although this legislation varies from province to province or territory, in *none* of these extensive legislative frameworks is there a specific provision from which one can infer that the legal effect of an advance directive is influenced by the question of whether the patient, who issued the living will, is pregnant or not. Thus, it seems that without any specific regulations for pregnant incompetent women, Canadian law treats the incompetent pregnant woman, who issued an advance directive while competent, in the same way as it treats other incompetent patients: that is, it respects the patient's right to control his or her care. However, the legal structure of living will legislation regarding incompetent pregnant women is different in the US than in Canada. I will turn now to describe the American legislation.

United States

Legislation model

Generally, in the US, living will legislation of states differs from the Canadian legislation in its allowance of use of a living will only when a patient is terminally ill, or after a prognosis showing that the patient would not recover. Although all states allow the patient to reject 'life-support', the majority of them do not allow the withdrawal of food and water.

Legally, where a patient has completed an advance directive, the provider is obligated to abide by the patient's wish to the extent that the wishes stated in the advance directive can be understood. With the directions of the Patient Self Determination Act (1990), health care facilities[7] should give patients information, inquire if the patient has an advance directive, and provide education to the public about advance directives. In any event, advance directives serve as a guideline for decision-making.

While all the states in the US have enacted some form of advance directive legislation, only 34 of them contemplate the validity of the advance directive when a woman is pregnant.[8] Each of these statutes has specific guidelines as to the applicability of an advance directive when a woman who makes the advance directive, is pregnant. As these guidelines reflect a practical balance between the constitutional rights of a pregnant incompetent woman and the interests of the state in protecting potential life (or, even further, the interests of a fetus), the requirements represented in each of the statutes are different from one state to another. Nevertheless, they can be roughly divided into the following six categories:

1) *Total disregard of an advance directive during the entire pregnancy.* This category is the most frequent, appearing in 17 states.[9] Statutes under this category declare that an advance directive of a person, who becomes pregnant, has no effect during pregnancy.

2) *Possibility/Probability/Medical certainty that the fetus will develop to live birth.* Some states have legislation that does not give effect to an advance directive if it is probable,[10] possible,[11] or supported by medical certainty[12] that the fetus will develop to live birth.[13]

3) *Viability of the fetus.* Two states mention the viability criterion as a limit of the effect of the advance directive. Colorado requires fetal viability before voiding an advance care directive. Georgia requires that the fetus be non-viable for the discontinuation of medical treatment.[14]

4) *Physical harm/pain to the pregnant woman.* In addition to the requirement of reasonable medical certainty that the fetus will develop to live birth, Pennsylvania and South Dakota ask for the assurance that physical harm or pain to the woman can be alleviated.

5) *Rebutable presumption of continuation of treatment.* The Minnesota advance directive law offers a unique approach. In 1998, the Minnesota legislature fundamentally revised its existing advance directive law (*Durable Power of Attorney for Health Care*, 1998). Prior to 1998, Minnesota's pregnancy provision provided that:

> In the case of a living will of a patient that the attending physician knows is pregnant, the living will must not be given effect as long as it is possible that the fetus could develop to the point of live birth with continued application of life-sustaining treatment.[15]

With the 1998 amendment, the current pregnancy provision states that:

> When a patient lacks decision-making capacity and is pregnant, and in reasonable medical judgment there is real possibility that if health care to sustain her life and the life of the fetus is provided the fetus could survive to the point of live birth,[16] *the health care provider shall presume that the patient would have wanted such health care to be provided, even if the withholding or withdrawal of such health care would be authorized were she not pregnant. This presumption is negated by health care directive provision ... or in the absence of such provisions, by clear and convincing evidence that the patient's wishes, while competent, were to the contrary* [my emphasis].[17]

Hence, the new approach acknowledges the interest of the state in potential fetal life, while still preserving the pregnant patient's right to withdraw treatment. It also encourages health professionals to discuss the issue with women, who are or could become pregnant. This view goes beyond simply making the living will void with pregnancy. It attempts to balance the woman's rights with the state's interest in protecting the life of the fetus.

6) *Probability that the fetus would not be born alive.* In Ohio, life-sustaining treatment can be withheld or withdrawn, if 'the declarant's attending physician and one other physician who has examined the declarant determine, to a reasonable degree of medical certainty and in accordance with reasonable medical standards, that the fetus would not be born alive' (Ohio Rev., 1992, § 2133.06).

The various forms of restricting the woman's right to control her care just because she is pregnant are troubling. Not only are women deprived of their right to determine their own treatment when incompetent, in some states this deprivation is regardless of the stage of the incompetent woman's pregnancy and heedless of whether or not the fetus is viable. This seems illogical: if the woman was competent, she could abort her child without hesitation, at least in her first trimester, but if she becomes incompetent during the first trimester, she cannot ask to withdraw life-sustaining treatment, and is thus compelled to save her pre-viable fetus's life.

The constitutionality of pregnancy clauses in the US

More disturbing than the fact that pregnancy clauses exist is the fact that they were not found to be unconstitutional by US jurisprudence. While the issue of constitutionality of pregnancy clauses has been raised in three judicial opinions, in none of these cases was there any substantial debate over the constitutional questions raised by pregnancy clauses nor the serious implications these causes have on women on general.

In *University Health Services v. Piazzi* (1986), the Supreme Court of Georgia implied that it would follow the pregnancy clause of Georgia, notwithstanding the objections of the patient's family. The court granted a hospital petition to continue life-support procedures on a brain-dead pregnant woman, *contrary to the request of the patient's husband and family*. The woman's wishes were unknown, and no living will was involved in this issue. The court held that according to the law of Georgia, the woman was dead and therefore had no protectable privacy interest. In addition, the court ruled that because the pregnancy clause of the Georgia legislation determined that the living will would be ineffective during pregnancy, the woman's wishes regarding it were irrelevant. The *Piazzi* ruling has led commentators to assume that the court's reliance upon the living will statute indicates that it might reject the claim that the pregnancy clause is unconstitutional (Dyke, 1990, p. 871). The court, nevertheless, did not state that it was unconstitutional.

It is important to notice that *Piazzi* did not leave any directive. Still, the court relied in its ruling on the Georgia pregnancy clause. One can argue that the court relied on the pregnancy clause because the woman was already dead. It is not clear whether the court would have mentioned it, let alone indirectly validated its constitutional content, had she been alive.

The second case in which the constitutionality of pregnancy clauses has been raised was *DiNino v. State* (1984). In *DiNino*, the plaintiff executed a living will, adding a sentence declaring that the directive was her final expression of her 'legal right to consent to termination of any pregnancy', and that contrary to the Washington Natural Death Act, it would 'still have full force and effect during the course of her pregnancy'. DiNino and her physician, who had reservations about including her directive in her medical file, sought a judgment declaring that her directive was valid, and that no physician would be liable for obeying it. DiNino argued that her constitutional right to privacy was otherwise being infringed in two respects. First, the provision directly inhibited her right to choose to have an abortion and second, it directly infringed her right to choose to forego medical treatment. It is interesting to note that in its argument, the state conceded that an individual could draft an advance directive that contains a properly worded abortion provision, or alternatively, delete the pregnancy provision of the model directive.

The Superior Court (King County) granted DiNino partial summary judgment, declaring the pregnancy provision of the Natural Death Act unconstitutional because, as drafted, the subsection inhibited a woman's right to exercise control over her reproductive decisions and, therefore, violated DiNino's fundamental right of privacy. The Superior Court, however, denied the declaration of validity of a woman's directive because this directive attempted to exercise full control over DiNino's reproductive decisions *beyond the point where the state has a legitimate interest in such decisions.* Both DiNino and the state appealed to the Supreme Court of Washington.

On appeal, the majority opinion written by Justice Brachtenbach held that the controversy was not 'justiciable' in the meaning of the Uniform Declaratory Judgments Act, under which DiNino and her physician brought the suit against the state of Washington, since the plaintiff was neither pregnant nor terminally ill, and thus her arguments concerning the unconstitutionality of the Natural Death Act pregnancy provision were 'purely hypothetical and speculative'. The only issue causing controversy was whether Ms. DiNino could draft a declaration that differed in its terms from that provided in the Natural Death Act. Since the state was willing to concede that the form could differ or be absent from the pregnancy provision – a fact which undermines the state's objective in enacting the pregnancy provision in the first place, the court concluded that 'in the abstract, the NDA itself does not *directly* infringe any constitutional rights as claimed by the respondents' (*DiNino v. State*, 1984).

Although the court admitted that the constitutional rights allegedly infringed upon are important, it did not find the case to be one of 'broad overriding public import' and, hence, did not think an advisory opinion on the constitutionality of Washington living will provision would be 'beneficial to the public or to other branches of government'. However, despite the fact that the court refused to express any opinion regarding the validity of DiNino's directive and the constitutionality of the Washington pregnancy provision, it implied that in a real controversy, DiNino's advance directive would have been effective. The court said: 'We express no opinion as to the validity of DiNino's directive as drafted, for this must await a factual controversy. However, under the facts presented, the respondents, as well as this court, can only speculate as to the possible impact of the NDA on an individual who is pregnant and is in a terminal condition' (*DiNino v. State*, 1984, p. 331).

In his dissenting opinion, Justice Dimmik explained why it is logically wrong to hold, as the majority did, that there is no justiciability at the time a woman drafts a directive under the Natural Death Act (NDA). In his words:

By the majority's reasoning, a woman must be pregnant and terminally ill before the issue is ripe for determination. Whatever the impact of the NDA in that circumstance, the woman whose directive will then be 'justiciable' will never benefit from a ruling on the matter. In fact, the case would run a very real danger of being declared moot before a judicial decision could be made. And if, in its discretion, the court chooses to address the issues on mooted facts, would that determination be based on any less speculation than a determination under the circumstances now before us?[18]

Justice Dimmik's vision was realized six years later when the court of appeal of the District of Columbia acknowledged, in one of the leading decisions in the US, the right of a pregnant woman to refuse a cesarean section that was needed to save the life of her 23-week fetus (*In Re A.C.*, 1990). The woman could no longer benefit from the court's decision because she and her fetus died two days after the forced medical treatment. One has to seriously ask whether moot cases are an appropriate forum in which courts should decide these life-and-death issues.

The constitutional challenge of a pregnancy provision identical to the one raised in *DiNino* was again unsuccessful in the case of *Gabrynowicz v. Heitkamp* (1995). In *Gabrynowicz*, the plaintiffs challenged the Uniform Rights of the Terminally Ill Act of North Dakota that invalidated an advance directive at pregnancy.[19] The plaintiffs were husband and wife. The woman sought to execute a living will and durable power of attorney (for her husband) with the hope that it would have the same effect whether she was pregnant or not. The plaintiffs argued that North Dakota's pregnancy clauses are unconstitutional as they 1) impose undue burdens on the right to terminate pregnancy and make medical decisions under the First, Fourth, Ninth, and Fourteenth Amendments; 2) deprive women of liberty (bodily integrity) without due process, violating the Fourteenth Amendment; 3) discriminate on the basis of gender, violating the equal protection guarantee of the Fourteenth Amendment; 4) require an expression of adherence to the state's policy of protecting fetal life, violating the right to make and decline to make an expression of belief under the First and Fourteenth Amendments; and 5) violate the right to free exercise of religion under the First and Fourteenth Amendments.

However, like the majority opinion in *DiNino*, the court chose not to discuss the constitutionality questions and dismissed the plaintiffs' motion out of technical reasons of standing and ripeness. The court held that at the time of the claim Ms. Gabrynowicz was neither pregnant nor incompetent. Hence, the court did not see any 'realistic danger' that the statute in question would directly injure the plaintiffs. The court acknowledged that section 23–06.4–07(3) of the statute authorizes medical treatment of a pregnant patient without distinguishing on the basis of fetal viability, and so admitted that at least some of the rights alleged by Ms. Gabrynowicz could be implicated. Nevertheless, the court still considered these questions to be abstract and non-justiciable.

Indeed, at the time of the trial, Ms. Gabrynowicz did not issue an advance directive and in that sense her case was less ripe than DiNino's. However, both women were fertile: they were ready to become pregnant and fully aware of the consequences of their proposed (present or future) directives. It is not clear why the courts avoided any substantial discussion of their matters under the premise that they were not yet ready. Is a state of loss of competency in which the woman's wishes cannot be directly examined a better one from which to evaluate her constitutional rights than a state of full competency? Alternatively, did DiNino or Gabrynowicz have to actually become pregnant to have their claims heard? What if the validity of their advance directives is an important factor in their decision of whether or not to conceive? Can the courts avoid these women's basic rights as competent healthy persons to make choices concerning their health, body, and reproduction?

Moreover, in *DiNino*, the court stated that Ms. DiNino or her physician had to make a better effort to look for another physician who would be willing to place the directive in her file. The court thus concluded that the real controversy was between DiNino and her physician. But is the question before the court really about who gets to file the directive? Does DiNino's physician have a duty to look for another physician who will agree to file her directive? Will the latter be immune from any possible liability? These questions definitely show that the courts' ruling on these matters is far from convincing.

As I mentioned above, Canada does not make pregnancy an exception to the individual's right to control her care. The English law has apparently gone through the same direction. Moreover, it considered the American approach, and rejected it. This will be discussed in the next section.

United Kingdom

Advanced directives are valid in English law provided they are made freely, without undue influence. It is also necessary that the person who issued an advance directive is competent, and had received sufficient information that applies to the circumstances, which subsequently arise. However, it seems that an enduring power of attorney would not have effect with regard to the medical treatment of brain-dead women: the Enduring Power of Attorney Act 1985 does not empower attorneys to make health care decisions, and their power is limited to financial decisions only.[20]

If a pregnant woman temporarily loses capacity, an advance directive would be effective, only if it specifically addressed the possibility of pregnancy. In case of doubt, scholars have argued that a directive refusing all of the recommended forms of medical treatment is unlikely to be respected, because the courts it may be assumed that the woman had not addressed her mind to the circumstances which have arisen (Peart *et al.*, 2000, p. 279). This also seems to be the case in Ireland. According to the literature, due to the constitutional well recognized rights of the unborn, Courts in Ireland will tend to ignore any advance directive that is issued and protect the life of the unborn child, unless there existed a 'grave, real and substantial risk to the life of the incompetent mother' (Sheikh and Cusack, 2001, p. 83).

However, this view of the literature is not supported in legislation, nor in English case law. Moreover, in its Report on Mental Incapacity, the English Law Commission *disagreed* with the US approach of suspending the effectiveness of living wills during pregnancies. It has recommended that women of childbearing capacity should address their minds to the possibility of a pregnancy if they wish to execute advance directives.[21] In section 5.25 to the report, the Law Commission said:

> We do not accept that a woman's right to determine the sorts of bodily interference which she will tolerate somehow evaporates as soon as she becomes pregnant. There can, on the other hand, be no objection to acknowledging that many women do in fact alter their views as to the interventions they find acceptable as a direct result of the fact that they are carrying a child.[22]

The Law Commission view is in accordance with the ethical guidelines on this matter. In a supplement to its previous report, the College of Obstetrics and Gynecologists stated that if the incompetent pregnant woman, who was fully informed, refused treatment during pregnancy in advance, her wishes should be respected *even at the expense of the fetus*. However, if the woman referred in her advance directive to some forms of treatment but had no opportunity to discuss treatment during pregnancy, and if pregnancy is not mentioned in the directive, 'the directive could be declared invalid because the circumstances at the critical time of decision were not clearly envisaged when the directive was made'.[23]

So far, I have discussed the existing laws in Canada, US, and the UK. As we do not have evidence that Canada considered the American approach and rejected it by *deliberately* avoiding the enactment of pregnancy clauses in advance directive legislation, an overview of the arguments which support and oppose pregnancy clauses is necessary to form a proper policy on this issue.

ARGUMENTS FOR LIVING WILL PREGNANCY LIMITATION

Balance of interests

Pregnancy clauses in living will legislation reflect an outcome of a balance between a woman's *right* to refuse treatment and control her future care, and the state's *interest* in saving the life of a fetus or in the fetus's interest for life (if it exists). Like any other balance, this balance has different outcomes depending on the proportionate weight given to the interests involved. As shown above, no unified approach or coherent solution has been offered by making such a balance. In some states, the fetus is given full protection and the mother's interests are struck for the full term of a pregnancy. In others, additional proof of the fetus's healthy development or viability is needed in order to restrain the mother.

Balancing the woman's rights with the state's (or the fetus's) interests can raise objections under four potential sources: 1) the subject of the interests involved, 2) the outcomes of the balance compared to similar conflicting situations, 3) the special place given to the fetus's interest to life, and (4) the process of balancing in itself between the 'parties' involved.

Subject of interests

One cannot ignore the jurisprudential questions of balancing between *rights* of a *living person* and the *interests* of an *abstract* called the state or, more problematic, the fetus itself. As will be elaborated on in chapter 5, while many are willing to concede that an individual life begins at fertilization, only a few argue that there is a psychological human being at fertilization. In addition, it is commonly believed that in order for one to have interests or rights, one has to be morally and legally classified as a 'person'. Applying the requirements set in the literature for moral personality (self-consciousness, rationality, capacity for moral judgments and communication etc.) also leads to the conclusion that the fetus is not a 'person'. My analysis in chapter 5 further shows that courts in the US and Canada have been reluctant to declare the fetus a person in the various opportunities they had.

Indeed, applying the criteria for 'human being' and 'person' can also lead to the unsettling determination that an incompetent, and certainly a brain-dead, pregnant woman is neither a human being nor a person. Still there is a difference between these categories. Unlike the fetus, an incompetent or even a deceased pregnant woman has held the status of personhood and humanness earlier in life. She is perceived and described as such. Her 'story of life' does not end with her biological condition of incompetency. Equating her with a fetus, thereby making her a 'non-person', would be stripping away a status that was previously recognized rather than declining to bestow a new one.

Even if we claim that an incompetent or a brain-dead pregnant woman is still a person, does it follow that it is the *same* person who issued the advance directive? While our intuition leads us to acknowledge personal identity in the first situation, we may be more careful as to the second. Within the personal identity query rests the assumption that if the criteria for personal identity include the 'preservation of the individual's ... entire complement of mental traits and capacities' (Green and Wikler, 1980, p. 125), and if brain-death is the irreversible loss of brain functions, then a prior directive has no moral authority to govern treatment decisions for the new person or the nonperson that the incompetent patient has become (Dresser, 1990, p. 432). A more moderate opinion suggests that although some cognitively impaired patients might be regarded as new persons, loss of personal identity should be taken to *diminish but not invalidate* the moral authority of a prior directive for individuals who, according to this view, have become nonpersons (Buchanan and Brock, 1989, p. 185).

The argument from personal identity is committed to a radical distinction between the death of a person (represented by the death of its brain as the locus of his or her psychological capacities) and the death of the body. Although the person might no longer exist, her body does. When 'maintained' on life-support, the brain-dead woman's body even 'lives'. But our intuition supports a different view. As will be further elaborated in chapter 5, our recognition of every other person depends upon recognition of an array of physical characteristics, which are *distinctive* features during life that are not extinguished immediately upon death (especially brain death). There is a spatial-temporal continuity of the physical body that leads one to *believe* that it is the *same* body that exists. Hence, what is done to a dead body has relevance for *our feeling about that person when alive*. The cadaver and the person are inseparable.

But are psychological capacities, memories, and mental traits so important that without them one can be claimed not to exist? Of course, one cannot ignore the 'slippery slope' peril of such an argument, which can easily apply to various living people with mental impairments, such as adults with severe dementia or anencephalic infants. One can also hypothesize a situation in which such mental capacities are transferred from a body (plus mental capacities) 'A' to a body 'B', whose brain has been cleared of its previous memories through a sophisticated physiological process (Agich and Jones, 1986, p. 273). Would we still argue that 'A' and 'B' are the same persons only because they share similar (subjective) mental capacities?

Additionally, the self who issued the directive has interests in how he or she is treated which survive the loss of personal identity. In fact, by issuing an advance directive one gives an implied consent to the validation of its wishes by the survival of his or her interests after death. The surviving of our interest in the future regardless of our condition in that future has an important value. As will be further elaborated in chapter 5, it gives meaning to our actions at present.

Moreover, what makes X the same person today that she was last week is some important connection between experiences at these two points in time that justifies saying that X had *both* experiences. The argument for personal identity assumes that the connection between these experiences is located within the psychological states of the *self* who has these experiences. But there can be another possibility. The connection between these experiences can be *maintained externally to the experienced self*, and can be regarded from the perspectives of others. This is especially true in brain death where the 'dead' appears to be alive, warm, pink, breathing, and in possession of a beating heart. In chapter 5, it will be argued that the brain-dead person represents an array of built-in memories from which they can never be completely separated by those who remember them while 'alive'. One who is brain-dead is the subject of a history in which choices, actions, and relationships play a central part. We cannot speak exclusively about one without reference to the other.

Different outcomes for similar situations

Even assuming that the mother and the fetus (or the state on its behalf) are of the same moral status, a second problem arises with the balance offered in pregnancy clauses. The analysis made in chapters 1 and 2 of this book suggests that the same balance between the same 'persons' concerning the same interests/rights is resolved *differently* in cases of abortion and in cases of bodily intervention, which are directly related to the pregnant woman's physical condition, i.e. with regard to cesarean sections and blood transfusion. Is there a justification for these different results?

Abortions   It is clear from *Roe v. Wade* (1973) that at the foundation of any balance of interests between (or within) the pregnant mother and her fetus is the assumption that the answer to the abortion dilemma lies in the moral status of the fetus. This moral status is derived from a biological development, which has been roughly determined by *Roe* as the point of viability. *Roe* is still the leading case in abortion law at the US and also seems to enjoy public support to this date.[24]

Two basic ideas have been identified in chapter 1 considering the Canadian abortion law. The first is the idea of freedom of choice (rather than privacy, as in the American context) as an almost absolute principle. It is the woman's right to fully control her body, so that even the biological father of the fetus cannot interfere with such a right. The second idea is the resistance of courts to interpret existing law in a way that would confer upon the fetus a legal substantial status prior to birth. The outcome is respect for the woman's choice and her right to make decisions concerning her body even during pregnancy.

Also shown in chapter 1 of this book is that Canadian abortion law demonstrates a weaker tendency to protect the potential life of a fetus than the American approach. Nor is the trimester framework a mandatory guideline in the ethical dilemma. Following *R. v. Morgentaler* (1988), it is reasonable to assume that the more developed the fetus, the less inclination there would be to terminate the pregnancy. More flexibility in this regard is expected in Canada.

Pregnancy clauses go beyond (or below) the viability criteria. Most of the pregnancy clauses do not distinguish between a woman who is in the earlier stages of pregnancy, and who could, therefore, have chosen to have an abortion if competent, and between those in the later stages, for whom abortion might be prohibited under state law. By not considering the developmental stage of pregnancy, the right of pregnant women to control their bodies and health-related choices is strictly infringed by these clauses. Thus, the incompetent pregnant mother's interests are given less weight than those in the abortion situation, without any legal justification (Mahoney, 1989, p. 225). In addition, pregnancy clauses accord much weight to interest in the life of the fetus and its moral status, far beyond that which is already determined in abortion cases.

General interventions during pregnancy The state's interest in the potential life of the fetus has shaped the scope of the procreative autonomy of pregnant women in areas other than abortion. In chapter 2 it was discussed how a growing number of courts have found that protection of the fetus justifies the imposition of medical treatment upon a non-consenting mother. Courts have ordered pregnant patients to undergo medical treatment, blood transfusions, or cesarean sections in order to benefit the fetus.

Analysing cases of bodily interventions with regard to pregnant women has brought me to the conclusion that despite the severity of the interference in the woman's right to self-determination and bodily integrity, in most cases courts try to balance the woman's interests with the state interest in protecting the unborn, viable, fetus. Nevertheless, courts demonstrate a tendency to protect the woman's right to refuse treatment with less interference than in abortion-law, along with an inclination to ask for a more serious harm to the fetus, if at all, in order to allow such an interference with the pregnant woman's liberties.

The analysis in the previous chapter also showed that whether through an advance directive or other methods used to infer the woman's opinion about the case, obtaining the woman's consent is a precondition for any potential intervention with her body. Also suggested in these cases is that the death of a fetus is not necessarily considered to be an unbearable result by the law, especially if the bodily intervention with regard to the pregnant woman, which could have saved the fetus's life, is done without her approval.

The limits imposed by pregnancy clauses are much more severe than in the cases analysed above. In contrast to the *Re A.C.* case (1990), discussed in the previous chapter, the balance reflected in these clauses does *not* demonstrate that interference with the woman's prior wishes is justified only when the interest to life is compelling. The fact that pregnancy clauses exist deviates from the courts' willingness to equate a competent patient's right to self-determination with that of an incompetent one. Moreover, the emphasis of pregnancy clauses on the interests of the fetus (derived from its moral status) should be questioned in light of these and other established decisions, according to which a fetus has interests only once it is born. Most pregnancy clauses do not ask, like in the *Baby Boy Doe* case (1994), for a proof of harm to the fetus, and, in contrast to the *M.B.* case (1997), the idea behind them is that a woman's right to refuse to consent to medical treatment is not absolute.

The interest to life

At the heart of the balance of interests provided by pregnancy clauses lies the interest/right of the fetus to life. Aside from the above general analysis of whether a fetus can be a subject of interest as a philosophical concept and when in 'conflict' with its mother, a special legal examination of the interest to life is required. In chapter 5, such an examination will be made. It is sufficient to argue here, that from a legal standpoint there exists no protractible interest to life for the fetus neither under the Canadian Charter of Rights and Freedoms, nor under the interpretation of the European Convention of Human Rights.[25] Incorporating such an interest to the balancing process appears to have no legal substantial sufficient support.

The process of balancing

A balance on its own seems to be a weak justification for the outcomes of such a balance. As will be shown in chapter 5, the notion of independent fetal rights or interests to be balanced with (or against) the pregnant woman's rights or interests is predicated on an idea of a disembodied fetus, separate and apart from the woman's body that sustains it. Iris Young puts it nicely: 'The dominant culture projects pregnancy as a time of quiet waiting. We refer to the woman as 'expecting', as though this new life were flying in from another planet and she sat in her rocking chair by the window, occasionally moving the curtain aside to see whether the ship is coming' (Young, 1990, p. 167). This dualistic view, which posits a maternal-fetal conflict, not only assumes antagonistic rights between a pregnant woman and her fetus but also lends itself to advocating a range of state policies and legal interventions that are inherently adversarial in their approach to regulating the lives of pregnant women (Dyke, 1990, p. 886).

Implying the woman's wish to bring her fetus to term

One of the arguments that supports the constitutionality of pregnancy clauses in living will legislation is that, in contrast to *Roe v. Wade*, which dealt with a case of a healthy woman who did not want to give birth and to care for the children that the abortion laws sought to force on them, a mother in a terminal condition who has signed a living will would likely have wanted the child to be born (or she would already have terminated the pregnancy) and she would not have to care for it (Gelfand, 1987, p. 780).

The evidence for such an argument is hard to come by. If it is only an implied impression, or even a legal presumption, then it is not enough to block the fundamental interests of the mother. Of course, the fact that a woman decides to continue a pregnancy to term is not conclusive. As will be explained in the discussion of implied consent in chapter 5, a pregnant woman may continue her pregnancy not as a result of deliberate choice but because of lack of access to therapeutic abortion, or because of cultural, social, personal, or family constraints. A physician cannot simply assume the woman would want her pregnancy continued after she becomes incompetent based on the fact that she is pregnant.

But more importantly, the argument for implied consent does not apply when the mother has explicitly written in her advance directive, as in the *DiNino* case, that she would want to withdraw life-sustaining treatment even in case of pregnancy. Would one still claim that she wanted to bring the child to full term? Or is she not allowed to issue such a directive in the first place? If the latter is correct, this argument still does not explain why the woman cannot choose to control her treatment in such a way.

A matter of privacy

Some have addressed the constitutionality of the pregnancy clauses as a matter of privacy (Dyke, 1990, p. 873). According to this view, if the privacy right is broad enough to grant women complete autonomy regarding reproductive decisions, pregnancy clauses are unconstitutional for attempting to restrict this autonomy. On the other hand, if the right to privacy is limited to the extent that a pregnant woman must forfeit her right to choose and to make decisions to the state, pregnancy clauses seem to be constitutional.

According to this argument we should decide first on the extent of the right to privacy, and only after doing so can we justify (or not) the existence of pregnancy clauses. Basically, this argument attracts an objection similar to the argument against balancing of interests, discussed above. In addition to the fact that this argument does not really provide an answer but rather shifts our attention to privacy questions, and even assuming that it is a matter of privacy, why does the 'same privacy' that a pregnant woman enjoys lead to a different conclusion when the woman's wishes to abort her fetus or when a bodily intervention is being considered with respect to her? Is there a reasonable justification for narrowing the extent of the right to privacy when the woman puts her wishes in writing?

In the Canadian context it is more appropriate to talk about the right to refuse life-sustaining medical treatment. This right has been well-developed in Canadian Law (*Malette v. Shulman*, 1990;[26] *Nancy B. v. Hotel-Dieu de Quebec et al.*, 1992[27]). No doubt, the right to refuse life-sustaining treatment lies at the 'very heart' of an individual's right to be free from any interventions when it comes to making important personal decisions. If the law truly wishes to protect this sanctified and elementary right of a human being, it should let the competent woman make the decision by herself and be responsible for it, instead of patronizing her when it seems that there is no meaningful interest against her decision to die. Moreover, the situation in which the right to refuse life-sustaining treatment allegedly endangers the life of the fetus, is test-case for the legal protection of the woman's right to self-determination. Just as it cannot be claimed that one has freedom of speech if they are restrained from saying irritating and annoying things, a woman cannot be claimed to hold a right to self-determination (or privacy) if her most important decisions in life could eventually be dominated by a group of judges or legislators. I see no reason to restrict her right due to pregnancy, especially when she chose to execute it while competent and healthy.

Authorizing an unlawful act

An additional argument that is brought in favor of pregnancy clauses is that doctors, who comply with a pregnant woman's request to withdraw life-sustaining treatment, knowing that it would kill the unborn child, would be committing a criminal offence.[28] Pregnancy clauses are needed because an advance directive cannot authorize the performance of an unlawful act.

The possibility of criminal liability seems to be extremely rare. There are terminological reasons as well as valuable policy considerations for rejecting the anticipation of criminal liability.[29] But more substantially, doctors, who follow their patient's wishes and have successfully gone through the process of an advance directive seem to be immune from criminal or civil liability and can be solely bound by professional practice standards. This is exactly one of the purposes of advance directives. If an act of withdrawing life-sustaining treatment from a patient were lawful, we would not have asked for it to be done through the mechanism of an advance directive. Advance directives are necessary to perform actions that would otherwise have been unlawful.

Furthermore, the House of Lords in the case of *Anthony Bland* went further to state that avoiding a request to withdraw life-sustaining treatment is perhaps an unlawful act by itself (*Airedale N.H.S. Trust v. Bland*, 1993). The court stated:

> If there comes a stage where the responsible doctor comes to reasonable conclusion …
> that further continuance of an intrusive life support system is not in the best interests
> of the patient, he can no longer lawfully continue that life support system: to do so
> would constitute the crime of battery and the tort of trespass to the person.[30]

Apart from the flaws that exist in the arguments supporting pregnancy clauses in living will legislation, there are sound independent reasons to oppose such clauses. I will turn to discuss these now.

ARGUMENTS AGAINST LIVING WILL PREGNANCY LEGISLATION

Self-control and medical care

Disregard for the pregnant woman's advance directives derogates the woman-patient's rights of self-determination and bodily integrity with respect to a deeply personal and self-defining decision. As discussed in chapter 2, the right of individuals to self-determination in health care is firmly rooted in the common law. It is founded on the fundamental right to be left alone, tied to the right to privacy,[31] and 'turns on the subjective wishes of the patient rather than on public opinion, state or familial preferences, or any objective test' (*In re Guardianship of Browning*, 1989, p. 273). Pregnancy provisions infringe on a woman's right to refuse medical treatment on the basis of her pregnant status. Pregnancy clauses deprive the woman of an interest in protecting what and who is most important to her, exactly when those values are infinite. They directly contravene the woman's express wish for privacy and personal autonomy (MacAvoy-Smitzer, 1987).

An argument for equality

While discussing pregnancy clauses, Anne Lederman brings into consideration a case of a newborn child whose father is in a terminal or vegetative condition, supported by artificial means (Lederman, 1994, pp. 369–70; Mahoney, 1989, pp. 230–1). In Lederman's example:

> Prior to his condition, the child's father executed a living will in which he asked to withdraw all life-sustaining treatment if he is in a state similar to the current one. The newborn son suffers from a disease treatable only by transplanting several organs and the father is the *only* acceptable donor. However, the baby cannot accept the organs immediately, and there is no way to store the organs outside the father's body. It is clear that without the organ donation the boy will die.[32]

Lederman asks whether, in this difficult situation, the state's interest in preserving life justifies the imposition of life-sustaining treatment upon the father so that his organs may be harvested for his newborn child at a later date. She gives a negative answer to this question. Lederman's answer correctly reflects the legal view on this matter. In contrast to pregnancy clauses, neither living will legislation nor court decisions require a father in such circumstances to continue treatment so that his body may be used for the child. Indeed, in contrast to civil law, common law courts do not compel one person to permit a significant intrusion upon his or her bodily integrity for the benefit of another person's health (*In re A.C.*, 1990, pp. 1243–4), even in cases where denying aid would result in *the death* of the endangered person. In *McFall v. Shimp* (1978), a Pittsburgh judge refused to order bone marrow transplant to a young man dying from cancer from his cousin, who was the only compatible potential donor located, but disagreed to donate. The court ruled that:

> The common law has consistently held to a rule which provides that one human being is under no legal compulsion to give aid or to take action to save another human being or to rescue … . For our law to *compel* defendant to submit to an intrusion of his body would change every concept and principle upon which our society is founded. To do so would defeat the sanctity of the individual, and would impose a rule which would know no limits, and one could not imagine where the line would be drawn.[33]

A pregnant woman does not and should not owe a 'duty to rescue' her fetus. The argument here is that state's interest in the life of the fetus should be equal to its interest in any other individual in need of immediate rescue, and not more than that. It is clear from the example that living will legislation imposes a greater obligation on the pregnant woman than it does on the father of a born child whose existence depends upon the organ donation from his father.

Not only do pregnancy clauses discriminate on a sexual basis (between incompetent women and incompetent men), but they also discriminate on the basis of incompetency (between a competent pregnant woman and an incompetent pregnant woman). Whereas a competent pregnant woman may choose to have an abortion with little restriction on her rights (especially before viability of the fetus), an incompetent pregnant woman cannot terminate her pregnancy, even before viability. This is so only because of her incompetency, and regardless of her or her relatives' view on this issue.

Finally, pregnancy clauses discriminate women on the basis of their *pregnancy* (between an incompetent pregnant woman and an incompetent non-pregnant woman). While an incompetent woman's directive to have life-support withdrawn would be effectuated, such a directive, when issued by a pregnant incompetent woman, would not be valid. Therefore, pregnancy clauses deny women the equal right of choice that is enjoyed by both men and other women, whether competent or incompetent.[34]

Trivializing the mother's choice

The mother's decision not to be maintained on artificial life-support requires her to confront herself with the most frightening and enigmatic concept of her own mortality. According to this argument, the seriousness of such a consideration makes it unlikely that she makes the choice easily. Pregnancy clauses trivialize the significance of the mother's self-defining and conscientious choice by automatically overriding it (Lederman, 1994, pp. 370–1). The mother may have been fully aware of her pregnancy but failed to specifically include it in her advance directive, or she may have been unaware of her pregnancy before she became incompetent. In either of these cases, the importance of the woman's decision, which is reflected in issuing the advance directive itself, provides a solid moral reason to support an implementation of her living will even when pregnant.

Ignoring the woman's family

It is reasonable to assume that the pregnant woman, as a competent adult, executed the living will solely out of concern for her family, regardless of fear of her own suffering or experience when her living will became operative. Under this argument, it is possible that she believed that maintaining her on life-sustaining care would devastate her family's financial and emotional resources, preventing them from caring for themselves and for each other. Therefore, disregarding the pregnant patient's directives ignores the cost of whatever harms the woman feared would come to pass to her family. Pregnancy clauses in living will legislation ignore not only the woman's wishes with respect to herself but also with respect to her family.

Involuntary servitude

The Thirteenth Amendment to the US Constitution declares:

> Neither slavery nor involuntary servitude, except as punishment for crime whereof the party shall have been duly convicted, shall exist within the United States, or any place subject to their jurisdiction.[35]

In Canada, the Charter of Rights and Freedoms does not provide a specific prohibition against slavery, though this can be based on the 'right to life, liberty and security of the person' under section 7 of the Charter (Canadian Charter of Rights and Freedoms, 1982, section 7).

Timothy Burch argues that pregnancy clauses reduce incompetent pregnant women to a state of slavery and involuntary servitude (Burch, 1995). In his view:

> Just as the African American woman's body was controlled by her master in all respects including reproduction, so is the body of an incompetent pregnant woman controlled by its new master – the state ... a state order to remain attached to medical machines and produce a child must also be considered a form of involuntary servitude prohibited by the Thirteenth Amendment.[36]

Ignoring the woman's advance directives and treating her body without due respect for her wishes amounts to a form of slavery. This form of 'involuntary servitude' is definitely reflected in the case of a brain-dead pregnant woman, who is being maintained purely for the sake of her fetus. Even if Burch's argument is far reaching, it still gives us a flavor of the resistance we should feel when considering imposing such medical procedure against a patient's expressed wishes.

CONCLUSION

The most important role of advance directives, in my view, is that they help to focus medical decisions along the patient's wishes. Dr. William Molloy conducted a survey, asking 909 people questions related to care and advance directives. Over 90 per cent of them said it was extremely important for them to be able to decide their treatment. Over 90 per cent of them were concerned that they would receive treatment without their consent, or that treatment would be too aggressive. When asked whether they would want to have their health care choices documented, almost 90 per cent said they would (Molloy, 1993, p. 218).

What do these big numbers from Molly's survey teach us? They surely serve as an indication of the importance of living wills regardless of the physical state of the incompetent person. Most of all, living wills provide a means of exercising some degree of control over medical care. But they also facilitate the process of decision-making in times of crisis and emergencies. By doing this, not only do they honour the patient's wishes but they respect the patient's family as well. In addition, they provide sense of security for physicians, enabling them to fulfill the patient's wishes without being threatened of lawsuit or prosecution.

A woman's decision to issue an advance directive and to have it effectuated implicates her fundamental right to make decisions regarding procreation, family relationships and bodily integrity. These are the most intimate and personal choices a person makes in a lifetime, and they are central to personal dignity and autonomy and to the 'liberty' interest that is protected under the Canadian Constitution.

Pregnancy clauses that exist under the American law should not be a model for Canadian law. Not only do they infringe on a woman's right to refuse medical treatment just because she is pregnant, and hence discriminate them from other non-pregnant women on the basis of their pregnancy, but they also discriminate them on a gender basis and on the basis of their incompetency. Pregnancy clauses also trivialize the significance of the mother's self-defining and conscientious choice by automatically overriding it. They ignore the pregnant woman's family, pretending to protect potential life without even drawing the line at the viability of the fetus. Finally, they control the woman's body, devalue it, and bring it to a state of involuntary servitude. The woman's wishes are automatically ignored just because she is pregnant.

The original intent of living will statutes was to permit the 'natural death' of persons who would otherwise linger for years on life-support in a vegetative but 'alive' state (Gelfand, 1987, p. 742). Pregnancy clauses totally disregard the wishes of the woman and her loved ones. Such legislation compels providers to force intensive and intrusive treatment upon a woman, inflicting exactly the sort of indignity upon the patient and anguish upon her family and friends, that 'Do Not Resuscitate' orders and living wills are meant to protect us against.

However, it is not enough to conclude that Canada should not follow the American model of pregnancy clauses. A more active step should be taken, similar to that in the UK, so that the American model should be publicly discussed and rejected. No doubt should be left in such an important area. What then should be the proper way to deal with incompetency during pregnancy with respect to Canadian women who issue an advance directive?

Timothy Burch suggests that physicians should consult with or defer the decision-making to the family or friends of the pregnant woman, instead of allowing the state to intervene in legislation (Burch, 1995, p. 565). However, this suggestion ignores the woman's wishes, reflected in her advance directive. Moreover, it is not clear from his proposal what is the mechanism for such decision-making in case of a conflict between the woman's directive and the family or friend's wishes. Whose view outweighs?

Gregory Gelfand offers a model of living will legislation that would include a pregnancy clause (Gelfand, 1987, pp. 802–21). According to his suggestion, if a patient is not in pain, a fetus that has not already been aborted should no longer be eligible for abortion. In cases where the patient is in pain, however, the balance shifts in favour of the patient, *even if the fetus is beyond the second trimester*. Because of the conflicting interests involved, Gelfand suggests calling upon the court at this stage to make any further decision (Gelfand, 1987, pp. 816–17).

Gelfand's model seems to be problematic. The keypoint of his suggestion is the woman's ability to feel pain. I find it odd that a terminally ill patient who feels pain but is, for example, two weeks from full-term can decide to withdraw life-sustaining treatment, whereas an incompetent mother, who, for instance, has just entered her second trimester, cannot ask for it. Why not respect the woman's prior decisions if one can infer from them the woman's view regarding life-sustaining treatment in case of incompetency during pregnancy? This brings me to my preferred suggestion.

Pregnant women and the proxies they appoint to make decisions about their care should have *full information* and an opportunity to make decisions about continuing pregnancy under circumstances where the pregnant woman might face health problems. This could be done by supplying forms for living wills (Weisbrad, 1995) as well as educational and explanatory material developed for patients in early stages of pregnancy and doctors. These materials would include the various kinds of treatment for which pregnant women may choose to give special instructions. When necessary, statutes should also require that women clearly state in their advance directive what is to happen if they become incompetent while pregnant. If a competent woman follows this suggestion, then her wishes must be effectuated at pregnancy with no exceptions, as in other situations when incompetency arises.

Until this happens, I would suggest upholding the living will of a woman even at pregnancy, especially in the first and second trimester when the state cannot claim to have any interest in potential life (as discussed in chapter 1). If the woman who issued the advance directive becomes incompetent in her third trimester, I would suggest consulting her family and friends to try to ascertain *her* views and ideology. In any event, I would not recommend having a mandatory provision that would invalidate the woman's directive solely on the basis of the gestational age of her fetus.

If there is no advance directive or durable power of attorney for health care decisions (specifically for maternal incompetency, or in general when the fetus is in its third trimester), directions must be sought from previously expressed statements of the pregnant woman. Due to the undignified nature I see in the medical treatment proposed, the assessment by the surrogate as to what the deceased's wishes were should be obtained through clear and convincing evidence.

Besides the weakness of arguments that support pregnancy limitation in living wills and the strength of those opposing it, there is a significant reason that Canada should not choose the American model. As shown in the two previous chapters, Canadian abortion law and the general law that governs legal interventions with regard to pregnant women seem to place more emphasis on the pregnant woman's wishes and her rights to self-determination, and tend to give less weight to considerations of the fetus's potential life than the American approach. Canada's avoidance from enacting pregnancy clauses in the many forms of living will legislation that exist in the country, strengthens my interpretation of the way in which a pregnant woman is regarded under the Canadian law. My recommendation is consistent with this interpretation. It is helpful to keep this in mind for the discussion in the next chapter, where I analyse the case of a brain-dead pregnant woman from a different angle, *i.e.* from the perspective of the dead.

NOTES

1   Capacity usually means the ability to understand the significant benefits, risks and alternatives to proposed health care and to make and communicate a health care decision.
2   The argument assumes that the now-incompetent patient is the same person who previously authored that directive. However, one can argue that for some patients we cannot make this claim because incompetence brings a loss of psychological continuity and connectedness with the prior competent self, thereby destroying the conditions necessary for personal identity. At the heart of this argument is the assumption that psychological continuity is an essential feature of the 'unity relation', that allows us to say that the stages of a person's life are stages of the *same* person's life. Thus, the argument goes, a prior directive has no moral authority to govern treatment decisions for the *new person* or the *nonperson* that the incompetent patient has become (Dresser, 1990). A more moderate opinion suggests that although some cognitively impaired patients might be regarded as new persons, loss of personal identity should be taken to *diminish but not invalidate* the moral authority of a prior directive for individuals who, according to this view, have become nonpersons (Buchanan and Brock, 1989, p. 185). This personal identity challenge to the effect of advance directives plays a more important role when a person is dead than when she is in a coma or suffers from a partial disfunction of the brain. With the death of a person, we can allegedly no longer argue that it is a new person. We might argue that it is a nonperson, as such having lesser significant moral status. Although the person might no longer exist, her body does. When 'maintained' on life-support, the brain-dead woman's body even 'lives'. Thus, the argument from personal identity is also committed to a radical distinction between the death of a person and the death of the body. I will elaborate on these issues in my fifth chapter.
3   Meisel rightly mentions that advance directives will not always avoid the need for judicial proceedings. For example, when an advance directive does not designate a proxy but merely gives instructions, a surrogate will still need to be designated by the court. Another situation that would necessitate a judicial intervention would be

when a third party (a family member or a friend of the patient) is dissatisfied with the patient's designation of a proxy through the advance directive.

4 Meisel, however, correctly asserts that it is not clear whether it costs less to treat patients near the ends of their lives who have advance directives than to treat those who do not.

5 Nevertheless, a criticism can be raised regarding the extent to which living wills promote an incompetent patient's right of self determination, since they reflect only the individual's past preferences and values as a once-competent adult and fail to incorporate the now-incompetent individual's interest. See *supra* note 2.

6 For an exhaustive description of this legislation see www.utoronto.ca/jcb/main.html, accessed on 1 May 2004.

7 This term applies to hospitals, nursing facilities, home health care providers, hospice programs, and health maintenance organizations.

8 These states are: Alabama, Alaska, Arizona, Arkansas, California, Colorado, Connecticut, Delaware, Florida, Georgia, Hawaii, Idaho, Illinois, Indiana, Kansas, Kentucky, Minnesota, Montana, Nebraska, Nevada, New Hampshire, North Dakota, Ohio, Oklahoma, Pennsylvania, Rhode Island, South Carolina, South Dakota, Texas, Utah, Washington, Wisconsin, Wyoming (Jerdee, 2000).

9 Alabama, California, Connecticut, Hawaii, Idaho, Indiana, Kansas, Montana, New Hampshire, Ohio, Oklahoma, South Carolina, Texas, Utah, Washington, Wisconsin, Wyoming. Interesting to note here that in Oregon, § 127.540 to the Oregon Review Statute, 1990 mentions abortions as one of the things to which the durable power of attorney is not authorized to consent.

10 Alaska, Delaware, Montana, Nebraska, Nevada, and Rhode Island. This is also the language of the *Uniform Rights of Terminally Ill Act* of 1989, which reads: 'Life sustaining treatment must not be withheld or withdrawn pursuant to a declaration from an individual known to the attending physician to be pregnant so long as it is probable that the fetus will develop to the point of live birth with continued application of life-sustaining treatment.'

11 Arizona, Arkansas, Illinois, Minnesota.

12 Kentucky, North Dakota.

13 For the difficulties in interpreting the language of the ambiguous terms 'probable' and 'possible' in this regard see Jerdee, 2000, pp. 996–7.

14 The Georgia Natural Death Act served as an inspiration to the court in the *Piazzi* case (*University Health Services, Inc. v. Piazzi*, 1986), thereby ordering to maintain Donna Piazzi (who had not left any directive at issue) on life-support. See *infra* my discussion on this case in section 2.

15 Minn. Stat. § 145B.13 subd. 3 (1998).

16 The language of the Minnesota statute is also far from being clear. The possibility that the fetus will develop to the point of live birth arguably encompasses the period before and after fetal viability. Of course, one could also argue that there is always a possibility of live birth of a fetus, when a woman is pregnant, and that this possibility ends only with the termination of pregnancy.

17 Minn. Stat. § 145C.10 (g). For discussion on the new law in Minnesota see Blumer, 1998.

18 *DiNino v. State*, 1984, p. 333.

19 Additionally, section 23–06.4–07(3) to the statute provided that: 'Notwithstanding a declaration executed under this chapter, medical treatment must be provided to a pregnant patient with a terminal condition unless ... such medical treatment will not maintain the patient in such a way as to permit the continuing development and live birth of the unborn child or will be physically harmful or unreasonably painful to the patient or will prolong severe pain that cannot be alleviated by medication.'

20 Nevertheless, the English government announced in 1999 that it intends to put in place a new system of Continuing Power of Attorney that would enable adults to delegate decision-making powers on healthcare to proxies (Peart *et al.*, 2000, p. 277).
21 Loss of capacity from a cerebral injury can occur under two typical situations: patients in a permanent vegetative state (PVS) and patients who are brain stem dead. Peart *et al.* (2000) report that in England, a diagnosis of PVS cannot be confirmed until the patient has been insentient for at least 12 months. So, PVS patients are unlikely to be pregnant unless they were raped in the nine months before the diagnosis of PVS. In contrast, Peart *et al.* mention that in Virginia (US), the diagnosis of PVS can be made after only one month of insentience.
22 *Report of the Law Commission on Mental Incapacity* 1995, London: H.M.S.O, § 5.25.
23 Section 3.4.2 to the supplement. See *Ethical Guidelines on Court-Authorised Obstetric Intervention: a Consideration of the Law and Ethics* from 1996, available at http://www. rcog.org.uk/guidelines.asp?PageID=109&GuidelineID=33, accessed on 26th April 2004.
24 A recent poll in the US shows that 52 per cent of Americans agreed and 37 per cent disagreed, with the result of *Roe v. Wade* (1973), while 50 per cent identified themselves as pro-choice and 42 per cent as pro-life (Jost, 2002, p. 644).
25 See *infra* my discussion in chapter 5.
26 In this case, the Ontario Court of Appeal upheld a finding of battery against a physician who had administered blood transfusions to an incompetent patient who was in a life-threatening condition. Although the physician was aware that the patient had signed a Jehovah's Witness medical alert card, refusing blood under *any* circumstances, he ignored the directive in order to save her life.
27 In 1992, the *Nancy B.* case explicitly recognized the right of a mentally competent patient to refuse artificial life-support and thereby hasten death. Nancy B. was totally and permanently paralyzed and unable to breathe on her own due to a neurological disease she suffered from. The court ruled she could be disconnected from the respiratory, acknowledging that such an act would lead to her death. The court ruled that if Nancy died after the respiratory was stopped it would not be an act of suicide, rather nature taking its course.
28 This argument especially applies when the fetus is viable. See, for example, in the UK, section 1 of the *Infant Life (Preservation) Act* 1929: 'Any person who with intent to destroy the life of a child capable of being born alive, by any wilful act causes a child to die before it has an existence independent of its mother, shall be guilty of a felony, to wit a child destruction.'
29 There are three main arguments against criminal liability. First, the requisite of intent is lacking. The doctor does not intend to procure an abortion or destroy the life of a child capable of being born alive. The intention is to withdraw treatment from the woman *in accordance with her request*. Second, it seems that criminal liability in this context requires some positive act. If a treatment is withdrawn because its continuation is considered futile, death is caused not by the discontinuation of treatment but by the preexisting condition from which the patient was suffering. Third, patients are entitled not only to withdraw treatment but also to request withdrawal of treatment provided they are competent when making the decision. To deny a pregnant woman this right, the argument goes is to override her autonomy and subject her interests to those of her fetus (Peart *et al.*, 2000, p. 282).
30 *Airedale N.H.S. Trust v. Bland*, 1993, p. 883.
31 The right to privacy extends also to allow *a patient's surrogate* the right to refuse medical treatment for the patient (*In re Quinlan*, 1976). It has been suggested that the privacy interest in bodily integrity is even more fundamental than the privacy interest in terminating pregnancy (MacAvoy-Smitzer, 1987, p. 1290).

32 Lederman, 1994, pp. 369–70.
33 *McFall v. Shimp*, 1978, p. 91.
34 For a feminist critique, including an argument for equality, see the excellent piece by Taylor, 1997. See also Rothenberg, 1996, pp. 76–7.
35 U.S. Const. amend. XIII, §. 1.
36 Burch, 1995, p. 555.

Chapter 4

Human Tissue Gift Law

So far, I have considered the post-mortem pregnancy as a type of a pregnancy case. I looked at it through the lens of discussions surrounding abortion, bodily interventions with pregnant women and the specific provisions of advance directive legislation relating to incompetent pregnant women. In this chapter, I will focus on the post-mortem component. I will question whether the dilemma of maintaining a brain-dead pregnant woman on life-support for the sake of her fetus is covered, and therefore could be resolved by the law governing other medical procedures performed on the newly-dead patients, especially procedures undertaken for altruistic reasons. One such procedure is maintaining the 'newly-dead' on life-support for the extraction of organs, for transplantation. I will refer to such a procedure as it is usually referred to, namely as a post-mortem gift.

Cadavers of organ donors are usually maintained on 'life-support' after death if their organs cannot be removed immediately. Human Tissue Gift acts are the legal mechanism designed to regulate the use of cadavers for therapeutic purposes, medical education or scientific research and to determine the conditions under which they can be used.[1] The background for this law was the shortage of organs for transplantation, and the need to legalize the removal of these organs from the deceased. The transfer of human tissue is considered a gift, not a sale. Commercial exchanges of human tissues are invalid in most jurisdictions, and are considered contrary to public policy.

THE REGULATION OF POST-MORTEM GIFTS

Canada

Human Tissue Gift Acts exist widely in Canada.[2] In Alberta, Ontario, British Columbia and most of the other provinces, any adult person can consent in writing at any time, or orally, in the presence of at least two witnesses during his last illness, 'that his body, or the part or parts of it specified in the consent, be used after his death for therapeutic purposes, medical education or scientific research'.[3]

When a person has not given consent under the circumstances above, or in the opinion of a physician is incapable of giving consent by reason of injury or disease and his death is imminent, the law authorizes the spouse of the patient, her adult children, adult siblings, adult next of kin, or, finally, the person 'lawfully in possession of the body' to consent on behalf of her for the same purposes.[4] In any case, consent cannot be given if there is reason to believe that the deceased would have objected.

Interesting to our case are the different ways by which the law defines 'human tissue' under this legislation. In most of the provinces and territories of Canada the term 'tissue' includes an organ, but does not include any skin, bone, blood, blood constituent or other tissue, that is 'replaceable by natural processes of repair'. However, in Ontario, Manitoba and Prince Edwards Island 'tissue' means a part of a living or dead human body and includes an organ but, does not include bone marrow, spermatozoa, an ovum, an embryo, *a fetus*, blood or blood constituents.

In the province of Quebec, there is no special statute under this model of Tissue Gift Acts. Article 11 to the Civil Code of Quebec (1991) provides the general principle of consent. It requests consent for 'care of any nature, whether for examination, specimen taking, removal of tissue, treatment or any other act'. Article 19 to the code is more specific. It deals with 'alienation of the body', but applies to *inter-vivos* gifts. In a strange way, the code does not cover the issue of post-mortem gifts, that is the donations of organs from the dead. Article 11 also asks that the risk incurred on the patient is not disproportionate to the benefit that may reasonably be anticipated. Finally, the law in Quebec does not use the term 'human tissue', instead it requires that the body part would be capable of regeneration. It is clear thus that a fetus cannot be interpreted under such a definition.

United States

The 'Human Tissue Gift Acts' model, which deals with disposing of the body and its parts after death, is not unique to the Canadian legal system. In the US, the Uniform Anatomical Gift Act (1987) expressly grants the right to the next-of-kin to control disposal of the body, in conformity with the common law. The act was enacted mainly in response to the need for more family donations of organs and to the medical profession's uncertainty about whose consent was necessary for donations and other 'gifts' from the dead. This 'model' of statute, or one that is very similar to it, has been adopted by most of the states in the US. It includes provisions that govern how individuals can give their bodies to medical schools or hospitals for various purposes, and also has provisions that allow family members to make those decisions on behalf of the deceased.

United Kingdom

In the UK, section 1(1) of the Human Tissue Act (1961) provides that if any person, either in writing or orally, in the presence of at least two witnesses, has expressed a request that his body be used after his death for therapeutic purposes, medical education or research, the person 'lawfully in possession of his body'[5] may, unless he has reason to believe that the request was subsequently withdrawn, authorize the removal from the body of any part, in accordance with the request (Human Tissue Act, 1961, sections 1–4). The law also provides that the person 'lawfully in possession of the body' may authorize the removal of any part from the body for use for the said purposes if, there is no reason to believe that the deceased had expressed an objection to this, or that the surviving spouse or any surviving relative of the deceased objects to the body being so dealt with.

A new law in England is now being considered in the English Parliament. The Human Tissue Bill [Bill 9] that, if accepted, will replace the Human Tissue Act 1961, aims 'to provide a consistent legislative framework for issues relating to whole body donations and the taking, storage and use of human organs and tissues' (Human Tissue Bill, 2004). The bill sets forth in section 1(a), the requirement of consent for the storage of a body of a deceased for purposes mentioned in the schedule to the bill. These purposes include, *inter alia*, anatomical examination, determining the cause of death, education and training that are health related, transplantation etc. Maintaining a body of a dead pregnant woman is not mentioned within the human tissue framework.

According to this new law, when the medical procedure performed on the dead does not involve storage for use, or use, for the purpose of anatomical examination or public display, the general rule is that the person's express consent given while alive will prevail (Human Tissue Bill, 2004, section 5(a)). However, when an express consent from the dead is difficult to find, consent given under an earlier appointment will be valid if it related to the specified activity (Human Tissue Bill, 2004, section 5(b)(2)).[6] If no appointment has been made by the deceased, 'a person who stood in a qualifying relationship' with the deceased is authorized to give or refuse to give consent on behalf of the dead (Human Tissue Bill, 2004, section 5(c)).

Some commentators have argued that maintaining the brain-dead pregnant woman on life support for the sake of her fetus can be considered as another form of post-mortem gift. Erich Loewy, for example, claimed that maintaining the dead woman for short period of time is just another way 'of valuing the living more than the dead, reality more than its symbol' (Loewy, 1987, p. 1099). In his view, it honors the memory of the deceased, supports their symbolic ongoing membership in the just community and affirms our ongoing concern for the living. I will turn now to discuss the various proposals in the literature to apply post-mortem gift law to the case of a brain-dead pregnant woman.

APPLYING POST-MORTEM GIFT LAWS TO BRAIN-DEAD PREGNANT WOMEN

Suggestions

In a very controversial article, Jay Kantor and Iffath Abbasi Hoskins argue that there are three possible models for analysing the ethical dilemmas concerning maternal brain-death (Kantor *et al.*, 1993). In the first model, we should treat the dead woman as if she were alive in a state of acute disease. This model provides her with the same rights and duties toward the fetus as the ones held by a living woman. In the second model, the pregnant woman is considered a mere incubator for her fetus, enjoying no rights relating to the treatment of her body. She is treated like an object rather than a person. Hence, any duties toward her are not owed to her for who she is, rather they are posed for the persons who are affected by how she – as an object – is being treated (Kantor *et al.*, 1993, p. 311). In the third model, the brain-dead pregnant woman is viewed like a cadaver-organ-donor. Her being maintained on 'life-support' is analogous to keeping a dead patient's somatic functions for organ removal (Kantor *et al.*, 1993, pp. 311–12).

After correctly eliminating the first two models, Kantor *et al.* argue that we should adopt the third model (Kantor *et al.*, 1993, p. 312). In both cases, it is argued, 'treatment' is provided for the sake of another person, prolongation of somatic functions may continue for some time, and consent requirements are less strict than those required for procedures performed on a living person. Kantor and Hoskins claim that as in the organ-donor model, where 'the family may have future legal responsibilities to the recipient, which would be absent when donation is done' (Kantor *et al.*, 1993, p. 312), the family of the pregnant woman will usually have close emotional ties to both the donor and the recipient.

The consequences of applying the third model to the case of a brain-dead pregnant woman, according to Kantor and Hoskins, are that if it is impossible to obtain direct evidence of the deceased's wishes, health care providers should search for 'a weak' substituted judgment about the woman's values that could lead to an inference about her wishes for the fetus. When in doubt, pregnancy should continue until a reasonable effort has been made to determine the woman's wishes (Kantor *et al.*, 1993, p. 313).

A similar, though less explicit view can be found in Nicola Peart and colleagues. These scholars claim that maintaining the woman's bodily functions until the fetus is delivered is a therapeutic purpose. Their explanation for such a conclusion seems more odd than the conclusion itself. They argue that since the woman has no 'real' interests so that the medical procedure is neither for her best interests nor against her best interests it is reasonable to say that it is for 'therapeutic' purposes (Peart *et al.*, 2000, p. 295). If the woman expressed the wish to have her bodily functions maintained until the birth of her fetus, Peart *et al.* suggest treating such a directive under the Human Tissue Act 1961 (Peart *et al.*, 2000, p. 283). They argue that a pregnant woman's directive, which complies with the formalities of this act, could be regarded as a request that her body be maintained after her death for the delivery of her fetus (Peart *et al.*, 2000, p. 283).

Nevertheless, Peart *et al.* claim that there is no legal duty to comply with the woman's request, so that even if an advance directive is covered by the Human Tissue Act it would still have a very limited effect (Peart *et al.*, 2000, pp. 283–4). Its only legal effect, they explain, would be that the person who is 'lawfully in possession of her body' would not be required to consult with her relatives – an otherwise necessary requirement when there is no explicit request from the deceased (Peart *et al.*, 2000, p. 284).

A third approach regarding the analogy between maternal brain-death and keeping the patient's body for organ transplantation is expressed by Robert

Veatch. Veatch suggests that if a woman signed an organ donation card and died while pregnant, it would be ethically permissible to sustain the pregnancy even over the objections of her family (Veatch, 1982, p. 1102). It seems that in Veatch's view, maintaining the mother on life-support is permissible only with indirect (but conceptually related) evidence that the woman asked to donate her body, or part of it, for the sake of others in need.

Discussion

I find the organ donor model inapplicable to the case of a brain-dead pregnant woman, and in this book I wish to offer a fourth model, which takes into consideration the specific circumstances of the dilemma of whether to maintain a brain-dead pregnant woman on life-support for the delivery of her fetus or not. In order to understand why the donor model does not fit into this dilemma, it is important to realize first the idea behind this model.

The idea of organ donations from the dead seeks to promote the welfare of an existing human being, who is in need of immediate therapy by way of transplantation. Its first and foremost aim is to save the life of the sick. The dilemma discussed in this book usually occurs when the fetus is premature and can only be delivered by cesarean section, so that the only possible way to keep the fetus alive (rather than save his life) is by maintaining the dead mother artificially until the point when it becomes possible to deliver the fetus successfully. As will be elaborated in my next chapter, the fetus is not 'sick' nor does it enjoy any moral status similar to an existing person. No wonder then that the organ donation model does not include the situation of post-mortem pregnancy. This is why the Israeli legislator for example chose to add the situation of post-mortem pregnancy to this model while regulating its performance (The Anatomy and Pathology Act, 1963, section 6C). The assumption was that maintaining a brain-dead pregnant woman on life-support is *not* a regular 'treatment' permitted under this model.

Human tissue gift laws provide the means of effecting an anatomical gift (usually an organ donation), the persons who may consent to such a gift, and the specific circumstances under which the gift should be given. In *Lyon v. United States* (1994), the court explained the purpose of such law:

> The Uniform Anatomical Gift Act is clearly designed to balance two competing policy interests. There is the need for donations of eyes and other organs for transplantation and research purposes. Time is usually of the essence in securing donated organs at the time of the donor's death. The act allows hospitals and physicians to ascertain with a high degree of certainty when someone is willing to donate organs, and to arrange for the prompt removal and preservation of donated organs. The act also recognizes the religious and moral sensibilities of those who do not wish to donate organs. The act does not compel organ donations nor does it establish a presumption that organs will be donated.[7]

It is clear that the first and major interest standing behind the establishment of organ donation laws does not apply to the case of post-mortem pregnancy. Treating the body of a brain-dead pregnant woman evokes approximately the same sensibilities and psychological inclinations as those existing in any other procedures performed on a body of a deceased. But the fact that the woman is pregnant adds more agony to her grieving relatives and friends and in a way magnifies the 'illusion' created by the lively appearance of the patient and the reality of her being dead.

Applying the human tissue gift model to the case of a brain-dead pregnant woman brings too many uncertainties. It is not clear what is the 'gift', and who is the 'recipient' of it. Assuming that the 'gift' is the fetus, the result of the 'donation' seems to be odd: the recipient (fetus) is the gift in itself. This is not the case in organ donation where the gift is only 'part' of the recipient. Moreover, the fetus, as a potential life and potential person, cannot be considered a 'Human Tissue' neither because of its moral stance, nor due to the fact that it is not 'replaceable by natural process of repair'. Finally, as I described above, in some of the provinces in Canada (such as Ontario, Prince Edwards Island and Manitoba) and in the new English law, the fetus is explicitly excluded from post-mortem gift statutes. Applying the donor model directly conflicts with the existing law.

But regardless of the legal difficulties of such an application, the rationale for it is also flawed. Applying this model to the case of a dead pregnant woman treats the mother and the fetus as two separate entities, a donor and a recipient, ignoring the unique symbiotic relationship between them (or within the mother) (Glover, 1993, p. 344). In organ donation, the relationship between the donor and the recipient is formed with the death of the donor. It does not exist before. Unless the parties were cast in the film *21 Grams*,[8] this relationship also does not exist after the act of donation. In our case, the apparent relationship between the alleged 'donor' and 'recipient' already exists. It is an inherent biological bond. As Jacqueline Glover nicely articulates, 'for organ donation, the relationship is a new one. One person dies and then becomes a donor to a recipient. A pregnant woman is already in relationship with her "recipient", and upon death, the "donation" continues' (Glover, 1993, p. 344).

It is difficult to compare the brain-dead mother to a 'donor'. Unlike a donor, who is only to be remembered as a distant and non-identifiable 'other' by those related to the organ recipient, the mother will always be present as a wife, a daughter, a sister, and a friend of the future child and of the family members. Indeed, 'we cannot reduce the moral question to one of self-determination, nor can we reduce the complex relationships involved to a model of donation of organs among strangers' (Glover, 1993, p. 343).

It is also difficult to compare the fetus to a 'recipient', whose moral status is of an already existing living being. Furthermore, the medical procedure is different in the two situations. Maintaining a cadaver for organ donation lasts for a much shorter time than maintaining a brain-dead pregnant woman on life-support. On this basis, one cannot accept Peart *et al.*'s reasoning that the process of maintaining a dead woman on life-support should be considered a 'therapeutic purpose'. As Richard Paige correctly argues, the term 'therapeutic purposes' meant to permit ventilation of a corpse, usually for several days, until a recipient of organs is found (Paige, 2000, p. 5). In addition, organs donated from the deceased serve as cure and treatment for the recipient. One cannot really argue that this is the case with a brain-dead pregnant woman.

Furthermore, in the case of maternal brain-death we are dealing with a shared genetic material, rather than a tissue. This 'proposed gift' is closer to 'a person' than a mere gamete, and is farther than being a 'replaceable' tissue. The idea of giving it as a gift, which implies that it is subject to a property or quasi-property interest seems far and does not fit to the existing law (*Moore v. Regents of the University of California*, 1990[9]). Indeed, the American case of *Hecht v. Superior Court* (1993)[10] as well as the French case of *Parpalaix v. CECOS* (1984)[11] and of *Mme Claire G v. CECOS* (1991)[12] regarded gametes as property or quasi-property. However, when dealt with the status of embryos, the US case of *Davis v. Davis* (1990) concluded that embryos are not strictly speaking, either 'persons' or 'property', but occupy an interim category that entitles them to special respect because of their potential for human life. The closer we get to the living creature of a fetus, the more we are reluctant to regard it as property.

Kantor and Hoskins argue for future legal responsibilities that the donor may owe the recipient. Nevertheless, it is not clear what these responsibilities are in a system that holds no duty to rescue others in general, and that respects the obtaining of express or presumed consent for organ donation, specifically. Even if such responsibilities exist, it is difficult to compare them to 'close emotional ties' of the family of the pregnant woman. Moreover, as I will show in chapter 7, a pregnant woman's ethical obligations toward her fetus end upon her death. No comparison of such potential responsibilities to the case of organ donation is valid any more with the death of the pregnant woman.

Finally, from a practical reason, it is difficult to see how applying the organ donor model to brain-dead pregnant women promotes the proposed procedure. Although this model seems to confer wide discretion to next of kin by empowering them to give consent on behalf of the deceased in organ donation, neither partners, nor indeed the intending donor, can insist either that an organ should be removed or that it should be used in a general or a specific way. The wording 'may', in the new English law, support such a reading (Paige, 2000). Thus, the partner of a deceased woman or her other relatives would not truly benefit from this analogy, as it would still be impermissible to require the mother's death, or to maintain her on life-support for the successful delivery of her fetus.

CONCLUSION

In this chapter, the law of 'post-mortem gift' ('Human Tissue Law') has been reviewed. This law provides the mechanism to permit the use of cadavers for therapeutic purposes, medical education or scientific research. After describing the Canadian, American and English legal frameworks on this issue, three main proposals from the literature to apply the donor organ model to the case of a brain-dead pregnant woman were discussed.

Analysing these proposals resulted in the conclusion that due to difficulties in the language of existing law and substantive differences in the rationales of both processes and their participants (donor/recipient/mother/fetus), the organ-donor model should not and cannot be applied to the case of a dead pregnant woman. As Hilde Nelson writes, it is one thing to have organs taken out of one's body before burial, and quite another to have that body subjected to unremitting intensive treatment for weeks and even months (Nelson, 1994, p. 259).

Nevertheless, discussion of post-mortem gift law indicates the importance that the law attaches to the body of a deceased. If the deceased did not ask that his or her body be used for any of the purposes mentioned in law, no other person is entitled to ask for it, especially if there is reason to believe that the deceased would have objected. Promoting respect for the deceased's wishes generally and respect for the pregnant woman's choices and right to self-determination specifically were the conclusions developed in this book earlier following the interpretation of the Canadian abortion law (chapter 1) and the law governing bodily interventions with pregnant women in general (chapter 2). These were also identified in the fact that unlike the US, Canada seemed to avoid enacting pregnancy clauses, in its advance directive legislation (chapter 3). With these discussions behind, I will turn to consider in the next chapter the core issues that are raised in the context of the dilemma of whether or not to maintain a brain-dead pregnant woman on life-support.

NOTES

1   This legislation also deals with '*inter-vivos*' gifts for transplants, that is the extraction of organs from living persons for purposes of transplantation. I will not discuss this part, in my book.
2   See for Alberta, *Human Tissue Gift Act*, R.S.A. 2000, c. H-15; for British Columbia, *Human Tissue Gift Act*, R.S.B.C. 1996, c. 211; for Ontario, *Trillium Gift of Life Network Act*, R.S.O. 1990, c. H. 20; for Manitoba, *Human Tissue Gift Act*, S.M. 1987–8, c. 39; for New Brunswick, *Human Tissue Act*, S.N.B. 1986 c. H-12; for Prince Edwards Island, *Human Tissue Donation Act*, R.S.P.E.I. 1988, c. H-12.1; for Yukon, *Human Tissue Gift Act*, R.S.Y. 1986, c. 89; for Nova Scotia, *Human Tissue Gift Act*, R.S.N.S. 1989, c. 215; for Saskatchewan, *Human Tissue Act*, R.S.S. 1978, c. H-15; for Nunavut, *Human Tissue Act*, R.S.N. 1990, c. H-15; for Northwest Territories, *Human Tissue Act*, R.N.W.T. 1988, c. H-6.
3   See, for example, *Human Tissue Gift Act*, R.S.A. 2000, c. H-15, s. 4(1).
4   Ibid. s. 5(1). The Ontario statute adds the same-sex partner to the list of the people who can make decisions on behalf of the deceased.
5   There is some uncertainty as to who this person is. This person could be the executor nominated in a will, a close family member or the person in charge of the hospital where the body is laying. But there could be other persons who can fit this description.
6   Section 4 of the Bill provides the mechanism through which such an appointment is valid.
7   *Lyon v. United States*, 843 F. Supp. 531, 536 (D. Minn, 1994).
8   *21 Grams* (2003) Directed by Focus Features; Screenwriter: Alejandro Gonzalez Inarritu.
9   In this case, the plaintiff had his spleen removed as part of his treatment for a particular form of leukemia. On discovering that a cell line had been developed from this, which had the potential to generate a lot of money, Moore sued under a variety of headings. The Supreme Court of California held that there were no, or only very limited, property rights in any cells removed from the human body. The court dealt

with the case by applying the principle of consent to medical treatment rather than analysing it from property-law perspective.

10 In this case, William Kane had committed suicide and left behind vials of his sperm. Kane had also left instructions that the sperm was for the use of his partner, Deborah Hecht. Kane's existing child from his first marriage sought to challenge Hecht's right to use the sperm. The Court of Appeal ruled that sperm can be bequeathed in a will and that Kane had the capacity to decide whether to use his sperm or not.

11 In this case, Alain Parpalaix stored his sperm before beginning treatment for testicular cancer. After his death, his widow wanted to use his sperm for insemination, but her request was refused by the sperm bank. The refusal of the sperm bank was based on the assertion that sperm was an indivisible part of the body and could not be heritable property in the absence of specific instructions from the person with whom the bank contracted. The tribunal court held that by depositing the sperm, Alain Paraplaix's intentions were clear, and awarded the sperm to his wife.

12 In this case, having learned from the experience of the *Parpalaix* case, the sperm bank told Michel G., who was also about to undergo treatment for testicular cancer, and wished to store his sperm, that their policy was that posthumous insemination was unacceptable. Michel's widow wanted to obtain the sperm, but it was held that the legitimate desire to have a child does not create an indefensible right to a child.

Chapter 5

Maternal Brain-Death: The Main Issues

Up to this point, I approached the debate surrounding the question of whether to maintain a brain-dead pregnant woman on life-support by looking at comparable *situations*, dealing with medical interventions in the woman's pregnancy or in the deceased's body. In this chapter, I will discuss the main *issues* raised by the situation of maternal brain-death. These will include the moral and legal status of the fetus, the interest/right of the fetus to be born, the gestational age of the fetus, pragmatic obstacles to maintaining a dead pregnant woman on life-support, rights/interests of brain-dead people, the legal requirement for consent, rights of next-of-kin and friends of the deceased, and the physician-patient relationship.

THE LEGAL AND MORAL STATUS OF THE FETUS

> Like the family, the fetus is a condensed symbol. The fetus simultaneously stands for the desire to regain traditional society, and for hostility to feminism and freer sexuality which threaten that world ... Further, the desire to protect the fetus – itself thematized as a miraculous meeting of nature and God – is connected with the view that the world is changing in ominous and threatening ways, ways that even deny life itself the opportunity to come into being.[1]

Moral status

What is the moral status of the fetus? Literature is divided in this question, ranging from arguing that the fetus has full moral status as persons who have been already born, to holding that fetuses have only a partial moral status and, therefore a partial set of rights (Beauchamp and Walters, 1999, p. 191), or even a more extreme view, *i.e.* of Peter Singer, which holds that moral status depends on capacity for moral agency, hence fetuses are similar to animals corresponding to their gestational stage. I will examine this question from two perspectives: The fetus as a human being and as a person.

Human-being

Many are willing to argue that an individual life begins at fertilization, but not that there is a psychological human being at fertilization. The concept of humanity is a confusing one, as it can bear two distinct meanings. On the one hand, it can mean biological human life, that is a group of characteristics, which set the human species apart from non-human species. On the other hand, 'humanity' can be used to mean a way of life that is distinctively human, and characterized by psychological, rather than biological properties. These characteristics can consist of the ability to use symbols, to imagine, to love, and to engage in higher intellectual skills. In this regard, the fetus is human only under the first meaning.

Personhood

Another concept that is attached to the question concerning the moral status of the fetus is whether the fetus is a person. The literature suggests a list of demanding criteria for being a person. The list consists of the requirement for self-consciousness, freedom to act and the capacity to engage in purposeful sequences of actions, having reasons for actions and the ability to appreciate reasons for acting, ability to communicate with other persons using a language, capacity to make moral judgments, and rationality. There is a broad consensus that more than one of these criteria is necessary to qualify as a person and some insist that consciousness, reasoning, self-motivated activity, advanced communicative abilities, and the presence of self-concepts are at least jointly sufficient for being a person (Warren, 1984, p. 102). It is clear that the fetus lacks these criteria.

The law also regards the fetus as a non-person. Under *Roe v. Wade* (1973), the word 'person' as used in the Fourteenth Amendment does not include the 'unborn'. Since *Roe*, there have been many attempts in the US to amend the constitution to grant fetuses the status of persons, to persuade Congress to declare fetuses persons without a constitutional amendment, and even to include fetuses in the Civil Rights Act of 1964. These efforts were, however, all unsuccessful (Jordan, 1988, p. 1123). In the previous chapters, we saw that the Canadian courts were also reluctant to declare the fetus as a person (*R. v. Sullivan and Lemay*, 1991;[2] *Tremblay v. Daigle*, 1989[3]).

Legal status

At Common law, the fetus is not a person entitled to legal protection, although courts have consistently referred to the power of legislature specifically to address this issue (Rodgers, 2002, p. 342). When in conflict with its mother, the fetus has no independent right to protection, and the fetus's interests are usually protected under 'the umbrella' of the state. The fetus and the pregnant woman are one entity in fact as well as in law (*Winnipeg Child and Family Services v. D.F.G.*, 1997, p. 945). Though the fetus is protected by the criminal law,[4] and the civil law,[5] it has a peculiar status while it is *in uterus*. The fetus is regarded as a distinct organism living in symbiosis with its mother (Peart *et al.*, 2000, p. 287). Sometimes it is also referred to as an organism *sui generis*, by which it lacks the full attributes of a legal person prior to its birth

(*Paton v. Trustees of The British Pregnancy Advisory Service and Another*, 1978, p. 989; *Re F (in utero)*, 1988).[6]

The maternal-fetal relationship has been described as the 'not-one-but-not-two' model (Seymour, 2000, pp. 191–202). This model puts emphasis on the shared needs and interdependence of the woman and her fetus, whose relationship is characterized by connectedness, mutuality and reciprocity. This model of maternal-fetal relationship is the dominant one in Canada (*Winnipeg Child and Family Services v. D.F.G.*, 1997, p. 945; Randall, 1999) and in the UK (*A-G's Reference* (No. 3 of 1994), 1997, p. 943[7]).

The dependency relations between the mother and her fetus are important not only for the fetus, but also for the mother. While sharing her infertility problems with Lora Brown in the film '*The Hours*', Kitty sincerely admits: 'You can never call yourself a woman till you're a mother.' Being pregnant is what makes a woman to be a woman. It is related to her feeling of self – defining her sexuality and gender. As Ronald Dworkin writes:

> Her fetus is not merely 'in her' as an inanimate object might be, or something alive but alien that has been transplanted into her body. It is 'of her and is hers more than anyone's' because it is, more than anyone else's, her creation and her responsibility; it is alive because *she* has made it come alive [my emphasis].[8]

As I showed earlier, a descriptive analysis of the law leads to the conclusion that the fetus has no legal rights. A normative analysis can lead to the same result. The notion of independent fetal rights is predicated on an idea of disembodied fetus, which somehow floats in an existence separate and apart from the woman's body, which provides the fetus sustenance. Iris Young explains this mistaken idea. 'The dominant culture projects pregnancy as a time of quiet waiting. We refer to the woman as "expecting", as though this new life were flying in from another planet and she sat in her rocking chair by the window, occasionally moving the curtain aside to see whether the ship is coming' (Young, 1990, p. 167). This dualistic view, which posits a maternal-fetal conflict, not only assumes antagonistic rights between the pregnant woman and her fetus, but also lends itself to advocating a range of state policies and legal interventions (like the one in the *D.F.G.* case, 1997) that are inherently adversarial in their approach to regulating the lives of pregnant women. Indeed, as Molly Dyke argues when the state subordinates a pregnant woman's choice to the rights of her fetus, the state is viewing the woman and her fetus as two distinct entities with hostile interests (Dyke, 1990, p. 886). Recognizing fetal rights strips women of their autonomous agency and privacy that serve as key elements for their personhood. Women lose their right to effectively refuse even the most intrusive violations of their bodies, their ability to make non-coerced choices about everyday life.

Even if the fetus does not have rights, he or she may still have interests. One suggestion that has been offered in the literature is to claim that a fetus has no autonomy-based interests, but only beneficence-based interests (Chervenak and McCullough, 1993, p. 349). This is because the fetus lacks the capacity to generate its own values and beliefs, which, in turn, would generate autonomy-based obligations.

Alan Fleischman goes through this route. He proposes to abandon the 'rights' discourse and instead talk in utilitarian terms of interests (Fleischman, 1989, p. 254). In his view, the proper course of action is one that maximizes good consequences, achieved by an analysis of risks and benefits of treatment for the parties concerned, third parties and society in general.

However, as Fleischman points out himself, the flaw of such an approach lies in the difficulty to predict outcomes that derive from the fact that diagnostic and therapeutic procedures applied to the fetus involve significant uncertainty and clear risks to both the fetus and the pregnant woman.

Assuming that such an approach is feasible, I prefer to focus my analysis on a more concrete way. In my next section, I will examine one such beneficence-based interest/right, that is the interest/right to be born, and more generally, the interest/right to life.

INTEREST/RIGHT TO LIFE

If the fetus has right or interest to life, doctors might have a corresponding duty to maintain the dead woman on life-support for the delivery of the fetus (Peart *et al.*, 2000, p. 293).[9] What is the scope of the interest in protecting potential life? Is there a right to be born?

Section 7 of the Canadian Charter of Rights and Freedoms (1982) states that: 'Everyone has the right to life.' In other sections of the Charter, the subject of the rights is termed 'individual', 'person', or 'citizen'.[10] From a linguistic perspective, interpreting the term 'everyone' to also include the fetus can be bearable. However, when given the opportunity to broaden the right to life to fetuses, courts did not go in this direction, and no direct application of this section to the fetus has been made.

As I indicated above, the American courts also refused to include the fetus under the term 'person' in the Constitution, thereby preventing the fetus from holding legal rights. The same applies to Europe. While already-born persons have an absolute right to live under article 2(1) of the European Convention of Human Rights 1950, the European Commission held that a fetus may not have an interest to life, but if it does, it must be restrained by its mother's right to life (*Paton v. UK*, 1980, p. 415).

Indeed, the core element of the right to life is in the claim not to be killed *unjustly* (Thomson, 1999, p. 206). Letting the mother (continue to) die is not unjustly killing the fetus. The death of the mother ceased the potential life of her fetus. The decision not to maintain the dead woman on life-support does not directly violate the fetus's right to life.

An alternative claim would be that even if the fetus has right to life, this right is liberty (or negative) right, that is a right to be free from pressure, duress or control – not a right to require action such as maintaining the mother on life-support (McLean, 1999). Judith Jarvis Thomson argues that having a right to life does not guarantee having either a right to be given the use of, or a right to be allowed continued use of, another person's body – even if one needs it for life itself (Thomson, 1999, p. 206).

I would like to support this argument by joining the distinction the court made between negative and positive rights in the *L. and H.* case (*Child and Family Services of Manitoba v. L. and H.*, 1997). In this case, the patient, a three-month-old child, suffered from 'shaken baby syndrome' which resulted in a permanent vegetative state. The Child and Family Services of Manitoba joined the recommendation of the child's physician for a DNR order. The patient's parents refused this recommendation and the agency went to court to seek an approval for the order.

The agency won, and on appeal, the High Court made a distinction between two kinds of rights. The first is the 'negative' right to refuse treatment; *i.e.* that patients are empowered to tell their physician not to interfere with their body without consent. The second is the 'positive' right to demand medical treatment, which is less recognized by law, and only in situations related to public health and safety.

Applying this distinction to our case would make a dramatic difference between the argument of not killing intentionally the fetus and imposing a massive life-support 'treatment', which is not in the interest of the *patient* (the mother), for the potential life of the fetus.

Even if the fetus does not have a right to life, he or she may still have a right to be born. Morally, such a right carries less weight than the right to life. But more importantly, it assumes that the child to be born will have life full of equality. However, as D. Gareth Jones argues:

> Although the benefit to the fetus may initially appear substantial (its life may be saved, when without intervention it would die) the fact that it will most probably be born prematurely (with the attendant risk of health impairment and disability), and may subsequently require repeated and prolonged medical treatment leads one to question whether there is in fact a clear benefit to the fetus and subsequent child.[11]

It seems that in the case of post-mortem pregnancy the right to be born should be balanced with the outcomes of this birth when it occurs after the proposed medical procedure. This leads to the next examination concerning the gestational age of the fetus.

THE GESTATIONAL AGE OF THE FETUS

Children born from postmortem pregnancies will be premature – sometimes quite severely premature – and so are at risk for serious ailments, ranging from brain damage to lung disorders (Kantor and Hoskins, 1993, pp. 308–9). One can argue that even if there is a duty to maintain bodily functions for the sake of the fetus, it still depends on the stage of the fetus's development, when maternal brain-death occurs, and on the clinical prognosis for the fetus.[12] It is expected that the more mature the fetus is at that time, the greater its chances of being delivered healthy.[13]

Of course, having decisions related to the potential well being of the fetus is in itself debatable, as it is not clear whether a reduction in 'quality of life', produced by physical and mental disabilities, is an appropriate consideration for the decision to terminate pregnancy. Moreover, the following questions arise in this context: Is there enough scientific knowledge to establish the chances of survival? Are the courts equipped to assess an expert testimony on such medical knowledge? In the *Piazzi* case, the court was convinced by the experts' evidence that the fetus has high chances of survival. The fetus nevertheless survived for only two days (*University Health Services, Inc. v. Piazzi*, 1986).

PRAGMATIC OBSTACLES FOR THE PROPOSED MEDICAL PROCEDURE

When on life-support, brain-dead patients tend to run into a host of medical complications. They often develop 'cardiac asystole (cessation of the heartbeat) within seven days, despite continued full cardio-respiratory support' (Peart *et al.*, 2000, p. 294). Many suffer from hypotension, loss of central autoregulation (Vives *et al.*, 1996, p. 69), pituitary insufficiency, glucose intolerance, thermo-variability, infectious complications resulting from prolonged assisted mechanical ventilation, and chronic bladder instrumentation (Bernstein *et al.*, 1989, p. 436; Santos, 1993, p. 46; Kantor and Hoskins, 1993, pp. 308–9).

In addition, intensive medical care is necessary to ensure that the fetus's needs are met,[14] and, accordingly considerable effort and resources must be made.[15] An argument could be made that a just society cannot and should not afford to direct thousands of dollars per day for an indefinite number of weeks or months on the care of one individual under conditions of moderately scarce medical resources.

Insistence on continuation of pregnancy also brings emotional trauma and invasive publicity to families (Gallagher, 1989, p. 194). Not only must families and friends go through the premature death of the woman herself, but one can suggest that they are also subjected to the genuinely horrifying knowledge that her body is being appropriated by strangers against her explicit wishes, used as an object in their symbolic warfare. This emotional stress characterizes not only family members but also critical care nurses. In the next chapter I will bring direct examples for such a distressful experience.

Finally, mishandling or abuse of dead bodies can be punishable by criminal penalties (Gallagher, 1989; *Canadian Criminal Code*, 1985, section 182) and by tort liability for 'outrage' or reckless infliction of emotional distress (*Lacy v. Cooper Hospital: University Medical Center*, 1990). Caution from possible legal responsibility can also serve as a pragmatic obstacle to health-care providers thereby restraning their readiness to maintain the dead woman on life support.[16]

RIGHTS/INTERESTS OF THE BRAIN-DEAD MOTHER

Legal analysis

One of the claims which support the maintenance of a brain-dead pregnant patient on life-sustaining treatment, is that the patient is already dead.[17] If the woman is dead, the argument goes, she is not a person anymore (Peart *et al.*, 2000, p. 292). Nor does she have interests or rights (Field *et al.*, 1988, p. 821; Fost 1994, p. 31).[18] Questions of autonomy cease to have relevance (Peart *et al.*, 2000, p. 292; Field *et al.*, 1988, p. 821).

Indeed, brain-death is recognized as legal death. *The Uniform Determination of Death Act* (hereinafter: UDDA), proposed in 1980 by the President's Commission for the Study of Ethical Problems in Medicine and Biomedical and Behavioral Research follows the Harvard Medical School Ad Hoc Committee's recommendations in this matter[19] and provides a model for legislating the brain-cessation criterion as legal death (*Uniform Brain Death Act*, 1997). This model was endorsed by the American Medical Association and the American Bar Association and has been adopted in various forms of legislation by 44 states in the US (including the District of Columbia). In Canada, brain-death was also approved to be legal by the Canadian Congress Committee on Brain Death,[20] the Canadian Medical Association and the Canadian Neurocritical Care Group (Beaulieu *et al.*, 1999). Section 1 to the UDDA (1980) states that:

> An individual who has sustained either (1) irreversible cessation of circulatory and respiratory functions, or (2) irreversible cessation of all functions of the entire brain, including the brain stem, is dead.

However, one can still argue that the UDDA does not set the brain-cessation criterion as the *only* method of assessing death. Rather, brain-death is an *optional* criterion for determining legal death *within the discretion* of the patient's attending physician. The medical profession remains free to formulate acceptable medical practices and to utilize new medical biomedical knowledge, diagnostic tests and equipment. If this argument is sound, women diagnosable as brain dead can legally be treated as still alive because their heartbeat and respiration are artificially maintained.

The history of the UDDA may support such an argument. In the Bill of this act it was stated that death criteria should not prohibit 'the use of other medically recognized criteria for determining death, as long as such a determination is made in accordance with accepted medical standards' (section 2).[21] The original version of the statute specifically asked for *at least* one of the criterion for the determination of death, and in the explanation of the bill it was emphasized that the bill provides that each criterion is not exclusive in determining death, 'allowing for the exercise of medical discretion'.

Even if one does not accept the argument that a 'breathing' brain-dead patient should be treated as a living person, the view that a brain-dead patient is deprived of rights or interests, which is referred to by Finnerty *et al.* (1999) as 'the cadaveric model', is distressing. Such an approach goes against most of our societal norms, which accord great respect and reverence for the dead people and sanctity for their bodies. Moreover, it has far reaching dangerous implications. Dr. Guy Benrubi, writes in his comments to Finnerty *et al.*:

> If, in fact, we accept the cadaveric model, does that mean that anyone can harvest organs without permission? Does it mean that we will have harvesting companies who will be

lurking right outside emergency departments and following patients into the hospital? Would health maintenance organizations sign contracts with harvesting companies for exclusive harvesting use of organs in patients who die under their plan? Would people get discounts if they decide to sign up with certain harvesting providers once they sign with their health maintenance organization? Would we have harvesting companies contracting with the state to harvest organs from executed criminals, and would that, in fact, lead to an increased number of executions with harder chances for appeal?[22]

A milder approach to the 'cadavric model' consists of the claim that dead persons have rights, but they deserve less consideration than the rights of living persons. However, when trying to look more closely at the rights involved, it is difficult to make such an argument. The right to privacy, autonomy, but most importantly the right to be treated humanly with dignity are not subject to degrees of gradation. These are fundamental rights that, due to their nature, demand protection by strict scrutiny. In my view, they should not hinge upon the question of whether their potential holder is dead or alive.

On harming the dead

The inquiry concerning the interests of dead patients also relates to the distinction between harm and wrong. Usually, it is argued that since dead people do not experience pain, let alone aware of any feeling at all, they cannot be harmed. However, it is still possible to claim that dead people can be wronged. Consider, for example, the idea of lying. If we lie to our friends, they may not be harmed, but they can be wronged even when they do not find out about the lie. Morally we are doing something wrong. Likewise, the dead can be wronged even if they cannot be aware of it, and even if they did not give this a thought while alive, asking to be treated differently (Spike and Greenlaw, 1995, p. 293; Glover, 1993, p. 343).

Moreover, claiming that the dead do not have the ability to suffer or to feel pain can lead not only to the conclusion that dead cannot be harmed, but, conversely, to the outcome that maintaining the woman on life-support cannot be to her benefit or in her interest.

Indeed, experiencing harm does not necessitate temporal existence. In a remarkable article on death, Thomas Nagel refutes the view that our fear of and objection to, death derives from the belief that when we die, we cease to exist (Nagel, 1979). Nagel suggests two indications which support this conclusion. We do not regard the *temporary* suspension of life, even for substantial intervals, as *in itself* a misfortune. Second, we did not exist before we were born (or conceived), and yet few of us regard that as a misfortune. Nagel holds the position that most of good and ill fortune has as its subject a person identified by her *history and possibilities*, rather than merely by her categorical state of the moment. The idea that there necessarily is a temporal relation between the subject of a harm and the circumstances which constitute it is unconvincing indeed. As Nagel writes:

> There are goods and evils which are irreducibly relational: they are features of the relations between a person, with spatial and temporal boundaries of the usual sort, and circumstances which may not coincide with him either in space or in time.

A man's life includes much that does not take place within the boundaries of his body and his mind, and what happens to him can include much that does not take place within the boundaries of his life [my emphasis].[23]

Nagel's idea that certain good and bad things attach to *human* subjects atemporally and beyond their life span can also be seen in the writings of Immanuel Kant. While discussing the interest to good reputation after one's death, Kant explains that such an interest is an 'innate external belonging', which is attributed to its subject *as a person* no matter if she exists or not. In his words, 'for in the context of his relation to others, I actually regard every person simply in terms of his humanity, hence as *homo noumenon*' (Kant, 1996, pp. 76–7). No doubt, a brain-dead pregnant woman is still a member in the human society.

But the idea of harming the dead goes deeper. In his book, *Speaking for the Dead: Cadavers in Biology and Medicine*, D. Gareth Jones argues that a 'now-dead' person has interests that go beyond her lifetime, based on what he calls the intrinsic value of the cadaver (Jones, 2000; Jones, 1995). Jones claims that we cannot assume that because a woman was pregnant at the time of becoming brain-dead, she would inevitably want the pregnancy continued after her death. Maintaining a brain-dead woman on life-support without specific consent is, in his view, an act of disrespect towards the 'now-dead', treating her as no more than a human incubator (Jones, 2000).[24]

Nicola Peart *et al.* agree with Jones so long as the woman's wishes are known. However, if her wishes are unknown they do not consider that 'the moral obligation to respect cadavers is a strong enough ethical reason for discontinuing a treatment that would save the life of the fetus' (Peart *et al.*, 2000, p. 297). In their view, respecting the autonomy of the dead woman when her wishes are unknown is 'an unwarranted extension of the concept of autonomy, and it disregards the fact that the benefit of continuing treatment to the fetus outweighs any harm to the dead woman' (Peart *et al.*, 2000, p. 297).

The idea that dead people have interests is developed in Joel Geinberg's theory of Harm (Feinberg, 1984). By arguing that X has an interest one really means that X has a moral or legal claim (the latter is usually a legal right) for a specific outcome or condition. Once this claim is defeated or set back, a harm has been made to X (Feinberg, 1984, p. 33). According to Feinberg, interests can survive the death of a person (Feinberg, 1984, p. 83). Feinberg follows George Pitcher in arguing that interests harmed by posthumous events (including the harm of death itself) are not interests of the remaining body ('the *post-mortem* person'), rather they are interests of the living person who no longer exists ('the *ante-mortem* person') (Pitcher, 1984, p. 184;[25] Feinberg, 1984, p. 89; Scarre, 2003, p. 244). T. M. Wilkinson helps us understand the categories of *ante-mortem* and *post-mortem* person through our memories. When I remember my dead grandmother, says Wilkinson, I remember not the grandmother *as she is now* but the *living woman in the past* (Wilkinson, 2002, p. 34).

It is easy to see how the idea of posthumous interests can be further applied to a general theory of rights. By focusing on the preservation of well-being rather than on the exercise of choice, the interest theory of rights leaves open the possibility of ascribing legal rights to dead people (Kramer, 2001). Matthew Kramer follows this theory and applies it to the dead. He argues that because various aspects of the well-being of dead people can receive essential protection through legal norms, these creatures can be classified as potential right-holders. Ascribing such rights is possible, in his view, by subsuming the immediate aftermath of each dead person's life within the overall course of his or her existence – through highlighting the ways in which the dead person still exists after his or her death (*e.g.* the continuing influence of the dead person on other people and on the development of various events, the memories of him or her that reside in the minds of people who knew of him or her or knew him or her, and the array of possessions which she accumulated and then bequeathed or failed to bequeath) (Kramer, 2001). Although the appropriateness of classifying a dead person as a potential right-holder under this view will last for only a certain period of time, a 'recently dead' pregnant woman who is about to be maintained on life-sustaining treatment falls into this period of time.

Even if one does not agree that the newly-dead have rights as much as the living, one can still claim that some interests of the living person (such as in not being harmed) survive after death (Buchanan and Brock, 1989, p. 166).[26] Buchanan and Brock claim that surviving interests cannot be construed as rights of *self*-determination because this *self* no longer exists. Instead, they argue, the former self has a 'right of disposal' over 'what is to happen to one's living, non-person successor' – a right we should conceive 'as something like a property right in an external object' (Buchanan and Brock, 1989, p. 166). Of course, this right of disposal asserts interests in treatment decisions for the new (non) person as well as interests in disposition of the dead body.[27] Maintenance on life-support is one such decision.

More generally, the law's recognition in caring for the dying, along with freeing them from suffering rather than simply postponing their death reflects the fundamental respect that the law shares for the sanctity of life but also for the 'sanctity' of its end.[28] Not only when an individual is declared dead, is it the case that any 'best interests' that this individual had in receiving medical treatment can no longer (strictly speaking) exist, but the English case of *In re A.* (1993)[29] also established that treatment after death would be a 'continuing indignity' to the dead.

Performing procedures on the dead without consent may be considered contrary to public policy. This argument has been raised in the general context of posthumous reproduction and in the more particular case of the use of gametes of a deceased person. The English Warnock Committee who examined the English Human Fertilisation and Embryology Act stated in its report that the use by a widow of her dead husband's semen for AIH is a practice which 'we feel should be actively discouraged'.[30] In its response to the Warnock Report, the English government recognized that 'many people are uneasy about this practice' and did not feel it should be actively encouraged (McLean, 1999, p. 336). This uneasiness is probably the explanation for legally declaring the posthumous child as being fatherless.[31]

Moral intuitions

Our moral intuitions towards the dead consisting of 'feeling uneasy' are believed to have three major components (Jones, 2000, p. 42). An initial component is the close identification of people and their bodies. D. Gareth Jones argues that our recognition of each other depends upon recognition of an array of physical characteristics, which are distinctive features during life, and are not extinguished immediately upon death. Hence, what is done to a dead body effects *our feeling about that person when alive*. It is impossible to separate between the cadaver and the person she is.

The second component concerns other people's responses to the cadaver. By 'people', Jones refers to those who knew the deceased while alive and had memories of that person. According to this view, the cadaver represents an array of built-in memories that can never be completely separated from it. These memories convey an obligation to respect the deceased and its built-in associations. Disrespect of the cadaver, on the other hand, evokes a sense of revolution.

A third component concerns the deceased personal relationships with relatives or friends. A special role is given to the people who are now grieving the deceased. From that perspective, respect for the deceased is respect for the relative's (or the friend's) grief. Jones mentions that *the reality* of the cadaver also plays a substantial role during the grieving process.[32] More generally, the wrong that is done to the dead is experienced by others on behalf of the dead (Glover, 1993, p. 344).

Psychological inclinations toward the dead

Because of its strong moral base, respect for the dead is reflected in our daily psychological inclinations. Maintaining a brain-dead pregnant woman on life-support for the successful delivery of her fetus while her body is in a permanent process of deterioration, is a painful emotional act. The experience with the German case of Marion Ploch, for example can teach us a lesson about the public reaction to such a procedure. 'SS-Nazi Pig', 'Concentration Camp Dr. Mengele', 'Dr. Frankenstein', 'Zur Leichengymnastik ('To the Gymnastics for Corpses'), 'Now Human – Instead of Animal – Experiments' are only few examples of such a reaction (Anstotz, 1993, pp. 344–5). This psychological response can also reflect the view that people may not accept brain-death as death. They attribute a moral status of a living person to the newly-dead. The concept of human dignity keeps playing an important role here.

Talking about the dead

Of course, our psychological reaction toward the dead pre-assumes that the dead still exist in a significant way. The best manifestation for this is seen in our language. Our speech pre-assumes that people regularly continue to exist after death. We describe people who have just died exactly the same way, as they were present prior to their death. David-Hillel Ruben mentions three possible posthumous uses in our language (David-Hillel, 2003, p. 10). 'Posthumous reference' is when we refer to a person who no longer exists, and the property predicated to that person as something she had only when or while she existed, so the property is not predicated posthumously. Under such use of the language only the reference is posthumous.[33] An example David-Hillel brings for such a reference is '*Napoleon* was Emperor of France in 1808'. But there is also a stronger posthumous use of the language where both the reference and the predicated property to the subject are posthumous. In the sentence '*Napoleon* is *now being eulogized*', reference is made now to Napoleon (who no longer exists) but also a property ascribed to him (being eulogized) in the present tense. Thirdly, there could be posthumous predication only with no reference at all. 'There is one and only person who was an Emperor of France in 1808 and he is being eulogized now' is an example for such use. What is common to all these uses, explains David-Hillel, is that in discussing the deceased (Napoleon), we clearly have a particular subject in mind to refer to or to predicate with. Although it may no exist in 'reality', this subject is a very specific and concrete one.

When we refer and predicate a dead person, thereby ascribing her a certain property, we assert of her that she continues to have that property. Reference or ascription of properties to a specific subject does not become impossible when the referent or the ascribed subject ceases to exist. As Loren Lomasky explains:

> The proposition $F(a)$ succeeds in referring if a is/was/will be, and '$F(a)$' is true if, timelessly, F is a property of a. It is timelessly true of A that A has end E and it also is timelessly true that wrongful thwartings of E count as violating the rights of A.[34]

Moreover when we say, 'we love Socrates' we pre-assume in a way that Socrates still exists to be loved. We still maintain the *relationship* of love when one relata had died. The relationship between the living and the dead does not altogether cease upon death. It continues through the actions of the living as they carry out the wishes of the dead. Furthermore, we have a direct epistemic and cognizant contact with the dead. We know them and they are familiar to us in the same way we recognize many of the living persons, having at some time made their acquaintance.

Our way of talking about the dead in the present tense reflects, like every other mode of language, the way we think of them, namely as existent *in some way*. Surely, the exact way needs to be explored, but the fact that the dead *as a person* may not exist after biological death should not deter us from assuming her persistent existence for the purpose of holding interests (and being ascribed with properties). We say, 'God is good', 'Love is great', or 'Red is a royal color' even though we do not know if God, Love or Red exist at all. Likewise, for the purpose of our talking, thinking and ascribing properties to the dead we need not explore the physical status of this subject. It is sufficient to conclude some kind of posthumous existence (maybe in a weaker sense than the usual one) that is necessary for our language and thinking. As David-Hillel argues:

> But if a property is true of some object at t, then surely the object of which the property is true at t must itself exist at t, just in order to display or exemplify that property at that time.[35]

Religious convictions

Another possible explanation for our strong reaction toward the dead can be found in religious convictions. The feeling of 'continuing indignity' to the dead patient, presented by the *Re A.* case (1993) discussed above and in greater length in chapter 2, is indeed very strong. It also has religious perspectives. The notion of human dignity is premised on the idea that human beings deserve to be treated humanly as creatures, who are being observed by God, their creator. It is the nature of this *special interaction between creatures and creator* that shapes the duty to act with dignity toward the first. This duty does not derive from an isolated intrinsic value of human beings, as assumed under a secular regime. D. Gareth Jones elaborates on this point in the following way:

> All human beings are to be viewed as having an inalienable dignity, stemming from our creation by God and revealed supremely in the redemption made possible by Christ. It rests not on what human beings can accomplish in material, social or spiritual terms, but on the rock of God's love. Consequently human dignity is always based on what individuals are in the sight of God and never on what they may be able to do for society, for mankind, or even for God. From this follows that those who are of no functional value to society still retain a dignity, since they remain important *in this sight and purposes of God*. Elements of this dignity are also to be found in those who have died, but a short time ago were one of us.[36]

Indeed, in some cases religious convictions have made the legislator to insist on treating patients even when they can be considered legally dead. In New York and New Jersey, for example, the law now requires physicians to honor the objections of family members to cease treatment of their beloved ones and to continue medical care *despite evidence of loss of brain function*.[37] The background for this legislation was the tremendous effect of neurological death has on Orthodox Jewish community on the one hand, holding that one whose heart still beats and whose respiration continues is still alive, and on some Japanese on the other hand, adhering to an understanding according to which neurological death is an unnatural and premature death that would hasten destruction of the mind-body union (Olick, 1991, p. 277). The importance of religious beliefs and the idea of remaining 'in the sight of God' leads to another element of our attitudes towards the dead, namely the idea of bodily continuity and personal identity.

The idea of continuity

Bodily continuity

Although the pregnant woman is dead, under the proposed medical intervention, her body continues to be 'alive'. One might hold that the idea of bodily continuity is what ethically matters in personal identity over time. According to this argument, as long as the *same* body is living, the *same* person is 'alive'. In the Judeo-Christian tradition a man not only *has* a body, he *is* his body (May, 1973). Furthermore, death rituals tell us that the person dies when the person's *body* is declared dead, but not before, and only from that moment is it appropriate to dispose of the corpse. The distinction between the death of the body and the death of the person whose body it is is sharply reflected in brain-death where the body of the 'dead' is still living and breathing.

Presupposition of unity

But the sense of continuity in one's personality is not restricted only to the existence of one's body. It is broader. In fact, it is presupposed in every act we do. Not only do our present actions really impact on our future, but we also perceive them as such. Unless we function on that basis, we would not have been able to do anything at all. Our anticipation for the effect of our present actions in the future is the basis for performing them. This anticipation is an intrinsic nature of the human being. As Robert Olick argues:

> Why should I rise each morning and labor through the day if I will be a different person at the end of the day; if my weekly paycheck goes to the bank account of a future person who is not me; or if my pension, savings and investments will benefit a future person who is not me?[38]

It is a rational presupposition of the moral life that X's actions have meaning for a future person who will still be the same X. Whether the future is one where we see ourselves alive, or where we anticipate we will be dead, is irrelevant to the premise of this presupposition. Therefore, the presupposition of unity makes it difficult to think that once the woman is dead, she is no longer the same person she was.

Narrative embodied in a single life

Another viewpoint from which one can look at the brain-dead pregnant woman is through her history. Following Alasdair MacIntyre's conception of the unity of life as 'the unity of a narrative embodied in a single life' (MacIntyre, 1984, p. 218), we should see ourselves as subjects of history consisted of past, present and future experiences, in which choices, actions, and relationships play a central part. Robert Olick articulates this point while criticizing the opposite approach: 'the successor new person, S^2 has no personal history. His personal life begins as a severely demented dying patient whose life will be extremely short. He has no family, no friends, no one who has been a part of his life and is able to act on his behalf in a way that takes a personal history into account' (Olick, 2001, p. 148). According to this view, what makes the various stages of a person's life to be *her* life is a *narrative* that makes that life intelligible. This narrative includes aspects of our natures and attitudes, and it also involves our moral agency and responsibility.

On the one hand, the intelligibility of an individual's life story pre-assumes that the chapters of her life are part of that same life and hence, presupposes a form of personal identity over time. On the other hand, we cannot make sense of the stages of a person's life without this narrative. Narrative, intelligibility of one's life and personal identity coexist and interrelate with each other. There is no meaning to speak exclusively of on one of these concepts without referring to the others. Moreover, because a life of a person is connected in important ways to the lives of others, such as family members, friends, etc., the narrative of that person is *part of their narrative*. The brain-death of the pregnant woman is not just an event in *her* life; it is an event in the lives of family and friends as well. It is a story of her life but also of theirs.

The human body

Death carries with it a personal intrinsic value manifested in the human body. We regard a person and her body to be inseparable. Moreover, when we recognize each other, we identify each other's bodies or attributes relating to their bodily parts such as their unique voice, special shape, or particular smell. While this description applies ideally to living people, some important aspects of this recognition process continue following death. The significant value attached to such a phenomenon leads to what Robert Wennberg calls the 'overflow principle':

> We do not treat human corpses as garbage, because the corpse is closely associated with persons: it is the remains of a physical organism that at one time supported and made possible personal life.[39]

All that remains of the person is the cadaver, and yet our respect for that person and for the memory of that person leads to respect for the person's remains. Moreover, the body of a deceased serves an important role in the initial grieving process. Hence, we show disrespect to the 'newly-dead' when we allow the corpse to be medically treated in the absence of any consent on the person's part prior to death, or without the approval of close relatives.

Is the body of a dead pregnant woman different than other women's bodies and men's bodies? To help this discussion, it may be instructive to have a sense of what it means to be on 'life-support'. Without a sense of what it means to be under these physical conditions, it may be hard to fully appreciate the arguments concerning the medical 'treatment' or 'mistreatment' of the dead.

The *Karen Quinlan* case provides a nice illustration (*In re Quinlan*, 1976). Although Quinlan was in a vegetative state, at the time of her trial she had a catheter inserted in her bladder, a respirator tube in her trachea, and a nasal gastro feeding tube in her nose and throat. Karen had received over 300 blood gas tests, a brain scan, an angiogram, an electroencephalogram, a lumber tap, and several other tests. She was emaciated and in a classic 'decorticate posture', with her feet drawn up near the buttocks and extended, her forearms drawn in against the chest, her joints severely rigid and deformed, and her hands at right angles to the forearms. To handle the continual risk of infection, antibiotics were administered and tests for infection constantly made.

Karen was almost constantly sweating, often profusely and when body rashes occurred she was constantly being moved and bathed. Heat lamps were used to treat her skin lesions known as decubiti, or bed sores, that were generated by her constant repose. She went through awake-and-sleep cycles, made stereotyped cries, yawns, and spastic movements, but was never conscious. Can this be called a dignified treatment of a woman's body? Would we want all this for a potential life that might not even survive or in the better way would suffer from physical and mental disabilities for life? I believe we should be tougher in our decision to allow it.

CONSENT

The Rule

The notion of consent is a fundamental doctrine in law and biomedical ethics. Its origin lies in the common law maxim, according to which medical intervention (invasive or not) can only be provided where the consent of the individual (usually the patient) to be treated has been obtained (*Schloendorff v. New York Hospital*, 1914).[40] The requirement of consent derives from the 'greatest right' (*Pratt v. Davis*, 1995) – the right to inviolability of a person and to bodily integrity. It follows that there is no *prima facie* justification to violate this right with the death of a patient.

Moreover, the law regards the notion of consent not as a mere contract between the patient and the physician but as a *process* aiming to ensure that no treatment is performed without the agreement of the patient (Nelson, 2002, p. 114). The procedural character of the consent requirement has led courts to recognize the patient's right to withdraw treatment at any time or stage of the treatment after an initial consent was given (*Ciarlariello v. Schacter*, 1993, p. 136). This leads to the conclusion that the consent requirement is not determined by the doctor-patient relationship that allegedly ends with the patient's death. Instead, it has a deeper origin that rests in the respect for the patient and her body. In *Malette v. Shulman* (1990), the court held that, as a matter of common law, touching the body of a patient during medical treatment would constitute a battery if the patient did not consent to the intervention.

Exceptions to the Rule

Under the common law, two general exceptions exist to the rule of consent. According to the first, while a health-care provider is faced with a true emergency (usually not anticipated), she can administer treatment without express consent (*Marshall v. Curry*, 1933; *Murray v. McMurchy*, 1949; *Civil Code of Quebec*, 1991, section 13). Here, the treatment is usually necessary to save life or avoid health complications when the patient cannot provide consent. However, it is well established that the 'emergency exception' does not apply where the reason for undertaking the procedure without consent has more to do with convenience than with an immediate need for treatment (Nelson, 2002, p. 118).

According to the second exception, a treatment can be administered without consent if an explicit legislative provision mandates so (Nelson, 2002, p. 116). Generally, there are two sorts of legislation with regard to this exception: mental health legislation and public health legislation concerning, for example the prevention of spreading a communicable disease.[41]

Another common exception to the rule of consent is 'the best interests' test. According to this test, the proposed medical intervention should serve the interests *of the person on whom it is proposed*. Third party interests are technically irrelevant (McLean, 1999, pp. 329, 332).

Maintaining a brain-dead pregnant woman on life-support is not an emergency case that is necessary *for the patient* (the dead woman). Certainly, it does not aim to save the life of the patient. Although the goal of the medical procedure is to save the fetus's life, this was not the original purpose of the exception to the consent requirement.

Does the proposed medical procedure serve the brain-dead woman's interests, specifically her interest in having a child after her death?[42] I would hesitate giving an affirmative answer to this question. As Aziza-Shuster suggests, people need to produce merely for themselves, or there could be more to the reproductive experience than personal interests like rearing the child or being aware of the child's existence (Aziza-Shuster, 1994, p. 2184).[43] If this what stands behind the right to reproduce, then maintaining a brain-dead pregnant woman on life-support could not be considered as serving her interests.

Moreover, not only is there no explicit legislation that supports performing life-sustaining treatment on the pregnant woman without consent, there is one that legally forbids it. I will turn now to discuss the statutory provisions in this area.

Statutory requirements

The notion of consent has a place in Canadian legislation and all provincial acts clearly set forth this requirement. In the Province of Ontario,[44] for example a health provider, who proposes a treatment for a patient is not authorized to administer the treatment, and must take reasonable steps to ensure that it is not administered, unless '(a) he or she is of the opinion that the person is capable with respect to the treatment, and the person has given consent, or (b) He or she is of the opinion that the person is incapable with respect to the treatment, and the person's substitute decision-maker has given consent on the person's behalf' (*Health Care Consent Act*, 1996, section 10(1)). 'Treatment' here is defined very broadly as anything that is done for a therapeutic, preventive, palliative, diagnostic, cosmetic or other health-related purpose; it includes a course of treatment, plan of treatment or community treatment plan. Maintaining a brain-dead pregnant woman on life-support can, of course, fall into the definition of 'other health-related purpose'.

In the Province of British Columbia, the requirement of consent applies to any medical procedure, which is termed by the legislator a 'health care' (*Health Care (Consent) and Care Facility (Admission) Act*, 1996). However, such care is defined in the same way as in the Ontario legislation. Health care is divided into major procedures and minor ones (*Health Care (Consent) and Care Facility (Admission) Act*, 1996, section 1). The 'major' procedures include a surgery, any treatment involving a general anesthetic, major diagnostic or investigative procedures, or any health care designated by regulation as major health care. The 'minor' procedures include routine tests to determine if health care is necessary and routine dental treatment that prevents or treats a condition or injury caused by disease or trauma (*Health Care (Consent) and Care Facility (Admission) Act*, 1996, section 1).

The general rule in British Columbia is that a health-care provider must not provide any health care to an adult without the adult's consent (*Health Care (Consent) and Care Facility (Admission) Act*, 1996, section 5(1)). Further, if the patient is presently unable to give consent, the provider cannot decide whether to give or refuse substitute consent to the procedure unless having made every reasonable effort to obtain consent from the adult patient (*Health Care (Consent) and Care Facility (Admission) Act*, 1996, section 5(2)). However, with regard to major health care, a health-care provider may provide major health care to an adult without the adult's consent if after consulting with the adult's spouse, relative or friend or with any other person who has relevant information, the health-care provider decides that the adult needs the major health care and is incapable of giving or refusing consent to it (*Health Care (Consent) and Care Facility (Admission) Act*, 1996, section 11). In addition, the provider can make such a decision when the adult does not have a substitute decision-maker, guardian or representative who is authorized to consent to the major health care, or when someone chosen under section 16 has authority to consent to the major health care and gives substitute consent, and the health care provider complies with the conditions mentioned above (*Health Care (Consent) and Care Facility (Admission) Act*, 1996, section 14(1)(a)).

A sound interpretation of the statute in light of our case is that maintaining the brain-dead patient on life-support is similar to treatment which involves a general anesthetic, and thus, not only does it fall into the category of 'health care' but it also carries the characteristics (and hence the consequences) of statutorily defined 'major' health care, as opposed to 'minor'. In order to perform such a procedure without consent one must fulfill the exception requirements, stated above. Otherwise, the performance of the medical procedure may be illegal.

The law in the Province of Nova Scotia differs from that in British Columbia in a few ways (*Hospitals Act*, 1989). First, a 'patient' is defined as 'a person who receives diagnosis, lodging or treatment at or in a hospital'. The definition of treatment is broad and includes any treatment performed in the hospital. According to this definition, a patient does not necessarily have to be alive in order for her to be treated. The general rule states:

> [W]here a person in a hospital requires medical or surgical treatment and is incapable of consenting to the required medical or surgical treatment for any reason and such person does not have a guardian or there is no one recognized in law who can give consent on his behalf to the required medical or surgical treatment, then the Trial Division of the Supreme Court or a judge thereof may upon *ex parte* application by the Public Trustee authorize the required medical or surgical treatment.[45]

Under this section, a series of requirements must be fulfilled before performing any procedure and the health-care provider is not allowed to perform the treatment without consent. Instead, if consent cannot be obtained by the patient, the issue is decided by court (*Hospitals Act*, 1989, section 9(1)).

A different statutory model of consent is seen in the Province of Quebec. The general rule on consent in Quebec states that 'no person may be made to undergo care of any nature, whether for examination, specimen taking, removal of tissue, treatment or any other act, except with his consent' (*Civil Code of Quebec*, 1991, section 11). However, 'if the person concerned is incapable of giving or refusing his consent to care, a person authorized by law or by mandate given in anticipation of his incapacity may do so in his place' (*Civil Code of Quebec*, 1991, section 11). Similar to the Nova Scotia statute, the Quebec statute sets forth a broad definition for what is required for consent ('care of any nature'), that clearly can include maintaining the newly brain-dead pregnant woman on life-support by the successful delivery of her fetus.

In sum, Canadian's general consent legislation incorporated the common-law requirement of consent to medical treatment, usually performed by health-care provider, and defined these treatment in a broad way that can include the management of post-mortem pregnancy. According to this legislation, a health-care provider is not allowed to perform such treatment without obtaining consent of substitute decision-maker, family members, guardian or court. Of course, the requirement of consent set forth in the general consent legislation corresponds to the obligation to seek for express or substitute consent with regard to medical procedures performed on the deceased generally. The obligation of the latter has been discussed in great detail in the previous chapter of this book.

The requirement of consent is not only a legal requirement, but also an ethical one. But perhaps such a requirement can be satisfied merely by implying consent from the patient, or just presuming it? I will turn now to examine these questions.

Implied and Presumed Consent

Consent can be expressed or implied. An expressed consent from the dead can only be given by the patient before arriving to the hospital, either by directive or by signing a consent form. Implied consent is less clear and more complex. Some examples of implied consent will help. Consent can be implied from circumstances.[46] One example for such situation is that the medical procedure shall be done unless the patient or her next of kin objected to it ('opt-in').[47] Another example of implied consent is when a discussion takes place between the provider and the patient before the procedure begins which leads to the conclusion that the patient consented (*O'Bonsawin v. Paradis*, 1993). Thirdly, one can imply consent by a reasonable person test (Nelson, 2002, p. 114). Another possibility is that by signing or consenting to go through a certain procedure one may infer consent to undergo any other procedures may be necessary during the course of the main procedure consented to (*Villeneuve v. Sisters of St. Joseph of Diocese of Salut Ste. Marie*, 1972).

Stephen Wear *et al.* argue that implied consent might be assumed in the case of maternal brain-death, provided that the woman already invested months of pregnancy toward the birth of her fetus (Wear *et al.*, 1989). The circumstances of her being pregnant lead one to presume her consent to the medical procedure. Is being pregnant a sufficient circumstance to infer consent to serve as an incubator? In my view, there are general and specific reasons to reject such a conclusion.

Erin Nelson argues that express consent is preferable for two reasons (Nelson, 2002, p. 114). According to the first, implied consent leaves the patient out of the process and therefore is against the philosophy underlying the law with respect to consent. The second reason is that express consent provides better evidence (as opposed to reliance on implied consent) that the patient has given her permission for the proposed treatment. Indeed, when relying on implied consent it is essential that the circumstances from which the consent is inferred be clearly documented. One can question whether the practice of maintaining the brain-dead pregnant woman on life-support in the intensive care unit is one of the best circumstances under which to ask for documentation.

But besides the doubtful base upon which the implied consent rests, there are several specific reasons to ask for an explicit consent from the woman. Traditionally, our case does not fall into the classical category of either implied or presumed consent. Indeed, it is unreasonable to believe that, prior to the need of hospitalization, a young woman had already considered the situation of brain-death at pregnancy. Although there are various aspects of her 'narrative' that could give a sense to what she would have wanted, these aspects are not solely unique to the case of maternal brain-death and do not differ from ones that relate to other bodily interventions which do not involve the special issues raised by the first.

Secondly, there are many people who from an ideological, religious, or other personal belief strongly oppose any use or interference with their body after death. One cannot fully respect their convictions by only presuming or implying their consent rather than asking for it explicitly.

Thirdly, it is possible that the pregnancy was unintended and unwanted, or even forced on the woman. It certainly will not do to assume that because the woman did not have an abortion she has chosen to continue the pregnancy since her personal code, poverty, or lack of access to the procedure might have blocked this option. A decision to continue pregnancy to full term while alive is not a decision to continue pregnancy while dead. A physician cannot simply assume the woman would want her pregnancy continued after brain-death only from the fact that she is pregnant. Clear evidence is required to justify such an assumption.

Fourthly, from the perspective of the child and the woman's family, it is reasonable to think that the woman may not have wished to produce a motherless child, and burden her grieving partner or parents with sole care of a small infant. Neither may she have wanted to extend the grieving process for her family and friends, as they watch her body being artificially sustained for a period of weeks or even months (Jones, 2000, p. 98).

Therefore, analysis of the implied or presumed consent leads to the conclusion that substitutes for express consent are insufficient for processing the maintenance on life-support. As Hilde Nelson writes:

Even if in life and health she joyfully and willingly assented to the pregnancy, we cannot assume that now, under very different circumstances, she would desire intensive support of her cadaver to achieve that end. While she might have wanted, for example, to bring a third child into a close and loving two-parent family, she might not at all have wanted to burden with a third child a grieving single parent who is already overwhelmed by the care of the two who exist. Nor would she necessarily have wanted to produce a motherless child particularly if, as our catalog of cases suggests, the father's ability and willingness to rear the child can't be counted on.[48]

Obtaining express consent on behalf of the woman involves confronting her relatives and friends. I will now examine the role of this group in our case.

RIGHTS OF THE BIOLOGICAL FATHER, NEXT-OF-KIN, FAMILY AND FRIENDS

What right, if any does a biological father of the fetus, next-of-kin, other family member or friends of the pregnant patient have in the situation of maternal brain-death? In the previous chapter it was mentioned that the Human Tissue Gift Act includes a hierarchy for surrogate decision-making.[49] Should this model apply to post-mortem pregnancy as well? In his article, 'On Deliveries Carried Out on Corpses', Daniel Schafer discusses the importance of relatives in the process of obtaining informed consent for such medical treatment (Schafer, 1998).[50] But do relatives always have a right to decide? What is the source of such a right? Does it derive from their legal status as maternal and fetal surrogates, their quasi-property rights 'in the deceased', or their being the spokespersons for their own interests?

Stephen Wear *et al.* suggest two exceptions to the relative's power in the context of post-mortem pregnancy (Wear *et al.*, 1989). The first, where the family refuses to maintain the pregnant brain-dead on life support when extended support, 'even for a few *weeks*',[51] would markedly enhance the chance and quality of fetal survival. The second, when the family demands that the dead woman will receive life-sustaining treatment while fetal survival is unprecedented and, even if gained, would be accompanied by profound fetal morbidity.

John Robertson attempts to put the husband of the deceased at the picture, but accords him little weight (Robertson, 1994, p. 1053).[52] He argues that the husband of a brain-dead pregnant woman does not have the *power to control* 'the dispositions of human remains' (Robertson, 1994, p. 1053). Nor does his right to reproduce carry any right to have the body or resources provided for such a right (Robertson, 1994, p. 1055).[53] But what is the basis for the exceptions of Wear *et al.* and Robertson's arguments?

Case law supports the general view that the father of the child has no power to override the woman's autonomy regarding decisions on pregnancy (*Paton v. British Pregnancy Advisory Service Trustees and Another*, 1979, p. 281; *C. v. S*, 1988). My analysis in chapter 2 of this book concerning bodily interventions with pregnant women also revealed that the law keeps the biological father (genitor) out of the picture, even regarding complicated and hazardous decisions to the fetus, such as cesarean sections and blood transfusions.[54] This approach should apply also to the case of a brain-dead pregnant woman. Although she is not alive, the focus should be on the woman's wishes and ideology regarding pregnancy and the proposed medical intervention. The biological father should only be allowed to contribute to a full understanding of these and should be allowed to reflect on these, not determine this understanding.

Sometimes, it is the tragic event that makes the family members learn for their first time about the pregnancy.[55] When such circumstances occur, it is not reasonable to expect the family members to have a readily developed standpoint on the woman's pregnancy and the proposed medical treatment.

The more complicated situation is when a controversy takes place regarding the rights and duties family members and friends have once their loved one is dead. In the *Piazzi* case, for example, there was a controversy between the biological father of the fetus who asked for the dead pregnant woman to be kept 'alive' and the husband of the deceased who opposed it (*University Health Services, Inc. v. Piazzi*, 1986). In the *Mapes* case, there was a disagreement between the deceased's boyfriend and her parents. The boyfriend wanted to sue the hospital that has kept his comatose girlfriend on life-support for the delivery of their child, although the parents of the deceased had asked for such a treatment.[56] Sheikh and Cusack support Peart *et al.*'s view that 'the person responsible for burying the deceased, commonly the next-of-kin, would not be entitled to the possession of the body until the child is delivered or had died *in utero*' (Sheikh and Cusack, 2001, p. 80). Thus, in their view, it is the healthcare providers who will have the lawful retention of the deceased patient's body in the circumstances of being obliged to preserve the life of the unborn.

The Law Reform Commission of Canada, in its 1983 report, suggested that the physician of an incompetent patient should be the central figure in the decision-making process, and that, although there should be consultation with the patient's family, the ultimate responsibility must lie with the physician (Law Reform Commission of Canada, 1983, pp. 64–5).

Of course, an ideal model of decision-making for incompetent patients should reflect a consensus among health-care providers and the family. However, when such a consensus does not occur, I would hesitate to claim that it is the responsibility of a physician to have the final decision. Instead, I would support the view that the decision should reflect, as much as possible, the woman's wishes. When no such view can be identified, I would object to the procedure, unless two conditions are met: the fetus is in a very progressed stage of development (on the third trimester), and there exists at least one positive view that supports providing the woman with life-sustaining treatment. My suggestion is derived from my previous analysis of abortions law (chapter 1 of this book) and the legal view regarding bodily interventions on pregnant women (chapter 2 of this book), along with the requirement of consent and its application to the case of maternal brain-death.

THE PHYSICIAN-PATIENT RELATIONSHIP

In the past, while treating a pregnant patient, physicians could only treat the mother and had to assume that in maintaining her health, the fetus's health would be enhanced. The fetus itself was largely beyond, and in practice outside, the diagnostic and therapeutic scope of the physician. This therapeutic philosophy was merely a result of the fact that assessing fetal condition was made by indirect methods. Some examples for such methods include palpating the fetus through maternal abdominal wall and uterus, measuring hormonal milieu through maternal urine and serum, and estimating statistical risks from parental medical histories (Nelson, 1988).

However, advances in medical technologies and in the knowledge of fetal physiology have enabled physicians to see the fetus in a direct way. In this new age, physicians have been able to see the fetus in detail with ultrasound, assess its condition with amniocentesis and fetal heart rate monitoring and operating on it while *in uterus*. The medical ability to visualize the fetus shaped the discussion on separate moral and legal status to the fetus and was shaped by it. This has made physicians believe and act as the fetus was their 'second patient' (Nelson, 1988). The consequences of such an attitude is that if one of the patients dies, the doctor's duty to the other patient still remains, and what matters is the patient's best interest (Sheikh and Cusack, 2001, p. 79).

The medical model of maternal-fetal relationship has shifted emphasis from unity to duality (Mattingly, 1992).[57] This shift has also made a change in the physician-patient relationship. In this new situation, treatment that was administered for one patient could be contradictory for the other, yet both patients must be treated. The duality model has made conflicts between duties of beneficence and nonmaleficence that physicians owe to both patients.

Maintaining a brain-dead pregnant woman on life-support undermines the traditional physician-patient relationship. It makes physicians feel obligated to withdraw their commitment to act in the best interest of the patient, and instead become the fetus's practitioners, and that perspective seems to be problematic. Still, a question needs to be asked as to whether the description of a duty of care to only one patient ('the fetus') is correct and desirable. To answer this question one ought to inquire more about the nature of the relationship between the mother and the fetus. Such an inquiry will take place in the following two chapters of this book. In the next chapter, the dilemma of whether to maintain the woman on life-support will be analysed through the discussion of a relational feminist approach, which I find highly appealing. Chapter 6 of this book will follow on this analysis and examine the moral duties that the brain-dead pregnant woman owes to her fetus before and after her death.

NOTES

1   Hunter, 1981, p. 132.
2   In this case, two midwives assisted in a home birth but were unable to complete the delivery due to the woman's complications. On the way to hospital, the baby was delivered but not alive. The Supreme Court of Canada ruled that the midwives could not be convicted for criminal negligence causing death to the baby, as the term 'person' in section 203 of the *Criminal Code* (now 220) does not include a fetus not yet born alive.

3 In this case, a man attempted to get an injunction to prevent a woman from terminating her pregnancy on the grounds that the fetus was a 'human being' and had a 'right to life' under section 1 of *Quebec Charter of Human Rights and Freedoms*. The Supreme Court of Canada denied the injunction because the fetus was not recognized as a juridical person under Canadian law.

4 Especially with the enactment of statutes, which giving the fetus greater protection by recognizing the killing of a fetus as a crime *separate* from homicide. See, for example, in California, where the legislator went far beyond this protection of the fetus and defined murder as the 'unlawful killing of a human being, *or a fetus*, with malice aforethought' (*California Penal Code*, 1986, § 187).

5 Mainly through actions for prenatal injuries. For examples in the area of succession and workman's compensation, where the fetus' interests seem to be protected prior to birth (Peart *et al.*, 2000, p. 293); for a recognition of a duty of care owed to the fetus by an Australian court see *Watt v. Rama*, 1972; See in the UK, the *Congenital Disabilities (Civil Liability) Act 1976*, c. 28 § 1(1) which confers on a person the right to sue those who caused him or her injury before its birth; For a detailed discussion on the legal protection of the fetus see Jost, 2002.

6 In Israel, the *Capacity and Guardianship Law*, 1962 states in section 1 that every *person* is in capacity of having rights and obligations from birth till death. Nevertheless, section 33(a)(6) allows the nomination of a custodian for the fetus.

7 In this case, the House of Lords described the maternal-fetal relationship as one with 'an intimate bond', and that the mother and the fetus as two distinct organisms living *symbiotically*, rather than a single organism with two aspects. The court regarded the fetus as a unique organism and, thus was reluctant to apply to such an organism the principles of law evolving in relation to autonomous beings.

8 Dworkin, 1993, p. 55.

9 Another way to protect the fetus would be to claim that the fetus has an interest to be born healthy (Robertson, 1989, p. 261). This is an uncommon argument and I will not discuss it here. It is important to mention that when defined as an interest to be born healthy rather than as a right to life, the first has a weaker moral weight than the latter, and this is also acknowledged by Robertson himself, who asserts that this interest does not automatically override its mother's interests.

10 The same wording applies to the French version of the Charter. While the subject of the right to life is termed 'chacun', the Charter bears other subjects as well such as 'citoyen' and 'personne'.

11 Jones, 2000, p. 98.

12 However, sometimes it is difficult to assess a clinical prognosis to the fetus, or such an assessment could take days to weeks, while in the meantime, the dead woman has to be maintained 'alive' (Hill *et al.*, 1985).

13 But see Feldman *et al.*, 2000. In this report, the authors claim that successful outcomes can occur even when the brain injury of the mother occurs *much earlier* than 24 weeks of gestation.

14 See Finnerty *et al.*, 1999, p. 298. The authors explain: 'Cessation of spontaneous respiration (part of the definition of brain death) requires ventilatory support. Maternal blood pressure must be supported to avoid decreasing uteroplacental flow. Panhypopituitarism may develop with diabetes insipidus and adrenal insufficiency. Loss of hypothalamic thermoregulation may lead to either hypothermia or hyperthermia. Nutrition support, including parenteral nutrition, is important for fetal growth. Last, strict infection control precautions are necessary because sepsis develops more easily.'

15 The cost of maintaining a brain-dead pregnant woman over an extended period to produce a child is estimated at half a million US dollars or more (Finnerty *et al.*, 1999, p. 300). Maintaining Donna Piazzi cost at least 1,200$ (US) per day, and keeping her baby in the neonatal unit was 1,200$–3,800$ (US) a day (Jordan, 1988, p. 1110). See also Spike, 1999, p. 60. Spike estimates the cost of such a procedure to be at least 2000$ (US) a day, whereas Nelson estimates it is 3,200$ (US) per day (Nelson, 1994, p. 251). A possible solution to the high cost can be found in Pennsylvania where the law, which implicitly acknowledges its 'taking' of the incompetent pregnant woman's body by providing 'just compensation' in the form of payment for the expenses associated with continued medical care: 20 Pa. Cons. Stat. § 5414 (c)(1) (Supp. 1999).

16 Sometimes, the fear from future sanctions can result in an opposite response. As Dr. Walter Bishop advised physicians in an article he wrote on that subject: 'Perform the procedure even without consent, because (a) even if you are sued, the likelihood of being found liable is slim and (b) the courts may well hold next that you may be sued, if you fail to perform the section, by the legal representative of the child (and that case maybe yours)' (Bishop, 1978, p. 179).

17 But see Siegler and Wikler, 1982; Veatch, 1982. The authors discuss the confusion, occurring in situations of maternal brain death and the difficulty in talking about the woman as dead while maintained on life-support. Some authors suggest solving such a confusion by calling the 'newly dead', who is being maintained on life-support, a patient in 'a persistent brain death'. See Spike and Greenlaw, 1995, p. 292.

18 But see Wear *et al.*, 1989, p. 1728.

19 Ad Hoc Committee of the Harvard Medical School to Examine the Definition of Brain Death, 1968.

20 Canadian Congress Committee on Brain Death, 1988.

21 *Uniform Determination of Death Bill*, Senate File No. 209, S.J. 452 available at http://www.legis.state.ia.us/GA/78GA/Legislation/SF/00200/SF00209/Current.html, accessed on 17 August, 2003.

22 Benrubi, 1999, p. 302.

23 Nagel, 1979, p. 6.

24 Compare Jordan, 1988, p. 1154. Jordan correctly argues that in some circumstances the burden of maintaining a corporeal existence degrades the very humanity it normally serves.

25 Pitcher, though, defines harm in a different way than Feinberg. In his view, an event harms someone when 'it is contrary to one or many of his more important desires or interests' (Pitcher, 1984, p. 184). Still, both Feinberg and Pitcher identify the *ante-mortem* person as the subject of the surviving interests.

26 This is especially true with regard to interests in future child rearing. See MacAvoy-Smitzer, 1987, pp. 1297–8.

27 It is important to see the distinction they make between the self-determination interest of a self in what happens to the same self (person) from the interest of a self in what happens to a thing that is not only not the same self, but not self (person) at all. This distinction has a moral implication: the former interests have greater moral weight than the latter.

28 Sheila McLean even uses a stronger language when she argues that we have an interest in avoiding condoning an assault on the dead person (McLean, 1999, p. 341).

29 In this case, the hospital sought clarification over the disconnection from a ventilator of a child, who was declared brain stem dead. The court stated that '… it would be wholly contrary to the interests of A, as they may now be, for his body to be subjected to the continuing indignity to which it was currently subject. Moreover, it would be quite unfair to the nursing and medical staff of the hospital, who were finding it increasingly distressing to be caring for a dead child'.

30 *Report of The Committee of Inquiry into Human Fertilization and Embryology Cmnd.* (1984), 9314/1984 ¶ 109.
31 See *The Human Fertilisation and Embryology Act* 1990, (U.K.) 1990, c. 37, s. 28. But see *R v. Human Fertilisation and Embryology Authority, ex parte Blood* [1997] 2 All E R 687 (successful actions of a widow to export gametes of her dead husband outside the UK for insemination and to have the deceased husband registered as the child's father).
32 Some argue that maintaining the deceased on life-support helps the grieving process. It 'gives a family time to accept the reality of a sudden and unexpected event and to prepare for what would otherwise be a precipitous plunge into grief' (Spike and Greenlaw, 1995, p. 292; See also Ascioti, 1993, p. 47): 'The first 2 weeks after Sheila was declared brain-dead were the most difficult. Her husband visited daily. He was terribly distraught. Sometimes we'd find him lying next to Sheila, sobbing uncontrollably, his arms wrapped around her, clutching for the life that no longer existed.'
33 Of course, one can argue that the *act* of predicating a property to him *now* is also posthumous, whereas the *time* of the predicating act is not.
34 Lomasky, 1987, p. 219.
35 David-Hillel, 2003, p. 11.
36 Jones, 1995, p. 11.
37 New Jersey statute annotated, 26–6A-5, suppl 1994 (1987); New York Compilation Codes Regulations, Rules 7 REGS, title 10, section 400.16 (d), (e)(3)(1992).
38 Olick, 2001, p. 140.
39 Mentioned in Jones, 2000, p. 57.
40 See also *The Council of Europe Convention for the Protection of Human Rights and Dignity of Human Being with Regard to the Application of Biology and Medicine: Convention on Human Rights and Medicine* (European Treaty Series 164, 4.IV. 1997). This convention prescribes in article 5: 'An intervention in the health field may only be carried out after the person concerned has given free and informed consent to it. This person shall beforehand be given appropriate information as to the purpose and the nature of the intervention as well as on its consequences and risks.'
41 See, for instance, *Public Health Act*, 2000, sctions 29–36.
42 Even if one argues that dead people do not have rights, the argument for posthumous interests can still be claimed.
43 The right to posthumously reproduce will be discussed in chapter 8.
44 *Health Care Consent Act*, S.O. 1996, c. 2, Schedule A.
45 Hospitals Act, 1989, Section 9(1).
46 The first case that discussed it is *O'Brian v. Cunard Steamship* Co., 1891. See also *Reynen v. Antonenko*, 1975.
47 This form of consent is more common in Europe and especially with regard to organ transplantation (Wilcox, 2003, p. 938).
48 Nelson, 1994, p. 253.
49 The Hierarchy mentioned in the law is as follows: 1) a person designated orally or in writing in an advance-directive or durable power of attorney for health care decisions 2) a guardian authorized by the court 3) the spouse 4) an adult child or adult children of the patient 5) a parent or parents 6) an adult brother or sister 7) any other relative in order of blood relationship. But see Wear *et al.*, 1989, pp. 1728–9. The authors argue that preference should be given to what they call the 'husband-father'.
50 Sometimes, there is no time to ask the family and physicians make the decision alone, driven by the urge to save the fetus. In Israel, for example, it was reported in a recent case of a Bedouin dead woman whose physicians decided to deliver without

consulting the family members. The woman was in her eighth month of pregnancy when she died. Although in retrospect her family's objection to an autopsy could have revealed their attitude towards the delivery of a fetus from the deceased daughter, the physicians did not seek for their consent. The child died a day after its delivery – http://www.ynet.co.il/articles/1,7340, accessed on 13 May 2003; http://images.maariv. co.il/channels/1/ART/477/314.html, accessed on 15 May 2003.

51 Wear *et al.* clarify this term by providing an example of four weeks of maintaining the woman on life-support from the 22nd week of gestation to the 26th.

52 It is not clear, however why Robertson focuses on the husband rather than on the biological father of the fetus. In the *Piazzi* case (1986), for example, these were two different persons.

53 This seems also to be the view of Sheila McLean when she argues that the requirement of a partner of a deceased to use the gametes of the first is not denied to the survivor, merely the ability to do so with a specific person (now deceased): McLean, 1999, p. 341.

54 The case may be different with regard to research involving pregnant women and fetuses. The American rules with respect to research that 'holds out the prospect of direct benefit solely to the fetus' also ask for the consent of the father. However, when the father is unavailable, incompetent or temporary incapacitated the research can still be performed without his consent. *No parallel provision applies to the mother.* Hence, even in this area of intervention, obtaining consent from the mother seems to outweigh the same requirement as applies to the fetus's father. See *Code of Federal Regulations*, 2002, Title 45, Part 46, Subpart B § 46.204(e), available at http://www. access.gpo.gov/nara/cfr/waisidx_02/45cfr46_02.html, accessed on 1 May 2004.

55 See for example the two cases presented by Finnerty *et al.*, 1999.

56 Reported in the Daily Telegraph in 1996, mentioned in Paige, 2000.

57 Still, the 'Unity Model' is considered the dominant one by the medical profession. *The Ethical Guidelines on Court-Authorised Obstetric Intervention: A consideration of the Law and Ethics* from 1996 states that 'the aim of those who care for pregnant women must be to foster the greatest benefit to *both the mother and fetus* with the least risk to *both*' (sec. 4.3.1) and that 'in caring for the pregnant woman an obstetrician must respect the woman's legal right to choose or refuse any recommended course of action and *at the same time* maintain the medical obligation to promote the well being of the mother and the child' (sec. 4.3.5) (my emphasis) – http://www.rcog.org.uk, last visited on 5 January 2003.

Chapter 6

Relational Feminist Analysis

In this chapter, I intend to analyse the major concepts that relational feminist theory would raise with respect to the issue of maintaining a brain-dead pregnant woman on life-support. By applying some of the main concepts of relational feminist theory I will confront the traditional liberal theory. This latter theory regards a brain-dead pregnant woman in isolation from her family and separate from her fetus. As a dead person, the theory denies the pregnant-woman from any rights or interests and considers her to be non-autonomous, with doubt a person.

With the help of relational feminist theory, I would like to suggest some new ways to approach these issues, or better: a new language to talk about this situation. My analysis is based on the idea that the use of words and their divisions into categories construct the way we – social entities that communicate and interact with each other by language – think and decide in such cases.

The issue of maintaining a brain-dead pregnant woman on life-support touches upon many deeply rooted concepts. *Autonomy* is the most obvious one. The notion of autonomy is traditionally perceived as control over one-self. Such control or 'self-rule' implies an unconditional capacity to make personal decisions. It also involves a call to act with respect and humanity towards the autonomy holder. By applying feminist relational theory, my goal would be to establish a broader meaning to the concept autonomy, so that we would be able to argue that the brain-dead persons also enjoy some degree of autonomy. By arguing that the brain-dead persons are (partially) autonomous, I would claim that although their autonomy may be construed not as fully as living persons, it would definitely necessitate a special ethical position towards them that would prevent others from ignoring them as being 'legally' dead.

The second concept I will analyse is the metaphor of *field* which relational feminists adopt from contemporary theories in science and theology to capture the social component of autonomy and to explain how living creatures in the world co-exist. I will seek to apply the metaphor of field to the dilemma of 'prolonging' the life of a brain-dead pregnant woman. I would suggest looking for the field that consists of a dead patient that is shaped by the interactions surrounding her in this new and conflicting situation. By doing so, I will demonstrate the complexity of the dilemma I propose to examine, but more specifically, emphasize the different fields and social structures that operate simultaneously on the dead pregnant patient.

Boundary is the third concept that that will be examined in this chapter. I will analyse it from two perspectives: the boundary between the dead pregnant patient and the fetus, and the boundary between the dead pregnant patient (with the fetus) and the external world. The latter perspective will also be analysed by the fourth concept, the *human body*. I will argue that the *human body* (dead or alive) has a social role, and that due to this role, protection of the dead body is *a societal* value to be implemented in the same manner that applies to living persons. I will also demonstrate how this view is reflected in the law, which is a major participant in constructing this societal value.

My fifth concept will be *privacy*. In this part, I will introduce the notion of privacy, and I will discuss the dichotomy between the private-public domains. I will bring the relational feminist critique to this dichotomy, and I will examine its application in the situation of a brain-dead pregnant woman.

The final part of my analysis will be devoted to the concept of *property*. Two possible contexts for property claim would arise. The first will relate to potential claims of the dead patient's relatives concerning their 'property rights' in the body of a deceased. The second will involve the question of whether the fetus is a property of the dead pregnant patient. Before examining these questions, I will generally discuss the concept of property. I will, then apply the feminist' critique to regard potential life as property. The second part of my analysis will include a brief description of legal decisions that exemplify how courts mistakenly rule that next-of-kin have property rights in the body of the dead. I will provide an explanation for this error and will conclude by a call to reject the language of property in this regard.

AUTONOMY

Central to the debate over the use of a brain-dead body is the concept of autonomy. A major reason for many of the problems identified with the autonomy ideal, especially with regard to dead people is that the notion of autonomy is commonly understood to represent freedom of action for agents who are paradigmatically regarded as independent, self-interested, and self-sufficient.[1] As such, it is easy to categorize the dead as not being autonomous or as not being entitled to autonomy (due to their death).[2] The familiar critique, by feminists, to the liberal tradition of autonomy is that this latter theory takes atomistic individuals as the basic units of a political and legal theory, and, thus, fails to recognize the inherently social nature of human beings (Nedelsky, 1989, p. 8).[3]

The case of a brain-dead pregnant woman can support this criticism by demonstrating the fact that usually a brain-dead woman is not the only person at stake. She exists in a very special and unique *social context*. This context includes the fetus, who although, as demonstrated in chapter 5, does not enjoy a legal status as a person, its 'best interest' and the protection of its potential life are the most important factors in the decision as to what constitutes the 'right' thing to do with the dead pregnant patient.[4] It also includes the patient's parents, the biological father of the fetus, the 'legal' father of the fetus (if he is different from the 'biological' father), and other family members. Moreover, there are the health-care providers, who on the one hand face the emotional burden and the complex relations with the patient's families and friends, and who on the other hand might have a moral obligation to provide treatment to the fetus.

In addition to this, one should bear in mind that the decision whether to go on with the medical procedure is also influenced by the location of the intensive care unit, its staff, their professional knowledge and experience to perform such procedures, their ethical and religious convictions, the financial abilities of the patient's family and the unit's funding resources, the legal statutes and decisions that govern the specific jurisdiction where the patient is hospitalized, and so on. The fact that each of the parties involved has many directions of influence makes it impossible to examine the woman's autonomy in isolation from a constant and changing social interaction within which she is engaged.

In my view, the case of maintaining a brain-dead pregnant woman on life-support highlights the most powerful evidence in the social interaction people may have. This case reflects, maybe in the strongest way, that it is in the patient's own 'capacity', as a social brain-dead person, to shape the interaction with the social beings that surround her, and that are part of her unique social existence in the intensive care unit.

Interesting to point out here is the psychological and moral intuition family members and clinical care nurses have when interacting with brain-dead people. The application of the criteria of irreversible brain failure in defining death builds on advanced technology and expert knowledge, contrasting with everyday notions of death. People still tend to associate death with the 'lifeless' cold body lacking bodily signs of life, not with a warm, breathing, perspiring brain-dead person. Since the dividing line between a dying and a brain-dead 'patient' is not clear cut for most people, it is difficult for the families of some deceased, and to some extent of clinical care nurses, to accept such diagnosis, particularly when, for purposes of the delivery of the fetus, the deceased is actively monitored in the intensive unit and, if necessary, subject to cardiopulmonary 'resuscitation'.

Here are some examples of emotional reactions of clinical care nurses who were asked to care for brain-dead pregnant women (Diehl *et al.*, 1994, pp. 135–6):[5]

... Sometimes I forgot she was brain-dead and I would *talk to her* ...

(Ann Fetcho)

... I was always aware that I was caring for *two people* ... Usually when a person is declared brain-dead in our unit, the life support is discontinued. Keeping the mother alive was a double standard to me ...

(Jane Dilliard)

... I found it difficult to deal with the callous way that other care providers not involved in her direct care were reacting to her. They were so insensitive to her as *a human being* ... *I worried for her being alone. I gave her back rubs and touched her arm so she would know I was there* ... I have two children and I think about what I would want. Do I want ten thousand people trooping through my room every day when I am so vulnerable? I believe it was important to *treat her as a person* ...

(Debra J. Belles)

... *I talked to her and tried to make her look as good as she could for her own mother (the child's grandmother)* when she visited ...

(Theresa Mylet)

Indeed, treating the brain-dead woman with respect as a living person is, in my view, a direct outcome of the autonomy she enjoys as a person who interacts and engages in a social net of interrelations under these special circumstances. This view is not in accordance with the claim that an inseparable component of the capacity to autonomy, is the ability to feel autonomy (or more accurately to feel autonomous) (Nedelsky, 1989, p. 25). Jennifer Nedelsky argues that the focus on feeling or experience in this regard defines the party whose perspective is taken seriously, and 'by turning out attention in the right direction it enhances our ability to learn what fosters and constitutes autonomy' (Nedelsky, 1989, p. 25). She explains that the capacity of autonomy does not exist without the feeling of it, that the feeling of autonomy is our best way of understanding the structure of the social relations that support it, and that focusing on the feeling of autonomy defines as authoritative the voices of those whose autonomy is at issue (Nedelsky, 1989, p. 25).

I find this explanation troubling. First, it appears to rule out not only dead patients[6] from the categorization of 'autonomous' people, but also people with mental ailments, children, and maybe people whose intellectual or cognitive abilities to grasp and feel the 'sense' of autonomy are under-developed. In my view, people in all of these categories constitute, and are part of, a complex web of social interactions that shape and form their capacity for autonomy, at least in its weakest form the result of which necessitates acting towards these autonomous persons with respect and humanity.[7] Thus, I find that what is important in autonomy is not the passive feeling of the capacity to autonomy but that which gives (or potentially can give) the feeling of autonomy or the sense of it, namely the capacity to engage in meaningful relations even when one is considered legally dead.

Second, the component of 'feeling autonomous' seems also problematic for its subjective nature. Jennifer Nedelsky mentions one form of this problem. She acknowledges that relations that foster the feeling of autonomy may vary considerably across cultures and over time within one culture (Nedelsky, 1989, pp. 25–6). Judy Scales-Trent, while referring to the white men who came to Williamsburg to learn about the racist history there asks: 'How hard is it for them to exercise autonomy within a culture that works so hard to create and maintain categories we call "race"? ... given this context, to what extent can white Americans distinguish their own norms from those strong social norms that structure their consciousness?' (Scales-Trent, 1999, p. 863). And Cynthia Willett also writes: 'Many of us are overwhelmed by social forces that restrict our ability to feel what we want to feel, to express our deepest desires, and to hold on to our most precious relationships. Moreover, it is not clear that the legal protection of a private "sanctuary" could provide a realistic barrier against hyper-modern forms of social power' (Willett, 2001, p. 170). Another form of this claim can be reflected in our difficulties to understand, compare, and evaluate feelings in general given their complexities.

Since our perceptions of acting towards people is deeply rooted, *inter alia*, in the notion of autonomy I would not recommend forming a new concept of autonomy that would apply to brain-dead people. Hence, my suggestion would be to reconceive the common notion of autonomy deriving from an insulated perspective of the self by focusing on the social structure that fosters and enhances the capacity to (actually *or potentially*) feel autonomous. By this, I will ask to abandon the subjective component concerning the actual feeling of autonomy for, as illustrated it creates serious difficulties to infer autonomy in many important situations like the one in the case of a brain-dead pregnant woman.

Another critique that feminists raise against the liberal notion of autonomy lies in the traditional view that autonomy is an individual value, and thus takes the meaning of autonomy from the recognition of and respect for the inherit individuality of each person. According to this critique, when autonomy is identified with individual independence and security from collective power (such as the power of the state or the patient's family to insist on maintaining the brain-dead pregnant woman on life-sustaining treatment for the future interests of the fetus), the choice left is between admitting collective control and preserving autonomy in any given realm of life (Nedelsky, 1989, p. 14).

Here again I find the feminists' answer convincing: the dichotomy between autonomy and collective power forecloses a whole range of social arrangements (Nedelsky, 1989, p. 14). I have mentioned above some of the complex webs of interconnections that form the social behavior and decision-making in the case of a brain-dead pregnant woman. This process of decision-making is characterized by free choice.[8] Choice is impossible in dichotomy. A liberal approach would probably state that, once dead, the pregnant woman is not autonomous, and thus, the only other option that is left is to maintain her for the collective, or other individuals' purposes.

However, as one can see, in reality, this is not so. The story doesn't end with the woman's death. Actually, it starts then. It is influenced by the woman's past interactions but also by her present ones. While she is laying in bed and is pronounced brain-dead a series of complex inter-relations affect her situation. She is regarded formally and legally dead, but she is perceived emotionally and psychologically alive. She is considered a motionless and lifeless creature, but she raises strong reactions towards her. She is still a mother, a wife, a daughter, a friend, a co-worker and a patient. All of these factors shape the decision of whether to maintain her 'alive' (just) for the sake of the fetus, or not.

THE FIELD METAPHOR

The complex interactions that characterize our case can also reflect, in my opinion, the metaphor of 'field' which is emphasized by the feminist relational theory. By looking at contemporary theories in science and theology dealing with 'the creative forces of the universe', relational feminists find the metaphor of field to capture the social component of autonomy. Feminists revealed that in this literature discussing these theories the relational context was the key to articulating the nature of creativity that was in question. Thus, for example, Brian Goodwin's work, inspired, *inter alia*, by the Chaos theory, explicitly articulates the idea that the organism is the *'dynamic vehicle'* of biological emergence (Goodwin, 1994).[9] In this view, the organism is grounded in relationships, which operate at all different levels of our being. Goodwin's conclusion is that the capacity of a complex system to generate novelty is primarily a function of the way the different parts are related to one another and the dynamic organization of the whole, namely their interrelation.

Goodwin finds two properties for the 'field': 1) the behavior of a dynamic system that is 2) extended in space (Goodwin, 1994, p. 51). Relevant to our case is that the *system*, and not its parts or their properties is characterized by generativity. The creativity resides in the field and not in the particulars that are part of the field. Relational feminists will thus analogize and argue that the capacity for autonomy exists within certain kinds of social fields.

Applying this notion to our case leads to the conclusion that there is no meaning to search for autonomy *in* the dead woman. Rather, the autonomy is in the field that she constitutes and which is constituted by her. The case of maintaining a brain-dead pregnant woman on life-support deals with a very strong generative power. The thing that makes it strong is the deep contrast between the woman's death and the potential life of the newborn. This generative power is manifested by *all* interactions surrounding her in this new and conflicting situation. It is not the woman herself. It is the whole web of interrelations that shape, constitute, and that are also being shaped by this generative power. Goodwin advises us that the capacity for creative interaction ('self-organization') is the network of relationships. By this, Nedelsky adds, there may be a variety of forms of fields that generate creative capacity (Nedelsky, 1989, p. 56). Such a variety is best manifested in the difficult case that involves a brain-dead pregnant woman.

I will turn now to suggest that the physiological capability of maintaining a brain-dead pregnant woman 'alive', thereby fulfilling her *right to procreation* is also a form of respect for her autonomy. My suggestion is inspired by Brian Goodwin's comments on autonomy in biological creatures. Goodwin states that 'these properties of active self-maintenance, reproduction and regeneration express a quality of autonomy in organisms: they are due to processes that occur within organisms such that *the whole has characteristics distinctive to its particular species* [my emphasis]' (Goodwin, 1994, p. 175). Hence, advocacy to maintain the dead woman 'alive' cannot seriously be based on the claim that she does not have autonomy and at the same time that such a procedure is justified as a fulfillment of her right to procreate, and hence as a respect for her autonomy by bringing about an outcome she would have wanted. The origins of these two claims seem to contradict one another. This contradiction of course also emphasizes the complexity of this case: respect for autonomy can result in two opposite consequences. Nevertheless, it also suggests the variety of fields that one situation (brain death of a pregnant woman) involves.

I find the metaphor of field with its social emphasis very appealing to the specific situation of brain-death. I will turn now to devote a special discussion on this specific state. Advancement in biological and medical knowledge has led to a conception of death as *a process* characterized by more or less recognizable stages with diffuse boundaries. Death is a *social* process conceptualized as the progressive ceasing of social functions (such as producing and consuming for instance). This process is social since it is defined in corresponding social rules associated with each stage of 'social death', each of which indicates the appropriate treatment towards the body during this process.

More specifically, defining death according to the complete and irreversible cessation of neurological signs, namely brain death, implies abandoning the concept of death but also the concept of a 'moment' of death. Although from a legal perspective death is a moment in time, in a brain-death the procedural character of death becomes more manifest, since no precise moment of death can be determined (something extending both forward and backward from the moment of a verbal declaration of death).

The concepts of living/dead/corpse are thus social categories corresponding to different stages that each involves particular sets of relations. Therefore, in order to effectively address the question of whether a brain-dead pregnant woman should be maintained 'alive' or not, we need to move away from the familiar Western understanding of autonomy, which regards the self as a special kind of 'property' to be preserved, and we should import the notion of field with its social understanding.

The metaphor of field helps us build a *relational conception* of the self. Under this conception, relational selves are inherently social beings that are shaped within and modified by a web of interconnected relationships. The continuation that is reflected in the process of dying, especially when a brain dead pregnant woman is on the one hand legally dead, but on the other hand capable of being maintained 'alive' for the delivery of her fetus, can be better conceptualized under this new metaphor.

BOUNDARY

The case of a brain-dead pregnant woman enables us to carefully examine the notion of boundary in two contexts: boundary between the brain dead pregnant woman and the fetus; boundary between the brain-dead pregnant woman (with the fetus) and the external world. Few words on the metaphor of boundary are necessary.

Boundaries serve as the means of comprehending and securing the basic values of freedom or autonomy (the latter – in its traditional meaning) (Nedelsky, 1990, p. 162). The metaphor of boundary is closely related to the notion of property and privacy. Jennifer Nedelsky describes the evolution of the concept of boundary by discussing the symbolism of property in the American constitutionalism as an important means of having control over one's life, of expressing oneself, and of protecting oneself from the power of others. She concludes her analysis by arguing that property helped construct the idea that the most autonomous man is the most perfectly isolated. Given that autonomy is a capacity (as opposed to a static condition), it must be perceived as a developmental stage (Nedelsky, 1990).

Relational feminists see the construction of relationship essential for this development (Nedelsky, 1990, p. 167). By this, the metaphor of boundary, serving the idea that what fosters autonomy is the protection against intrusion, seems inappropriate for relational feminists (Nedelsky, 1990, p. 167). The argument is that the metaphor of boundary consistently inhibits our capacity to focus on the relationships it is in fact structuring. Hence, Jennifer Nedelsky's suggestion is to go behind the boundary metaphor and to unpack what it stands for (Nedelsky, 1990, p. 172). Is she right?

I agree that if one sees the construction of relationship as what enhances autonomy, the metaphor of boundary is not useful. However, Jennifer Nedelsky's suggestion is unclear to me. She acknowledges that one of the general problems with the boundary metaphor is that it 'obscures the questions it was intended to answer, it closes down rather than invites inquiry' (Nedelsky, 1990, p. 173). Moreover, when discussing boundaries with regard to child-parent relationship she writes:

> ... They focus the mind on barriers, rules, and separateness, perhaps even oppositional separateness. They do not direct attention to the nature of the relationship between the parent and the child ... ; in addition, boundary imagery teaches both parents and children that security lies in walls ... boundaries structure relationships, but they do not help us to understand or evaluate those structures, and often the structures are undesirable.[10]

Nedelsky's conclusion is that 'the imagery acknowledged with the boundary is too well-established, too wall-like, to closely tied to a separative self' (Nedelsky, 1990, p. 175). Therefore, she calls us to look behind the metaphor of boundary. But how can this new metaphor of 'looking behind' (the old metaphor) be done? And if this is her conclusion, why stay with the metaphor of boundary at all? Why abandon it? Perhaps the reason Professor Nedelsky wants to leave the metaphor of boundary and only change its conventional interpretation is the same reason that makes her stay with the notion of autonomy – that is the fact that these notions and categories are so deeply rooted in our tradition that one can not abandon them from our daily discourse and thinking. Such a reason has made Sara Hoagland assert a more radical argument; that not only one cannot abandon these categories but one cannot also change their (traditionally accepted) meaning (Hoagland, 1990).

In regard to the category of boundary, I would like to suggest a probably radical argument, but opposite to Hoagland's argument. I think we should seek to completely abandon the notion of boundary while talking about and thinking of autonomy in its relational meaning. Unlike the term 'autonomy' that can bear various interpretations, the category of boundary carries an inherent meaning of separateness that is contradictory to the social construction under the relational theory. I agree with Jennifer Nedelsky that our conceptions of boundaries structure relationships. But their structure of relationships is in light of what separates one from the other rather than what connects them. In my view, it is difficult to imagine a linguistic meaning to the metaphor of boundary that will emphasize the latter. It is more 'efficient' to adopt a new metaphor to the idea of developing relationship as a way to enhance autonomy, even within a gradual and long process of time. I believe that by using this new metaphor more frequently, the bricks of the wall surrounding the old metaphor will fall apart.

As the reader could probably guess so far, I do not think there are boundaries between the brain-dead mother and her fetus or between the brain-dead mother (with her fetus) and the rest of the world. Applying the feminist relational theory here will help me make my point.

The concept of boundary between the mother and the fetus touches upon the delicate problem of maternal-fetal conflict. This conflict is raising the following questions: What is the relation between the mother and the fetus? What does this relation entail on the moral and legal status of the fetus? While above I was concerned with the social relations a brain-dead woman has in general, here, I will focus on the relations between a brain-dead pregnant woman (with the emphasis of her being pregnant) and her fetus. I will try to answer the questions raised by looking at some of the literature of feminist relational theory.

Cynthia Willett's writing on the relations between the mother and her fetus appeal to me. Willett mentions some of the alternatives to the metaphor of boundary with regard to mother-child relation (Willett, 2001, pp. 164–5). Both the mother and the child are 'whole creatures' in 'communion' with one another; the mother is in a political and economic power in relationship with various others (including fathers, domestic workers, or employers), all of whom mediate her relationship with her child; the mother and the child enjoy a multifaceted social relationship. Thus Willet is arguing against separating the child from the mother.

Indeed, carrying a baby is perhaps the most intimate physical-emotional relationship there is (Nedelsky, 1993, p. 364). Mary Shanley describes the limits of the language to convey such a relationship (Shanely, 2001, pp. 112). She quotes Gwendolyn Brooks' poem on abortion, '*The Mother*':

> You are dead. / Or rather, or instead, / You were never made. / But that too, I am afraid, / Is faulty: oh, what shall I say, how is the truth to be said?

Shanley brings Barbara Johnson's analysis of that poem. Johnson notes that the poem continues to struggle to clarify the relation between '*I*' (the woman) and '*You*' (the fetus), but in the end, the language of the poem can no more distinguish between '*I*' and '*You*' than it can come up with a proper definition of life. Shanley also sheds light on the mother-fetus relation with Iris Young's writing (Shanley, 2001, p. 112–13). She quotes Young:

> ... While for observers pregnancy may appear to be a time of waiting and watching, when nothing happens, for the pregnant subject pregnancy has a temporality of movement, growth, and change ... the pregnant woman experiences herself as a source and participant in a creative process. Though she does not plan and direct it, neither does it merely wash over her; rather, *she is this process, this change.*

It is in these writings that I am inspired to argue for 'one entity' consisting of the mother and her fetus (especially in the case where the fetus is not yet viable). But also the law, that is part of the field in which the brain-dead mother (with her fetus's) interactions take place, structures these relationships and shapes this concept. The way the law grants rights to the fetus only after it has left the maternal environment including rights that relate to the time *prior* to its birth contributes to the perception of the fetus as integral part of the woman.

The same ideas are expressed in court cases. Many states in the US recognize (viable) unborn children as having rights to sue for stillbirth, but not for damages occurred before. In the Canadian *D.F.G.* case, discussed in more detail in chapter 2, the court ruled that the law does not recognize the unborn child as a legal or juridical person possessing rights (*Winnipeg Child and Family Services v. D.F.G.*, 1997). The court emphasized that:

> ... Before birth the mother and unborn child are one in the sense that 'the life of the foetus is intimately connected with, and cannot be regarded in isolation from, the life of the pregnant woman'. It is only after birth that the foetus assumes a separate personality. Accordingly, the law has always treated the mother and the unborn child as one. To sue a pregnant woman on behalf of her unborn foetus therefore posits the anomaly of one part of a legal and physical entity suing itself.[11]

Once the child is born, alive and viable, the law may recognize that its existence began before birth for certain limited purposes. While discussing the imposition of duty of care owed by the mother to her unborn, the court in *D.F.G.* held that such a duty may create a conflict between the pregnant woman as an autonomous decision-maker and her fetus.

In my opinion one cannot avoid this conflict when it is also considered with the 'best interests of the fetus' as an argument in favor of keeping the brain-dead pregnant woman 'alive'. Can we really speak of the interests of the fetus as separated from the interests of the mother? Surprisingly, the 'best interests of the fetus' rule is a very strong one. It derives from a fundamental concern to the fetus's future life – or more accurately, it is concerned with the quality of the growth and development of the fetus, which the pregnant woman is carrying.

In the case of a brain-dead pregnant woman the 'best interests of the fetus' rule seems to have a more important role. The chances that the fetus would survive *in utero* to 24 weeks are estimated at 50 per cent. To be born at 24 weeks carries a 75 per cent chance of either death or significant developmental disability after an ordeal in the intensive care unit, a 50 per cent chance of survival, and 50 per cent chance of significant disability for survivors (Spike, 1999). Applying the best interest standard here requires that we do everything in our power to maximize the length of time of *in utero* development, including the use of medical and surgical interventions. However, despite all these efforts the chance for a good medical outcome is at most 10–12.5 per cent (Spike, 1999). Can and should we act according to this rule and make every effort to save the fetus? Can one really conceive the interest of the fetus without considering those of its carrying mother? I think not.

Perhaps we should interpret this rule differently. We should not ask what the (sole) interests of the fetus are. Instead, we should ask for the respect and appreciation for the child to be born. By this, we will not be concentrating on the mere present survival of the fetus best assured by prolonging the time of its *in utero* development. Rather we would focus on the future conditions of its care taking, its welfare and its emotional and physical health.

Is there a boundary between the brain-dead pregnant woman (with the fetus) and the external world? I would like to answer this question from the unique perspective of the human body, to which I shall now turn.

THE HUMAN BODY

The issue of maintaining a brain dead pregnant woman 'alive' is strongly connected to the general concept of the human body. The body is a space whose relationship with others is governed by a matrix of rights and rules. In an earlier discussion, I supported the view that the human body (dead or alive) is socially constructed. As Cynthia Willett puts it:

> Sociality goes deeper into the natural realm than we have acknowledged. As human beings, we need to be loved and respected through the proper signs of touch and of the gaze. We experience these needs through our bodies. The body is itself part of our social presence. Respect for our body as part of our self is a need of our spirit. The mind/body divide not only removes us from the impact of the body on the mind; it removes us from social contact. This divide is useful to those who can find no other way to respond to the pathos of the social world than through stoic withdrawal.[12]

In the previous chapter I strongly argued that the need to be loved and to be respected does not end with a person's death. The body of a brain-dead woman still has a social function even when she is laying spiritless in the intensive care unit.

Here also the law is present in the field of interconnections with the human body. The law shapes this field by special rules and norms. It does not treat the person's 'body' only as an anatomical or physiological entity attached to the person. By forbidding the selling, destroying or giving away of the body, the body is understood by the law not as an object or simply a property, but as something that is socially constituted.

Hence, I will argue that protection of the dead body is *a societal* value to be implemented in the same manner that applies to living persons. To use Catherine Keller's words: 'our skin does not separate – it connects us to the world through a wondrous network of sensory awareness … through my sense I go into the world, and the world comes into me' (Nedelsky, 1990, p. 177). The skin of a brain-dead woman keeps interacting and structuring the (new) field in which she and her social environment are part of. Even though it may not actively connect the brain-dead pregnant woman with others, it still keeps her engaged with others, shapes their attitude towards her, and forms different reactions on them as well. Literary speaking, the skin of a brain-dead person remains warm. Her body is still sweating. She looks like a living person. The appearance of her existence is as strong as it was a few moments ago when she was alive. Through her skin she remains in the world. She remains intact.

PRIVACY

The case of maintaining a brain-dead pregnant woman on life-support for the successful delivery of her fetus emphasizes a strong sense of the notion of privacy. Is there a bigger interference to the privacy of a human being (dead or alive) than that of keeping their body alive for the sole benefit of others?

Indeed, privacy is strongly related to autonomy. In its original thinking individual autonomy was conceived of as protected by a bounded sphere, defined primarily by property where the state was not allowed to enter (Nedelsky, 1989, p. 17). In this regard, Judge Major's ruling in the *D.F.G.* case that 'once the mother decides to bear the child the state has an interest in trying to ensure the child's health'[13] is prima facie violating her privacy. Autonomy (to the individual) is conceptualized in the traditional liberal thinking as 'private' as opposed to the 'public' represented by the 'state' (or the power-holders). This individual-collective conflict can have a moral consequence.

However, our case challenges the dichotomies private-public, and individual-state. Although the hospital as a 'public' entity has the physical capacity to interfere with the pregnant woman's (perhaps) most private sphere, it will do so only with the consent or following the request of her substitute decision-makers. The latter are neither the 'state' nor do they belong to the 'public'. Thus the 'taking of property' (of the brain-dead woman) is a pure private act. The fact that her maintaining on 'life'-support cannot be directly performed by private actors but through the health-care system, does not categorize the act to a public act. One should stop focusing on the *players* of the act and instead concentrate on the act *itself*. In this regard, the dichotomy private-public can lead to wrong moral judgment on whether to allow the 'public' sphere to interfere with the 'private' sphere.

Another way to look at post-mortem pregnancy is by regarding the woman's family, friends and fetus – who all form and shape the interference with her privacy – as a collective. However, this collective should not be seen as a potential threat to the brain-dead pregnant woman (the individual), but somewhat a constitutive of her, and hence a source of her autonomy in her current special condition, as well as a danger to it (Nedelsky, 1989, p. 21).[14]

As Immanuel Kant asserts, privacy also entails relationships of respect. It is also strongly connected to the metaphor of boundary: where we treat bounded spheres as indexes of personhood, respecting those boundaries constitutes respecting persons (Nedelsky, 1990, p. 176). Because of the difficulties associated with the metaphor of boundaries, Jennifer Nedelsky suggests to focus directly on the patterns of relationship that foster and express respect for people's needs, rather than on 'respecting boundaries'. As I showed in this chapter, applying her suggestion to our case would clearly make a strong claim against keeping the pregnant woman 'alive' for the sake of her fetus.

I would like to end my discussion on the concept of privacy by looking again at the law. I want to demonstrate how it also shapes our attitudes in this regard. For this purpose I will analyse our case from an abortion-law perspective, but shed a feminist light to it.

The right to make decisions regarding one's own body, as abortion, is conceptually derived from the right to privacy. I would argue that if the pregnant woman were alive, she could choose to have an abortion before viability age. Courts acknowledge that there is a significant difference between the circumstance in which a woman chooses to abort a fetus and one where the fetus will develop to full term and will be born. This difference is reflected in the 'viability' criterion for abortions. According to this criterion, regarding which

I elaborated in my first chapter, no one could (legally) intervene to override a pregnant woman's wishes and force her to carry the pregnancy to term. The 'viability' criterion is a good example of how the law shapes the discourse of the boundary metaphor. The law is influencing the field in which it is part of. This field is broader than the one that encompasses the case of a brain-dead pregnant woman. It involves interactions and social interrelations in regard to the general concern about touching and physically intervening with a pregnant women's body within her first term. In my view, the analogy to abortion-law may be very useful.

While abortion involves the woman's decision regarding the best (or less worse) of two options, in our case we do not know if trying to save the baby adds to the tragedy in the woman's death or ameliorates it. In my view, keeping the pregnant woman alive would carry a significant emotional cost. The family will have to watch the slow deterioration of her body. The family will also worry about the fetus's survival. The nurses that will be involved in the prolonging process will also suffer from stress. The tragedy of losing the brain-dead pregnant woman and the fetus she carries at the same time will be seen, in retrospect as *one tragic event* mourned by the family as a group. Keeping alive a pregnant woman to save the fetus can thus result in experiencing two tragic events with a continuing sense of grief.

PROPERTY

Two possible contexts for property claim can arise in the case of maintaining a brain-dead pregnant woman 'alive'. The first relates to potential claims regarding the property interests that the next-of-kin have with respect to the deceased pregnant woman. The second involves the question of whether the fetus can be considered the property of the pregnant woman. Of course, one can connect these contexts and argue that if the woman's family has property interests in her, then, allegedly, they also have property interests in the fetus as well.

By determining if X has a property one has to ask what kinds of powers or entitlements should flow from defining an object as someone's property. By property I refer to that which is identifiable as 'ours' and cannot be taken from us without legitimate justification. As will be elaborated below, my definition represents the connection between property and what are seen as the sources of its security – law and government. As Nedelsky argues, property is a right that requires collective recognition and enforcement. It defines what the society (or the state) cannot touch without legitimate reason (Nedelsky, 1990, p. 162). Thus, it is defined as a sphere in which we can act largely unconstrained by collective demands and prohibitions.

Since it was established, property provided an ideal symbol for the conception of autonomy concerning the protection from intrusion of the collective. Traditionally, property helped build the image that autonomy goes together with isolation (Nedelsky, 1990, p. 166). Property is thus connected to the metaphor of boundary and conceived in terms that reflect this metaphor. It gives us control, and provides privacy and security to its holders.

I will turn now to analyse the two contexts of a property claim that apply to the case of maternal brain-death. I will start with the second context, which I find easier to deal with.

The idea of treating the fetus as property evokes concepts such as buying and selling, contracting etc. The application of these concepts to the human body is a major concern for feminism. The concern is mostly related to the objectification of women, treating them as 'baby-making' machines, the exploitation of poor women, and the increasingly destructive commodification of all living things (Nedelsky, 1993, p. 347). Jennifer Nedelsky specifically argues that treating potential life as property will undermine the sense of children as gift of life, and that a property regime for potential life will actually exacerbate the inequalities and the problems of alienation to which women are already subject (Nedelsky, 1993, pp. 349–50).

Claiming that potential life 'belongs' to the pregnant woman reflects the idea that she should feel attachment to that fetus. But to protect and to respect such an attachment which constitutes part of the woman's membership in the human community does not necessarily have to result in saying that she owns the fetus.[15] Protecting the feeling of attachment can be secured without using the ownership, possession and commerciality concepts associated with and derived from the notion of a property. The same argument should be made with regard to property interests held by the woman's family. I will turn to examine this claim now.

The right to property in the body of the deceased has a firm base in many rulings, especially in the US. In this regard, the law ascribes quasi-property interests to family members of a deceased, usually focused in due burial. I will briefly describe the legal analysis surrounding this issue. In my description, I would like to suggest that not only do courts mistakenly rule that next-of-kin have property rights in the dead, but the property reasoning of courts is getting much more frequent than it was, strengthening the 'property rights' of next-of-kin, rather than weakening them or transferring them to other category of rights.

In *State v. Powell* (1986), the Supreme Court of Florida challenged a law authorizing cornea removal by medical examiners without first consulting the next-of-kin. In *Powell*, the next-of-kin advanced two arguments. First, they argued that the law constituted an impermissible taking of private property (*State v. Powell*, 1986, p. 1191). The court examined at length the 'property right' of the next-of-kin in the body of a deceased and rejected the argument that there was an impermissible taking, concluding that cadavers are constitutionally protected private property (*State v. Powell*, 1986, p. 1192). The plaintiff then argued that the actions of the medical examiner deprived the next-of-kin of the fundamental liberty right to dispose of the decedent's remains. In rejecting this argument, the court declined to apply strict scrutiny and found that the right of next-of-kin to a tort claim for interference with burial does not rise to the constitutional dimension of a fundamental right traditionally protected under either the United States or Florida Constitution (*State v. Powell*, 1986, p. 1193). Instead, the court relied on the purpose of this law, and upheld it, finding that it was rationally related to the legitimate purpose of restoring sight to the blind (*State v. Powell*, 1986, pp. 1193–4).

Following the holding in *Powell*, the Supreme Court of Georgia similarly held that there was no constitutionally protected right in a decedent's body. In *Georgia Lions Eye Bank, INC. et al. v. Lavant* (1989), the mother of an infant, who had died of sudden infant death syndrome, brought a suit against a hospital and an eye bank for the wrongful removal of corneal tissue from the infant pursuant to Georgia statute authorizing removal for transplant of corneal tissue of decedents. Although the lower court held that the statute violated property interests protected under the due process clause in the American constitution, the Supreme Court of Georgia ruled that in Georgia, there is no constitutionally protected right in a decedent's body, and that the statute authorizing removal for transplant of corneal tissue of decedents, if no objection is made by decedent in his life or by his next-of-kin after death, is constitutional.

Over the years, however, the jurisprudence began to gravitate toward finding a constitutional right in the decedent's body. In *Brotherton v. Cleveland* (1991), the court has recognized a property claim with respect to a dead body. Mr. Brotherton was dead upon arrival at an Ohio hospital and the hospital asked the plaintiff, who was the widow of the deceased, to consent to donating her husband's organs. Based on the deceased's aversion to organ donation, plaintiff refused to give her permission. Because of the suspicious nature of Mr. Brothertone's death (suicide was suspected), an autopsy was performed. Despite plaintiff's objection, the coroner permitted the removal of the deceased's corneas. The plaintiff did not learn about the removal of corneas until she read the autopsy report. On behalf of herself and her children, the widow filed suit, alleging that her husband's corneas were removed without due process of law and in violation of the equal protection clause (*Brotherton v. Cleveland*, 1991, pp. 478–9). Using an analysis similar to that suggested by the plaintiffs in *Powell*, the court found that the removal of the corneas from the deceased is entitled to the protection of the Due Process Clause and thus invalidated the Ohio provision which was analogous to the Florida law and that was upheld by the court in *Powell* (*Brotherton v. Cleveland*, 1991, p. 483). Although the court acknowledged the difficulty in classifying the claim of the next-of-kin 'property', it maintained that the next-of-kin had a 'legitimate claim of entitlement' which rises to the level of constitutional protection (*Brotherton v. Cleveland*, 1991, pp. 480–2).

A stronger move toward construing a dead body as private property was made in a recent case in *Newman v. Sathyavaglswaran* (2002). In this case, the parents of deceased children brought action against a coroner, alleging deprivation of property without due process of law, premised on the removal of children's corneas without notice or consent (*Newman v. Sathyavaglswaran*, 2002, p. 788). The parents argued that by removing corneas without due notice there was a taking of their property without due process of law in and violation of the Fourteenth Amendment. After analysing the history of rules and concerning the possession and protection of dead bodies, and rejecting former decisions finding there were no rights with respect to dead bodies, the court held that 'serving a duty to protect the dignity of the human body in its final disposition that is deeply rooted in our legal history and social traditions, *the parents had exclusive and legitimate claims of entitlement to possess, control, dispose and prevent the violation of the corneas and other parts of the bodies of their deceased children* [my emphasis]' (*Newman v. Sathyavaglswaran*, 2002, p. 796). Hence, based on the parents' duties and their responsibilities after the death of their children, the court concluded that parents had property interests in the corneas of their deceased children protected by the Due Process Clause of the Fourteenth Amendment (*Newman v. Sathyavaglswaran*, 2002, pp. 796–7).

Analysing these cases results in the conclusion that there is a shift from the position that the next-of-kin have quasi-property rights in the body of the recently deceased, limited to possession of the body for purposes of burial with no protection under the Due Process clause, to a broader view acknowledging the next-of-kin's property rights in the body of the recently deceased to include the possession, control, disposal, and prevention of the violation of the body or its parts. Such a broad view offers increased protection of a dead body under the Due Process clause when the 'taking of the property' is done without due consent or notice.

But the shift to recognize a property right in the body of the deceased also reflects how the law not only shapes the field in which it is part of but how it is developed by the field in which it finds itself. The shift in the legal cases is also an example to the way the law provides a whole language to this field – a language of property rights.

However, I would argue that the language of property in these recent rulings is a basic conceptual error. Property is a set of legal rules and norms that structure power. The rules tell us who has to ask whom for what, and how powerful or powerless they will be in their request. As Jennifer Nedelsky explains, the error to use such language of property comes from the thought that whenever the issue at stake is who has control or authority to make decisions with respect to something, that something must be property (Nedelsky, 1993, p. 361).[16] In my view, we do not need the concept of property. It adds nothing desirable and it brings with it a whole set of presuppositions (such as those connected to commodification and objectification) which are inappropriate for human beings. Perhaps the notion of stewardship is better. Mary Lyndon Shanely suggests that 'a person's relationship to his or her genetic material is better thought of as a kind of stewardship than as ownership'. By this she emphasizes a turn away from 'those strands of the liberal tradition that emphasize the individual and property in the body, and towards those strands that rest on a deeper understanding of the person rooted in multiple and complex relationships to family and civil society' (Shanely, 2001, pp. 94–5). We should therefore reject the use of property language as dominating the relations between the pregnant woman and her family members (or next of kin) in this complex situation.

CONCLUSION

As shown feminist analysis of post-mortem pregnancy leads to the conclusion that in this chapter we need to look at things differently. We also have to constitute a change in our language, but not before a change in our way of thinking. Autonomy, field, boundary, human body, privacy and property are some of the main concepts that our case evokes. The relational feminist theory can do a good job in addressing these concepts, especially in cases where a dilemma of whether to maintain a brain-dead pregnant woman, alive or not, occurs.

In this chapter the important role of the law in each of these concepts was also emphasized. The law helps to define the field, which includes individuals' interactions with it. It defines the scope of the field one wants to focus on. An example for the latter is the *parens patriae* jurisdiction of the court that granting the power to step into the shoes of the parents and make orders in the best interests of the child. The law constructs and creates powers, norms, and boundaries to foster and enhance autonomy. Thus, for example, the law usually ignores the fact that individuals exist in families or relational contexts, it shapes the image of dependence as negatively compared with the desirable status of interdependence. It also provides a whole language to the field in which it acts.[17]

But the law is also part of the social field. As Cynthia Willett puts it, 'the function of law is to protect the social individual from violation, and to cultivate the erotic power of the individual-in-relationship-to-others' (Willett, 2001, p. 163).[18] The law never acts in a vacuum. It works in a more complicated ways to interact with many forces. It makes assumptions that are not outcomes of a logical or analytical process.

The language of law is that of rights and duties. The language of rights involves mutual relations. X has a right if Y has a duty to fulfill this right. X's right without Y's existence does not mean anything practically. Legal rights structure relationships of power, responsibility, trust, obligation, respect, and care-taking. Thus, it is the connections between people and their relationships to one another that matter in the sorts of issue for which we invoke legal rights. One cannot talk about the rights of the pregnant woman, the fetus, or the woman's family without engaging the relational discourse.

All of these factors should be considered. Relations are complex. No absolute answer or directive can be sought from analysing them. However, their importance to the human condition is so significant that not to consider them would be a terrible mistake but more importantly a basic misunderstanding of the human nature itself.

The mother-fetus relation is one set of human relations I described in this chapter. Let us now move to analyse the ethical duties of a pregnant woman to her fetus, formed under this special bond.

NOTES

1   Compare Martha Albertson who asserts that dependence is inherent to the human condition (Fineman, 2000, p. 18).
2   Such a conclusion mistakenly reflects the 'individualistic' value of autonomy: 'It is not even quite right to ask what are the conditions that create individual autonomy because the question implies that autonomy is some kind of essence, which while dependant upon certain conditions for its appearance, is, nevertheless intelligible in isolation from those conditions once it has made its appearance' (Nedelsky, 2002, p. 55).

3 Some argue that individuals experience a tension between the need for connection and the need for independence. Relational feminists oppose this dichotomy (Willett, 2001, p. 25).

4 I put 'best interests' in quotation marks since according to feminist relational approach there is no such a thing as the sole interest of the fetus. See my discussion on the maternal-fetus conflict, below.

5 Carol Diehl, JoAnn Haas, Karen Moore Schaefer, 'The Brain-Dead Pregnant Woman: Finding Meaning to Help Cope' (1994) 13(3) Dimens Crit Care 133 at 135–6 (my emphasis – D.S.).

6 By dead patients I refer specifically to the 'newly dead' that are in the intensive care unit, serving as mere 'objects' to such procedures as maintained on life support for the delivery of a fetus, organ transplantation, practise of resuscitation procedures, forensic examination, and the harvesting gametes or hormones etc.

7 An interesting question can arise with regard to the fetus. While the fetus does not engage in social interactions, to define its connection with the mother solely as a biological one can be underinclusive (especially compared to pregnant animals and their newborns). See *infra* my discussion on the maternal-fetal conflict.

8 However, this is not a simple conclusion as the more one emphasizes the way human beings are embedded in and constituted by web of relationships, the more one can run the risk of social determinism. The feminist relational theory attempts to solve this risk by importing the metaphor of 'field' that encompasses the idea of 'choice' and 'decision' merely from new theories in theology, physics and biology that deal with the 'creative forces' of the universe (Nedelsky, 1989).

9 Interesting to note that this model was found applicable even to ant colonies. The biological order of the organism reflected in its relational organization can also challenge the requirement of actual feeling of autonomy I have discussed above.

10 Nedelsky, 1990, p. 174.

11 Section 27 to Justice McLachlin's decision.

12 Willett, 2001, p. 214; see also Farley, 1997, p. 487: 'The body is a form of connection, a way of knowing pleasure and humiliation, of experiencing the self in others.' He further writes: 'the body is the lens through which we encounter the world: more than symbol. More than the bread and wine of Christ, the body is a knowing connection, it is the telling thing, the medium of experience, expression, being and knowing' (Farley, 1997, p. 488).

13 Section 95 of the Judge's decision (*Winnipeg Child and Family Services v. D.F.G.*, 1997).

14 See Willett, 2001, p. 170: 'we need to alter our focus from the individual-in-opposition-to-the-state to the individual-in-relationship with local and transnational systems of economic and cultural power'.

15 Jennifer Nedelsky makes the same argument more generally with regard to children: 'We say that children are ours', that they "belong" to us. But we do not confuse this sense of intimate connection with ownership' (Nedelsky, 1993, p. 358).

16 Here again the analogy to children is clear: 'the law confers a wide range of powers of control and decision-making authority upon parents with respect to their children. Yet we do not mistake children for property' (Nedelsky, 1993, p. 362).

17 For example see Reva Siegel who analyses the use of the 'privacy language' by the court as reasoning marital violence (Siegel, 1996).

18 Willett puts much weight on the notion of Eros. Joining the writings of Lorde and Walker, Willett regards love as a force for the expansion of the human personality in relationship to others. Eros in her view is primarily a source for, and not a primitive threat (as in the Freudian and post-Freudian thinking) to subjectivity.

Chapter 7

Ethical Duties of the Pregnant Mother

In her article on 'The Architect and The Bee: Some Reflections on Postmortem Pregnancy', Hilde Nelson raises the question of whether physicians have a legal duty to sustain pregnancies of women who die during the first or second trimester (Nelson, 1994). In order to answer this question, Nelson assumes four different grounds on which such a legal duty might rest. The duty might be a matter of respecting the woman's wishes, there may be a duty to the state to save the life of the fetus, a duty might be generally based on beneficence of the fetus, or one might find a duty of 'special relationship' between the mother and the fetus. In regard to the latter, Nelson argues that it is not clear at all how a relationship between 'such shadowy figures could breed special duties' (Nelson, 1994, p. 261). More generally, her conclusion is that there is no basis for a legal duty to continue pregnancy after the woman is dead (Nelson, 1994, p. 261).

In this chapter, I will look at the dilemma evoked by post-mortem pregnancy from the standpoint of the pregnant woman. I will do so by focusing on the fourth ground Nelson proposed as a basis for the duty to sustain pregnancy of a dead woman. In contrast to Nelson, I would claim that the special relations between the woman and her fetus (to which Nelson herself strongly argues) do provide such a moral duty. However, like Nelson, I would argue that this duty should be declined upon the termination of the relationship between the mother and her fetus with the mother's death. I will support my argument by analysing the special relationship between the mother and the fetus from four related ethical theories: ethics of relationships, responsibilities to society, ethics of families, and ethics of care. In the end, I will also bring a religious perspective that would support my practical conclusion.

THE NATURE OF THE MATERNAL-FETAL RELATIONSHIP

A legal duty to sustain pregnancy implies that there are two separate (legal) entities involved: the brain-dead pregnant woman on the one hand and her fetus on the other hand. The idea of separateness between the mother and the fetus touches upon the delicate problem of maternal-fetal conflict, which I addressed in chapter 5. This conflict is raising the following questions: What is the relation between the mother and the fetus? How does this relation affect the moral and legal status of the fetus? In this chapter, I will try to answer these questions by looking into the nature of the relationship between the mother and her fetus, and by inquiring about the moral and (perhaps) legal implications that such a relationship creates.

To understand the nature of the maternal-fetal relationship it will be useful to bring here a fascinating description about pregnancy written by Hilde Nelson in her article. By rejecting Marx's famous distinction between the architect and the bee, according to which the woman's activity of being pregnant is thought to follow its own preordained patterns, Nelson writes:

> In important ways, the pregnant woman more nearly resembles the architect than the bee. As is typical for her species, she both obeys the laws of nature and improves upon them, ordering and shaping what she finds in the natural world through her own intentional, creative activity. She transforms natural processes by valuing them or by imbuing them with meaning; out of the ordinary phenomenon of hunger, for example, she creates a dinner party. That is, she turns the need for food into an occasion for expressing friendship, or possibly furthering social ambition. Like the architect's, her edifices can be and often are purposeful and deliberate ... once having conceived the purposiveness continues: the woman creates a relationship with her fetus. It begins as an act of the woman's imagination, as soon as she knows or suspects she is pregnant. At that point she may be at odds with her own body, or she may be in a special harmony with it, as the newly formed fetus both is and is not a part of her own self. If she feels it as an intrusion she may figuratively push it away, distancing herself from it and perhaps aborting it or, after birth, neglecting it or giving it up for adoption. Or she may embrace it lovingly from the beginning, imagining its future and setting it within an existing web of relationships in which it will have a valuable place. Throughout the course of the pregnancy it becomes less and less her self and more and more its own. From the beginning it has a value independent of the meaning-system she weaves around it, but what she weaves also has value – the value of a painting or a song, and not just the value of the honeycomb ...[1]

Nelson's strong words go together with the feminist writings of Cynthia Willett, Mary Shanely and Barbara Johnson, discussed in the previous chapter. What follows from these writings is that the mother and the fetus are one entity or two creatures in a special relationship characterized far beyond the mere biological. This relationship has, in my view, a strong ethical implication. It creates special obligation to the fetus. The moral obligation to the fetus neither derives from the fetus' separate moral or legal status nor from the legal claims of the fetus as a potential right holder. It is also not deduced from the mother's traditional right to privacy, autonomy, or alike. Instead, the moral duty to the fetus is founded on the unique relationship between the mother and the fetus while due to the process of pregnancy. I will turn now to justify my argument by applying four different, though related, ethical theories: ethics of relationships, responsibilities to society, ethics of families, and ethics of care.

Before doing so, a clarification needs to be made. In this chapter, I am asking whether the mother owes a duty to the fetus so that it would be ethically justified to maintain the mother on 'life-support'. My query does not focus on the *consequences* of the proposed act. In this chapter, I am not dealing with the position that an action is morally right or wrong according to its consequences. I do not need to take here the account of what can reasonably be expected to produce the greatest balance of good or least balance of harm, in order to assess the best utilitarian outcome.[2] My only examination relates to the ethical obligation of the mother (and her physician's as a result) to sustain her pregnancy by artificial means of life-support until the fetus can be delivered successfully.

In this chapter I will follow Immanuel Kant's notion that an act is morally praiseworthy only if done neither for self-interested reasons nor as a result of a natural disposition, but rather from a *duty*.[3] That is, the person's motive for acting ethically must be the recognition of an act resting on duty. I will therefore focus on the centrality of the duty in the ethical judgment. More specifically, I will ask for the sources of such a duty, while discussing duties that derive from relations between the mother and the fetus.[4]

ETHICS OF RELATIONSHIP

The idea that duties can be derived from relationships between different creatures implies that moral responsibilities are neither corollaries of moral principles (like the principle of beneficence or autonomy) nor are they structured intuitively as 'rules of thumb' for determining sound deliberative conclusions. As shown in the previous chapter, under the Relational Feminist theory, moral responsibilities are a product of the multiplicity of relationships with particular persons that make up our lives. It is through the specific, concrete experience of engaging with persons in different settings of circumstances, and the connectedness shaped in these ways, along with the recognition of the intrinsic and unique value of persons involved that a relationship is formed such that responsibilities can be recognized.

Relationships between people and responsibilities accompanying them depend on the potentialities and possibilities that exist in the concrete circumstances within people's lives. For their intelligibility, relationships are believed to have a temporal dimension: they progress over time, sometimes growing, or just changing, sometimes declining, and sometimes ceasing to exist altogether.

The concept of a duty based on special relationship assumes that some people have a duty to undergo *more* than minimal risk on behalf of others because they have *willingly* consented to put themselves in a special relationship with those persons. The idea of special relationship is best shown in so-called 'fiduciary relationships'. One obvious example to a duty derived from a fiduciary relationship is the duty of physicians to treat their patients even when there is a risk of life-threatening infection to the provider herself. Another example for such relations would be the duty of firefighters and lifeguards to rescue and protect others even with the cost of endangering their own lives. But there are simpler examples and less sacrificing, i.e. those of 'trust duties' a lawyer owes toward her client. The assumption under this category of duties is that the moral duty derives from the willingness to undertake it and from the nature of the relationship that enables the fulfillment of this willingness.

Another possibility from which a duty can derive within a certain form of special relationship is *causality*. Under this source, a person is responsible for putting someone else at serious risk of harm, even unintentionally. A classic example would be the duty of a person who abandoned an open refrigerator in a vacant lot where the door was jammed shut over a trespasser.[5] Some claim that the parent's duties to care for their children are of this sort as well (Nelson, 1994, p. 260). In Immanuel Kant's view, it is the act of *procreation* that initiates this moral duty correlating with the child's 'original innate (not acquired) right' to the care of her parents. In Kant's own words:

> From a *practical point of view* it is a quite correct and even necessary idea to regard the act of procreation as one by which we have brought a person into the world without his consent and on our own initiative, for which deed the parents incur an obligation to make the child content with his condition so far as they can. They cannot destroy their child as if he were something they had *made* (since a being endowed with freedom cannot be a product of this kind) or as if he were their property, nor can they even just abandon him to chance, since they have brought not merely a worldly being but a citizen of the world into a condition which cannot now be indifferent to them even just according to concepts of rights [emphasis in original].[6]

Pregnancy satisfies the two forms of duties discussed above. The mother has willingly put herself in this special relationship with the fetus,[7] and she also has put her fetus in a causal risk of harm during pregnancy. The risk of harm is, of course, derived from the biological dependence of the fetus on its mother while in the uterus.

All of us suppose that we have a set of more or less well-defined specific moral responsibilities with respect to various particular persons with whom we are interrelated. Reflection on such relationships draws our attention to the importance of responding and behaving in ways appropriate to particular human beings generally and to members of a social community specifically.

People have intimate and non-intimate interconnections. In the intimate context, there are many moral duties, which we owe one another. Love, fidelity and solidarity are all examples of features grounded in the fine-grained particulars of lives lived in common. Reciprocity is ideally desired in these contexts but is not a necessary characterization of them. The mother-fetus relation is the best example for such intimate relations. In fact, it could be easily claimed that it is the most intimate relation one could have. On the other hand, in non-intimate contexts such as business, school, work, etc., we can claim the same kind of moral respect *that anyone else gets*; we can expect that our moral interests will be honored and our dignity observed in a way and to the extent we respect others.

Christopher Gowans argues for two kinds of considerations that our responsibilities in intimate contexts are rooted in (Gowans, 1994, p. 122). The first is the idea that each of the persons involved in these relationships has intrinsic and unique value. The idea that individuals are regarded as valuable in themselves implies that they are valued not only as a means to some further valued end or that they are valued not only by being a part of some valued whole. The second consideration is the recognition that some connection or another obtains between oneself and these intimates. Thus, for example, it is because Frances regards Tom as intrinsically and uniquely valuable, and because she *knows* he is her son and the person she has brought up for the past few years, that she *understands* herself to have special responsibilities towards him.

The idea of value derived from connection within relationship is associated to what Joel Feinberg calls 'other regarding' interest (Feinberg, 1984, p. 71). Feinberg argues that a person can invest a desire so strong, durable and stable in the well-being of others, that she comes to have an independent personal stake (interest) in it herself. It is a case of disinterested 'love' that is the basis for what Feinberg terms this 'other-regarding' interest. In Erich Fromm's words, a person is loved *for what she is*, or more accurately, *because she is* (Fromm, 1963, p. 33). Domestic relations such as the love of a parent to her child or one's love for one's spouse are usually the type of connections, which can provide this sort of interests.

Immanuel Kant's ethical theory regards respect for persons as an end in itself since a manifestation of respect for the moral law dictated by pure practical reasoning. Kant's universal principle of right is 'to act externally that the free use of your choice can coexist with the freedom of everyone in accordance with a universal law' (Kant, 1996, p. 24). In his view, what makes persons ends in themselves is a property *shared equally by all*: rationality and freedom. Since only this property is morally fundamental, nothing about persons that distinguishes them from one another is of deep moral relevance. Persons are intrinsically valuable, but are equally in being so.

In the Utilitarian tradition, persons are neither intrinsically valuable nor uniquely valuable. The Utilitarian view seeks to calculate and weigh the welfare of our actions, while each actor's actions are counted separately and in isolation to its interconnection to the others.[8] According to this view what ethically matters is the consequences of the act rather than its circumstances or the deontological status of its doers.

In both Kantian and Utilitarian traditions, whatever may be unique about individual persons cannot be of basic moral significance. In contrast to these two ethical theories, on the 'responsibilities to person' account we do not regard intimate parties as intrinsically valuable by application of an *a priori* moral law, but through the experience of concrete interactions. It is the context of our particular relations with other persons that matters to our morals. On this view, a person is not only intrinsically valuable in isolation to its surroundings. Instead, a person has an intrinsic value, which is different from that of everyone else. Still only by the fact that she comes to fully interact with others is her intrinsic value as a human being appreciated.

The uniqueness of persons can play different roles in deliberation. In the intimate relation contexts, for example in relations between family members or spouses, the specific ways in which a particular person is unique or valued are primarily important. In these contexts, we attempt to respond to what is uniquely valuable in these persons. As we move away from the paradigm of intimate relations, we are in less of a position to understand or appreciate much of what is uniquely valuable in a person. In the extreme cases, where there is no proximity in those relations, we can hardly respond to anything specific about the person or its value at all.

Being intrinsically and uniquely valuable creates the potentiality for responsibility. It establishes the assertion that there is a (specific and valuable) being for which one can have moral responsibilities. It does not by itself establish that someone, indeed that anyone, has responsibilities. These only arise when some connection is established between persons, for example, through family relationships, friendship, love, but also through common characteristics of people such as nationality, ethnicity or other shared background. The relationship can be innate or natural and involve no 'choice' with regard to at least one of the parties, or it can be 'artificial', though consented to by a way of agreement or actual behaviour.

On the basis of one or more of these various forms of connections, and typically the mutual recognition of the unique and intrinsic value of one another, a relationship between persons may be formed. Attached to such relationships is the understanding and appreciation of some form of responsibility by each person to the well being of the other. The nature and scope of the responsibilities, as well as the extent of their application on the parties involved and the degree to which they are well defined, varies with the nature of the relationship.

Of course, there is a great deal of diversity in the ways in which connections among us take place. This diversity results from the fact that our relationships depend upon social institutions that are both complex and variable across history and cultures. The different possibilities of our particular social world determine how we can come to be related to other persons. The implication of such diversity is a considerable variety among the moral responsibilities that arise from these relationships.

Applying the theory of responsibility in relationships to the relation between the mother and her fetus is highly appealing. Although the fetus is in an early stage of development, it has uniqueness. It was created in special context (time, place, emotional state, etc.), and it carries with it the special meaning of bringing a child into the world in the unique way of pregnancy, which I described above. As long as the mother is aware of this uniqueness, and as long as she acknowledges the value of her fetus and her relationship with the fetus, she is responsible for its well being. Thus, she cannot abort him out of her own discretion, and to the extent she can do so, she has a duty to refrain from smoking, drinking excessive amounts of alcohol, or taking recreational drugs. The moment she becomes brain-dead, she loses her ability to appreciate and understand that she has such a special relationship (and hence responsibilities) to her fetus. The second and perhaps the most important component of the source for her responsibility for the fetus no longer exists.

RESPONSIBILITIES TO SOCIETY

The duty of the mother to her fetus can also be justified by an ethic of responsibilities to society in general. Human flourishing requires more than individual relationships. It requires participation in collective forms of human activity. Moreover, many relationships between individual persons are possible and dependent upon some form of a collective. This elementary fact establishes the idea that we have responsibilities not only to individual persons, but also to social entities, which consist of persons brought together by a way of common interest, purpose, belief, aspiration, etc., but which nonetheless differ radically from persons.

Hence, there may be responsibilities to one's family (as a social entity), community, nation, religious institutions, profession, political party, and so on.

Social entities last longer than the persons who make them. Often, they are concerned with matters that transcend the needs of any specific individuals consisting of them, for example the general commitment the university has to promote general values as education and research. The obligation to advance these ends does not depend upon the participation of specific individuals although it cannot do without those. This is why our relationships with social institutions and groups and our responsibilities and duties owed to them are not reducible to our relationships with and responsibilities to particulars that form these institutions or groups. Responsibilities to a social entity thus should be thought of as something, which consists of persons assembled with some human interest.

A given relationship implies an understanding of the responsibilities that are constitutive of it. Many factors affect these features. Some of them include the nature of the persons consisting the social entities involved, the nature of the relationship within these persons, and the specific circumstances of these persons' lives (history, health, financial state, etc.). Other factors relate to broader circles of relationships that these persons have, and the possibilities that exist for these persons within the specific social institution or group.

One such important social entity is the family. The fetus, although not yet born, is part of the mother's family (new or existing one). From the mere fact of its existence *in uterus*, the fetus constructs this social entity, shapes it and gives it a new meaning, power-relation and form. Being part of it, on the one hand, and activating it on the other hand, the fetus's well-being is instrumental to the establishment of this new and developing social entity. The mother, as a moral agent, owes *a societal* duty to enhance this social entity and to care and provide it by, *inter alia*, being responsible for her fetus. In this view, the duty towards the fetus serves as a means to flourish the new social entity (the family).

However, families have intrinsic values in themselves and they differ from any other social institution. Families should be ethically respected not only since they are social entities like other entities. They are special. They represent a combination of the ideas discussed above, that is they are unique social entities, which constitute intimate relations within their members. Thus, they create special ethical obligations which I will consider now.

ETHICS FOR FAMILIES

What is so special in families? More than any other social entity families are characterized by the particular individuals that form them. The personal characterization of families makes this social institution irreplaceable by similarly (or even better) qualified people. Families function to foster the liberty and growth of their individual members, not as contributors to external ends, but mainly for the members themselves. Moreover, family members are 'stuck' with each other. We do not choose familial relations, nor can we replace family members with others. For this reason, we cannot tear apart our familial bonds.

From biological and historical perspectives, occupying family roles involves a variety of considerations we regard as morally significant. As mentioned above, families are social entities that consist of strong and unchangeable intimate relations. These relations provide a rich set of vulnerable situations and expectations, that when unfulfilled result in deep disappointment and sometimes a severe damage. Finally, families serve as our first and perhaps most fundamental guidance for our moral capacities, and they are also central to the evolvement of a child's conscience and sense of self. It is within families that children learn how to morally interact with others and to be ready for the 'real' life in which the successful development of social capacities is crucial for one's own survival.

Like traditional ethics in general, traditional medical ethics in particular is concerned with individuals. Under this view, it is morally wrong (if relevant at all) to take broader communal concerns into account while making treatment decisions for patients.[9] Nevertheless, it seems that medicine is not ethically devoted to all individuals. Only those people who have a doctor-patient relationship are subject to special moral concern. Medical ethics are, therefore, a contractual ethics in which all special duties flow from a relationship freely entered into by willing participants.[10]

Moreover, as Nelson and Nelson rightly claim, medical ethics, unlike general ethics, are grounded in a social practice, that is culture-specific traditions of the profession (Nelson and Nelson, 1995, pp. 57–9). This view is supported by contemporary calls for providers to regard their patients as active decision-makers who can (and should) often determine their medical interests for themselves, and who will not always opt for actions the physician suggests. Nelson and Nelson further argue that these calls are accompanied by the huge increase in medical-practice lawsuits that seems to have made a continuing threat to the professional career of physicians (Nelson and Nelson, 1995, p. 59).

Indeed, recent developments in the profession of medicine show that ethics of families have been well incorporated within medical ethics. It is believed that this process took place due to some important changes in the role of physicians, on the one hand, and in the centrality of families and communal needs, on the other hand. The most profound example for such a view is the fact that questions of justice in the allocation of medical resources (like in organ transplantation) have become very compelling. By dealing with such questions, providers are expected to make a balance of 'fairness' between the interests of their patients and the interests of society at large.

The implications of health care decisions are far beyond the patients themselves. As Eva Kittay beautifully writes when she discusses communitarianism and its effect on bioethics:

> We frequently speak as if the obligation to provide care to a particular person belonged to a given individual or, perhaps, to a family. But an individual in need of care is like a stone cast in the water. Those who feel the impact most immediately are in closest proximity, but the effects come in wider and wider ripples. Even though the well-being of an individual may be the immediate duty of those who are closest, it is the obligation of the larger society to assure that care can be and is provided.[11]

Along with this new trend in medical ethics are the centrality of the family and the increased role of the family in shaping the patients' attitude and decision-making. As the focus in the clinical area has extended from the patient to other family members (spouse, partner, parents), health-care providers face an inherent need to discuss their patient's health problems with people other than the patient herself.[12] The situation of a pregnant brain-dead woman is a classic example for such a complexity, as it always involves other family members as well. Sometimes, the attitudes of the patient's family members can vary among themselves. The case of Ellen Higgis that Jeffrey Spike brings in his article on maternal brain-death is an example of a real life situation in which Ellen's mother opposed to keeping Ellen 'alive' by artificial means but her father and his second wife asked the medical team to do just that (Spike, 1999).

ETHICS OF CARE

Another theory that can justify the argument for familial obligation to the fetus originates in ethics of care. The theory of ethics of care focuses on a set of character properties that are valued in close personal relationships. These properties include sympathy, compassion, fidelity, love, friendship, etc'.[13] Caring and compassion is also emphasized – though not exclusively – by virtue-ethics approaches (Pellegrino, 1995, p. 269). An ethics of care places greater emphasis on health-care providers' communication skills and emotional sensitivity as well as on the effects ethical issues have on relationships. It does so by abiding to five major principles on moral attention, sympathetic understanding, relationship awareness, accommodation and response (Manning, 1998, p. 98). Consequently, ethics emphasizing caring for others encourage the settlement of moral problems that give greater power to family members in health-care decision-making.

The Royal Commission on New Reproductive Technologies in Canada adopted the guidelines of ethics of care and regarded this theory as the most suitable in maternal-fetal conflicts. In its report, the commission concluded that:

> In line with the ethics of care, we believe that the best approach is to seek ways to ensure that the needs of both the woman and the fetus are met ... the ethic of care offers a means of avoiding the conflicts inherent in judicial intervention by promoting two fundamental values: respect for the rights and autonomy of the pregnant woman and concern for the health and well-being of the fetus. The best way to accomplish this is not by compelling pregnant women to behave in certain ways, but by providing a supportive and caring environment in which they can make informed decisions and choose from among realistic options before and during pregnancy.[14]

Hence, taking family seriously as an important social entity or for its intrinsic special values is also in accordance with ethics of care. As I showed above, ethics of families (as social entities and as special entities with intrinsic values), and ethics of care support the claim regarding the mother's duty to the fetus. However, with the mother's death, the mother does no longer take part in the familial obligations owed to the fetus like she did while alive. Her moral agency in this regard is over now, and she has no more obligations of care for her fetus. This practical conclusion will be finally supported by religious ethics, especially Catholic ethics.

RELIGION AND BIOETHICS

Religious ethical discussion is often conducted by reference to moral rules prohibiting or mandating the performance of certain types of actions. Much religious moral thought assesses actions in terms of the *intentions* embedded in them rather than in terms of what is done or what results (Brody, 1998, p. 44). As this chapter turns aside from examining the consequences of the proposed action of whether to maintain the brain-dead pregnant woman on life-support or not, religious moral thought is appealing to the discussion of the mother's moral duties toward her fetus. According to moral religious thought, the intention embedded in the action can substantially determine the moral permissibility of the action. The idea of intent, for example, can lead to different results when interpreting an act as 'letting die' rather than 'kill' – a distinction I touched upon in chapter 1 while discussing the issue of 'double effect'.[15] Examining our case through the lens of 'intent' leads to the conclusion that letting the mother (and her fetus) die peacefully does not amount to killing the fetus. By using the principle of 'double effect' it is possible to argue that the death of the fetus can be regarded as best foreseen but unintended result. Of course, this is different than (actively) performing an abortion on a living pregnant woman. In addition to the act of killing itself, this living woman continues to owe her fetus the moral duties discussed above, so that performing abortion is also morally wrong from the mother's perspective in terms of her moral obligations toward her fetus.

Respecting the secular principle of 'autonomy'[16] can find its companion in religious ethics in the concept of *fidelity* (Brody, 1998, p. 45). Much religious moral thought draws upon theological conceptions to develop an ideal of human relations. One such ideal is covenantal fidelity. According to this ideal, there is a covenant of fidelity between God and people, and this covenant mandates an obligation to act faithfully to each other. Hence, individuals entering into special relations with each other are bound by the requirements implied in this treaty of fidelity or faithfulness.

In the context of maternal brain-death, it is however difficult to speak of the pregnant woman's duty of fidelity to her fetus. Nevertheless, derived from the duty of fidelity is the physician's duty to respect the patient's wishes and be faithful to her, notwithstanding she holds the right to autonomy (and hence according to the traditional view, as soon as she dies, she no longer enjoys this 'right'). The woman's wishes should be respected and considered mainly because the physician has a duty of faithfulness towards her. This duty does not end while she is still a patient, laying in the intensive care unit, though brain-dead. Acting not in accordance with her prior wishes (including the situation in which she did not explicitly leave any directives regarding maternal death) violates the ideal of fidelity.

In addition to the notion of fidelity, there are other specific values that are fundamental to Catholic bioethics from which one can support the practical conclusion framed in this chapter, namely not to maintain a brain-dead pregnant woman on life-support. One important value is the belief in the sanctity of life. The value of a human life, as a creation of God is beyond human evaluation and authority.[17] According to this view, only God maintains dominion over this value. As Markwell and Brown explain, following on from this view is the idea that 'we are stewards, not owners of our own bodies and are accountable to God for the life that has been given to us' (Markwell and Brown, 2001, p. 189). Prolonging 'life' after a person is dead in this regard is 'playing God' perhaps in the extremist way. Moreover, according to the Catholic view, a person is a composite of body and soul, and as long as there is a living body (even with reduced mental capacities or with brain-death), there is still a person present. Hence, it seems that the Catholic tradition would hesitate to recognize, from the first place, that the brain-dead pregnant woman is dead.

Indeed, as Markwell and Brown argue, the process of maintaining a brain-dead pregnant woman on life-support for the delivery of her fetus, especially when the fetus is at the very early stage of development, constitutes extraordinary means, and therefore, is, from a religious perspective, wrong. There seems to be no moral obligation to sustain the woman's body for the sake of her unborn child under such an analysis (Markwell and Brown, 2001, pp. 191–2).

CONCLUSION

In this chapter, I examined whether a pregnant mother owes a duty to save the life of her fetus and to provide its well being. Such a moral duty has been shown to derive from the special and intimate relationship between the mother and the fetus. Two considerations support this duty based on the maternal-fetal relationship: the uniqueness of the fetus, and the mother's understanding and acknowledgement of such uniqueness. However, as argued in this chapter, when the mother is dead, the nature of the relationship changes, as she is no longer aware of her fetus nor does she appreciate her relationship with it. Also showed in this chapter is how responsibility to society in general, and to social entities, like families, in particular, constitutes a moral duty towards the fetus.

In addition to being social entities it was further demonstrated how the intrinsic values of families play an important role in forming the moral duty to the fetus. Nevertheless, it was argued that such an instrumental duty that enables the establishment of families no more exists as the pregnant woman is no longer socially and morally part of the family she had obligations to while alive. This argument was strengthened by applying ethics of care, and by analysing this practical conclusion from a religious perspective.

In sum, analysing maternal brain-death through the above ethical theories leads to the conclusion that a brain-dead pregnant woman has no moral duty to maintain the life of her fetus after her death, and that without any other prior intentions on her behalf, it would be impermissible to keep her on life-support for this purpose.

NOTES

1 Nelson, 1994, pp. 262–3.
2 See Beauchamp and Childress, 2001, p. 12.
3 'In ethics the *concept of duty* will lead to ends and will have to establish *maxims* with respect to ends we *ought* to set ourselves, grounding them in accordance with moral principles' (Kant, 1996, p. 147).
4 My inspiration for this analysis also comes from W. D. Ross's theory on *prima facie* duties. Ross's main argument is that some duties like fidelity, reparation, gratitude, beneficence, non-maleficence, justice and self-improvement are based in significant relations.
5 An Israeli case declared such a duty and found that the breach of that duty constitutes negligence under the private law. See 196/64 *The Attorney General v. Mordechai Bash*, 1964.
6 Kant, 1996, p. 64.
7 Nelson writes: 'women, unlike other animals, often are pregnant for a reason: they may conceive and carry a fetus because they want a special relationship that will last over time, or because they want an existing child to have a sibling, or because without children they would feel less firmly rooted in the world, or because they hope the baby's bone marrow will be a lifesaving match for a dying family member' (Nelson, 1994, p. 263).
8 For a different view see Mappes and DeGrazia, 2001, p. 16. Although not distinguishing between intimate relations and non-intimate relations, Mappes and DeGrazia claim that duties that derive from relations are consistent with Rule-Utilitarianism: 'Rule-Utilitarianism also seems to accord reasonably well with our experience of particular morally significant relationships. We commonly perceive ourselves as having special obligations arising out of our various morally significant relationships, and we think of these obligations as incompatible with functioning in the manner of an act-utilitarian. For example, parents have a special obligation to care for their children; physicians have a special obligation to act in the interests of their patients, and so forth. Such special obligations can be understood as having a rule-utilitarian foundation, as deriving from rules that, if generally followed, would maximize utility.'
9 Some, however, may argue that in addition to considering communal interests physicians have an obligation to save resources for society – an obligation that sometimes can compete with their own obligation to their patient. This makes them 'double agents' (Angell, 1993).
10 A stronger contrasting argument, which I will not develop here, would be that not only is medicine ethics not individualistic and impartial, but it tends to favor those who are powerful enough to enter into the doctor-patient relationship. Thus, it tends to favor those with more rather than less money, education, social standing, etc. (Nelson and Nelson, 1995, p. 57).
11 Kittay, 2001, p. 535. Some argue that health-care-decision making is not only a (neutral) matter of the society or the community in general, but that it is also and mainly influenced by our own culture, ideology, discourse and tradition: 'If we think of medical developments as simply putting difficult but discrete moral choices before us – how to best use this or that technology, whether to turn off a respirator, or whether to engage in a fetal therapy – we have already failed to see the presence of a still deeper question. That is really a twofold question: first, to what extent has the culture engendered by medicine already constrained our choice (forcing us, for instance, to consider the use of a respirator whether we want such a choice or not)? and second,

what kind of culture will we be engendering by the pattern of private decisions that eventually emerges from the need to make decisions?' (Callahan, 1994, p. 31).

12 Sometimes, sharing the patient's health problems with other family members can cause ethical dilemma. For example, when the physician discovers a new genetic disease, a question arises of whether the physician has a duty to contact other family members that may also be sick where the patient herself objects to telling her family.

13 Interesting to note here that the Latin word for cure is cura, which also means care.

14 Final Report of The Royal Commission on New Reproductive Technologies, 1994, p. 962.

15 One of the objections to Utilitarianism derives from this distinction and from the absence of components such as intention and responsibility. As Arras and Steinbock write: 'For nonconsequentialists, it can be very significant whether an outcome occurs because of something *I did*, whereas for consequentialists all that matters ultimately is *what happens*. This has led some consequentialists to reject a time-honored distinction in medicine between "killing" and "letting die"' (Arras and Steinbock, 2000, p. 11).

16 In this chapter, I did not focus on the principle of autonomy. A major reason for many of the problems identified with the autonomy ideal, especially with regard to dead people is that the notion of autonomy is commonly understood to represent freedom of action for agents who are paradigmatically regarded as independent, self-interested, and self-sufficient. As such, it is easy to categorize dead people as not being autonomous or as people who are not entitled to autonomy (due to their death). The familiar critique by Relational Feminists to this liberal approach to autonomy is that it takes atomistic individuals as the basic units of a political and legal theory, and, thus, fails to recognize the inherently social nature of human beings. See my discussion in chapter 6 of this book.

17 This is not exclusive to the Catholic tradition. In fact, all of the monotheistic religions (Judaism, Islam and Christianity) maintain that we have a duty to protect the life given to us by God.

Chapter 8

Conclusions and Suggestions

In this final chapter of the book, I will discuss the few reported legal cases which deal directly with maternal brain-death. I will examine in particular how and if these cases could apply to the Canadian legal system. In order to establish a proper legal opinion regarding the treatment of brain-dead pregnant women, I will also investigate whether an analogy from other situations of posthumous reproduction could be made. After discussing the proposals that have been made in the context of this dilemma, I will draw some conclusions and formulate some practical suggestions.

LEGAL CASES

Only three reported legal cases seem to deal directly with maintaining a brain-dead pregnant woman on life-support. Two of them are from Israel, while the third is an American case.

The Israeli cases

In Israel, the extraction of organ from the deceased for therapeutic purposes is permitted with the approval of three physicians, and with notification of family members of the deceased within five hours (or other reasonable time if a family member cannot be reached) after death (The *Anatomy and Pathology Act*, 1953, section 6). Under usual circumstances, the spouse of the deceased, her children, her parents or her siblings can give their consent to the surgery. The law specifically states that if the deceased objected while alive to the surgery, the post-mortem surgery will not be performed even if the deceased's next-of-kin agreed to do it. The opposite view applies as well: if the deceased agreed that the surgery would be performed after her death, the physicians are compelled to perform it even if the deceased's next-of-kin disapproves it.

However, the delivery of a fetus from a pregnant dead woman is an exception to this general rule, and physicians are exempted from going through the process of consent, or even notifying the family (The *Anatomy and Pathology Act* 1953, section 6C).[1] At the center of this exclusionary rule, Dr. Ruth Halperin-Kadary explains, is the perception that a delivery of a fetus, even from a dead woman, is not a surgery. Rather it is a natural and usual act, derived from the classical role of women to bring children to the world, which does not require any special procedure (Halperin-Kadary, 2002, p. 128).

One of the Israeli cases dealt with this particular issue. The case came to court when the husband of a pregnant woman, who was in a permanent vegetative state, asked for a declaration of the court that in case of brain-death the hospital would be compelled to immediately deliver the fetus (T.M.A.103/92, 1992). The woman was in her 28th week, and it was estimated that a delivery of the child under such circumstances would have a 20 per cent chance that the fetus would die, and a 40 per cent chance that the fetus would suffer from developmental complications. The husband's parents supported the view *not to maintain* the woman on life-support, while the woman's parents were divided on this question.

Although the court was not convinced that the deceased's mother was ready to rear the child to be born, and no other family member was found suitable to take care of the child, the court issued the order. The court emphasized the importance of saving the life of the fetus, and referred to section 6C of the Anatomy and Pathology Act 1953. Relying also on the Jewish law, the court stated that despite the uncertainty over whether the fetus has a right to life or not, if the fetus does not endanger the mother's life, there is a moral and perhaps a legal duty to save its life. Finally, the court referred to *Roe v. Wade* (1973), stating that the fact that the woman was on her third trimester made it easier for the court to intervene in her pregnancy.

However, in another case, when the husband of an eight-month brain-dead pregnant woman sought an order to deliver the fetus, the court refused to issue such an order (T.M.A. 38/89, 1989). In a two page decision, the court ruled that it was not authorized to accept the husband's petition, as it was formed under the Capacity and Guardianship Law 1967, and even substantially, the court found that such an order would not serve the interests of the pregnant woman. The husband testified that he could not rear the child, and it was not clear if there were good chances that the child-to-be-born would not be handicapped. Nevertheless, the court did not discuss the Anatomy and Pathology Act. It is not clear what the court would have ruled had it addressed that statute.

University Health Services v. Piazzi

In the *Piazzi* case, a Georgia court granted a hospital's petition to keep a brain-dead pregnant woman on life-support until the birth of her fetus, over the objections of her husband and family (*University Health Services, Inc. v. Piazzi*, 1986). Donna Piazzi had not drafted a living will or other health care directive embodying her intentions in such a situation, and the biological father of the fetus (who was not Donna's husband) favored continuing medical care to save the fetus.

After a short hearing of 45 minutes, the court determined that Donna Piazzi lacked the power to terminate life-sustaining medical treatment during her pregnancy even if she executed a living will, relying upon the pregnancy restriction in the Georgia Natural Death Act, which invalidated an advance directive at pregnancy.[2]

The court also rejected the argument that Donna possessed a constitutional right to refuse treatment and to terminate her pregnancy, concluding that these privacy rights extinguished when she became brain-dead. The court said: 'The privacy rights of the mother are not a factor in this case, because the mother is dead as defined by Georgia law ... and the United States Supreme Court decisions upholding the rights of women to abort non-viable fetuses are inapplicable because those decisions are based on the mother's right of privacy, which was extinguished upon the brain-death of Donna Piazzi' (*University Health Services, Inc. v. Piazzi*, 1986, p. 7). Finally, the court found that public policy in Georgia requires the maintenance of life-support systems for a brain-dead mother so long as there exists a reasonable possibility that the fetus can develop and survive.

Was there a reasonable possibility that Donna's fetus would develop and survive? The court believed there was. Reality, unfortunately, proved the opposite. The fetus died of multiple organ failure within 48 hours after its delivery (Jordan, 1988, p. 1110).

Application of legal cases

Unfortunately, the reported cases mentioned above do not really offer much insight into the legal solution to the maternal brain-death dilemma. Not only are the Israeli cases contradictory to each other, but they also stem from a legal system which has *specific* legislation on the issue of maternal brain-death. This is unique to the Israeli system. As argued earlier, section 6C of the Anatomy and Pathology Act 1953 is an exception to the rules concerning the treatment of the body of a deceased. Whether there is a justification for such an exception or not, it reflects an existing legal position. Canada does not have such legislation, and, in my view, cannot rely on these decisions.

We can also not rely on the *Piazzi* case. Besides the tragic outcome of the *Piazzi* decision, the court's ruling ignores some important issues that relate to the interests of the dead person discussed in chapter 5 to this book. Without any justification, the court immediately assumes that we should not care for those interests. But more importantly, the *Piazzi* decision rests on Georgia's pregnancy clause in its living will legislation. As discussed in chapter 3, Canada differs substantially from the American approach to pregnancy clauses in living will legislation. The different attitude is based on greater emphasis on respecting women's right to self-determination, and the strong arguments opposing to this discriminatory policy. Applying *Piazzi* would seem inappropriate for the Canadian legal system.

AN ANALOGY FROM POSTHUMOUS REPRODUCTION

Posthumous reproduction occurs when a child is born after one or more of the biological parents have died (Robertson, 1994, p. 1027). A distinction between men and women in this regard should be made. Posthumous reproduction by women involves extracting an egg from a woman *while she is alive*, fertilizing it with frozen sperm, and subsequently implanting it in a surrogate after the genetic contributor's death. Usually, when regulated, such a practice is not encouraged by the law. In Israel, for example, the *Regulations of the Health Security (In Vitro Fertilisation)* 1981 provide that there shall be no use of an ovum of a donor that has passed away. Nevertheless, a frozen ovum retrieved from a married woman, whose husband passed away, can be donated to another woman with the consent of the donating woman.

Posthumous reproduction by men involves retrieving sperm from a man *while alive*, freezing it, and using it for fertilization after the man has died. This is a more frequent procedure than posthumous reproduction by women and is usually more legally acceptable. The first reported legal case concerning this scenario is the French case of *Parpalaix v. CECOS* (1984). Alain Parpalaix, after being diagnosed with testicular cancer, deposited his sperm at a sperm bank for future use after his chemotherapy treatment. When Alain died, his wife wanted to use the sperm and the bank refused, arguing that the deceased did not leave any instructions on what should be done with his sperm after his death. The French court found that there was a fundamental right to procreate involved, and ordered the bank to return the vials of sperm to Alain's wife. Since the *Parpalaix* case, there have been a few more cases following request to retrieve or use a frozen sperm from a deceased.[3]

Posthumous reproduction can also occur when one or both of a stored frozen embryo's parents dies. The embryos may then be used by the surviving parent for reproduction, they can be donated to others for reproduction, discarded, or be used for stem-cell research. The latter usage is however illegal in Canada. The *Rios* case is the only reported legal case in which the genetic contributors of an embryo died. This case involved a wealthy Californian couple who received fertilization treatment in Australia, and consequently two embryos were frozen. Unfortunately, the Rios couple died in an airplane crash and had left no written instructions regarding the disposition or further use of their embryos. A massive public debate arose as to whether the embryos should be destroyed, made available for anonymous donation, or deliberately implanted so that they will be able to inherit an intestate share of the Rios's estate. The State of Victoria committee recommended the disinheritance of the embryos and their adoption by another couple.

According to a new legislation in Canada, posthumous reproduction is illegal, unless the deceased had specifically consented to it, prior to his or her death (*Assisted Human Reproductive Act*, 2004, section 8(1)). The new Act prohibits, at section 8(1), the use of 'reproductive material' for the purpose of creating an embryo, without written consent for that specific purpose. The same legal opinion has been expressed earlier by The Law Reform Commission of Canada: *Medically Assisted Procreation*. The commission concluded, in section 5(1) of its recommendations that 'Before conceiving embryos for future personal use, the person or persons with control should be required to make a written statement of intentions as to the fate of the embryos in such circumstances as the death of a person with control …' (Law Reform Commission of Canada, 1992). In Israel, there seems to be a different legal view depending on the gender of the genetic contributor. The *Regulations of Health Security (In Vitro Fertilisation)* 1981 state, in section 8(b)(2), that there shall be no use of a frozen embryo of a married couple if the wife died, whereas if the husband died, the frozen embryo can be implanted in the widow's uteros only one year after the death of her husband, and with a report obtained from a social-worker. Recent guidelines set by the Israeli attorney general on October 2003 call for a permissible attitude toward posthumous reproduction by men (mainly through a mechanism of presumed consent) including the extraction of sperm from the deceased (The Israeli Attorney General Guidelines no. 1.2202, 2003).

The arguments in favor of posthumous reproduction focus on the right to reproduce. No doubt, 'reproduction connects individuals with future generations and provides personal experiences of great moments in large part because persons reproducing see and have contact with offspring, or are at least aware that they exist' (Robertson, 1994, p. 1031; Antall, 1999, p. 227). It is argued that people who lose their spouses should not lose the opportunity to reproduce because of an unexpected death. Proponents of posthumous reproduction emphasize that this is the only way of having a child with (or from) the deceased.

Opponents of this approach argue, to the contrary, that only a few features of what is valued about reproductive experiences remain when the reproduction is posthumous. A large part of the decision to have a child involves the desire to rear and gestate a child and to be aware of such an experience. As Jeffery Spike writes, 'most pregnant women look forward to their motherhood, and a loving relationship with their baby, and not simply to giving birth and then giving the baby away, never to be seen again' (Spike, 1999, p. 64). In posthumous reproduction, a woman will be neither gestating nor rearing the child. Another argument against posthumous reproduction focuses on the psychological and financial well being of the child. It is argued that as a matter of public policy, children should have two parents whenever possible. To support such an argument studies are brought to show that children of single parents are disadvantaged in general, and children reared without mothers are even more disadvantaged, in particular. While single parents usually have the other parent available to be involved in the child's upbringing, both emotionally and financially, in posthumous reproduction there is one bereaved parent bringing a child into the world without the option of assistance from the other parent. In addition, there could be severe psychological implications to a child who learns he or she was born after the death of his or her parent (Landau, 1999).

An additional issue related to posthumous reproduction is harvesting gametes from a deceased. The harvesting question is more complicated than the use of gametes after the death of their contributors, as it involves a direct bodily intervention with the dead. Although this process mainly applies to harvesting sperm from the dead,[4] it is only a matter of time until harvesting ova becomes possible.

What makes these procedures even more problematic is the fact that the sperm only remains effective after freezing, if it was harvested within 24–36 hours after death. Hence, a decision has to be made quickly, and usually, there is no time to go to court. In practice, if a family member of the deceased asks for harvesting gametes, this would usually be allowed. Due to their emergency, only a few of these cases get to court. So far, there are no legal reported cases found in the Canadian, American, or English courts in this regard. The new law in Canada, nevertheless, prohibits the removal of human reproductive material for the purpose of creating an embryo after the 'donor' of such material has died unless a written consent for that purpose has been given (*Assisted Human Reproductive Act*, 2004, section 8(2)). Two legal reported cases are found in Israel, in which, due to time limits, orders to harvest the sperm were issued, without any legal discussion (1130/01, 2002; *Re German*, 2002).

Indeed, as Roxanne Mykitiuk and Albert Wallrap argue, if posthumous use of frozen is permitted only with the consent of the deceased, harvesting gametes from the deceased should be considered morally unacceptable without prior consent of the deceased (Mykitiuk and Wallrap, 2002, p. 410). As I mentioned above, this view is supported by the new legal regime in Canada.

An analogy from posthumous reproduction cases can be made to the case of a brain-dead pregnant woman. In the latter case, the arguments that oppose posthumous reproduction fully apply, whereas the argument that supports it seems less impressive. In contrast to the life of a child who is born posthumously by using a frozen gamete of a deceased, the physical and mental health of a child who is delivered in a cesarean section from a dead mother after being maintained on life-support, are at a high risk. This factor carries much weight in favor of the argument for the well being of the child. Not only will the rearing parent face the difficulties of a single parent (that would arguably affect the child's well being), but he will also have to cope with possible severe impairments of his child directly resulted from the proposed medical procedure.

Moreover, as opposed to a deceased who has only deposited his or her *gamete*, the brain-dead pregnant woman has already fulfilled her right to procreate while alive. She has knowingly gone through the process of pregnancy, and experiencing what it is like to be a mother to a potential *child*, created by *both* parents. The argument of the right to procreate is weaker in the case of maternal brain-death than in the 'regular' cases of posthumous reproduction.

Finally, one can hold that maintaining a brain-dead woman on life-support is a longer and a more undignified procedure to the deceased than a *one-time* surgical action of harvesting gamete from the dead, let alone permission to the spouse of a deceased to use his sperm that does not involve any physical intrusion with the dead. If the latter activity should be and is banned by law (unless the deceased has given his or her consent to it), then it is also necessary to approach the first at least with the same carefulness.

SUGGESTIONS

Some suggestions have been made in the literature regarding the management of pregnancy complicated by maternal brain-death. William Dillon *et al.* have suggested some guidelines for the medical team (Dillon *et al.*, 1982). According to these guidelines, in a pregnancy of less than 24 weeks, extraordinary measures need not be performed on the dead mother; in a pregnancy of 24–27 weeks, the mother should be maintained on life-support, and the fetus shall be immediately delivered by cesarean section when possible. Finally, in a pregnancy of greater than 28 weeks, if it is impossible to maintain the mother on life-support or if there are complications in the fetal development or health, the fetus should be delivered by cesarean section as soon as possible (Dillon *et al.*, 1982, p. 1091).

Jeffery Spike set two necessary conditions for maintaining the brain-dead pregnant woman on life-support. First, strong evidence that the deceased would have wanted to deliver a child posthumously, or, in the absence of such evidence, that the biological father of the fetus would want this. In the latter case, there also should be no evidence that this is contrary to the wishes of the deceased. Second, pregnancy is advanced to the point that the chance for a good fetal outcome, in terms of both fetal morbidity and mortality, is acceptable by a best interest standard (Spike, 1999, p. 64).

Nicola Peart and colleagues argue that regardless of the legal position, from an ethical perspective the woman's prior wishes cannot be irrelevant to any decision made by her family or health providers (Peart *et al.*, 2000, p. 284). They claim that since the woman has 'a personal investment' in the future of her fetus, her explicit request to continue pregnancy in the event of brain-death ought to be followed, when possible. If the woman's wishes are not known, Peart *et al.* argue that there is a *prima facie* obligation on the providers to act for the survival of the fetus without causing it damage. However, they further argue that if the pregnant woman's prior wishes are known, they must carry considerable weight (Peart *et al.*, 2000, p. 285). When a clear legal requirement on the medical staff or the family is absent, the woman's wishes ought to be respected (Peart *et al.*, 2000, p. 297).

Stephen Wear *et al.* suggest a test of 'clear and compelling fetal interest'. Only under such an interest would it be allowed to maintain a brain-dead pregnant woman, even when her family opposes to such a procedure (Wear *et al.*, 1989, pp. 1728–9).

The variety of suggestions reflects the fact that deciding how to deal with a pregnant brain-dead woman is a question of balance. Dillon *et al.* and Stephen Wear *et al.* give more weight to the interest of protecting the potential life, but they ignore the woman's interests. The suggestion of Dillon *et al.* is as arbitrary as the viability criteria, and Wear *et al.*'s test is obscure, as it is not clear if and when there is a compelling fetal interest. Peart *et al.* seem to offer a more reasonable balance, giving proper weight to the woman's interest. In my view, their guidelines are consistent with the main Canadian legal principals regarding interventions with pregnant women.

However, as showed in chapter 5 to this book, physicians have no *prima facie* obligation to save the fetus when the mother is dead. The fetus is not their patient. Their fiduciary duties to their patient (the pregnant mother) also *affect* the fetus, but not initiate a separate and autonomous set of duties to the fetus. These special duties, like any other physician-patient duties, are conditioned on the patient's health. When the patient dies, extinguishes all of the effect of such duties. Even if Peart *et al.* are right in arguing for such a *prima facie* duty, it seems strange that such a duty is dependant upon the question of whether the mother's prior wishes are known or not.

CONCLUSIONS

In my book, I have used James Nelson's model of 'casuistry of pregnancy', that is the making of moral judgments by noting similarities and differences between clear cases of admirable and defective maternal behavior in other women's experiences (Nelson, 1992, p. 326). Thus, I looked into situations of abortions and bodily interventions that affect pregnant women's life style and physical condition. In addition, I analysed the legal framework of pregnancy clauses in advance directive legislation, and I also examined the pregnant woman's ethical obligation toward her fetus under several ethical and religious theories.

Besides the 'maternal' component, I have also dealt with the 'brain-death' element. I discussed the tissue gift laws that regulate the use of corpses mainly for organ donations, and looked into the main moral, legal, psychological, religious, spiritual, and physical aspects of the question concerning the interests of dead people.

The moral and legal status of the fetus, as well as the jurisprudential question regarding the fetus's interest were also raised. Along with other issues, such as gestational age of the fetus, pragmatic obstacles to the medical intervention, legal requirement for consent, rights of next-of-kin and friends of the deceased, and the physician-patient relationship, I made an analogy from posthumous reproduction, and discussed the major suggestions to my research question.

Throughout this book, I have compared the Canadian legal system to the American, English and Israeli legal systems, and I have analysed the question of whether to maintain the dead woman 'alive' from a relational feminist approach.

At the end of my inquiry, I want to draw the following conclusions:

1) Maintaining a brain-dead pregnant woman in her first or second trimester is not what the court in *Roe v. Wade* (1973) meant to create. It is separating between the act of intervention with the woman's pregnancy and the state's interest that justify it. Moreover, the trimester approach in *Roe v. Wade* (1973) cannot apply to the case of a dead pregnant woman, as it addresses only the abortion context where the state must consider *both* an interest in maternal health and an interest in potential life.

2) As it appears from my analysis of the Canadian abortion-law and the law that governs bodily interventions with pregnant women's bodies, a pregnant woman has a protected right to fully control her body. This right is so explicit and so broadly interpreted that even the biological father of the fetus cannot interfere with such a right. Thus, seeking for the father's view can be only relevant if the biological father sheds light on the woman's view, but not otherwise.

3) Pregnancy clauses in advance directive legislation, which exist under the American law, should not serve as a model for Canadian law, which puts more emphasis on the woman's wishes and gives less weight to the consideration of the fetus's potential life than the American approach.

4) Canadian courts refused to interpret the existing law in a way that would confer the fetus a legal substantial status prior to birth. The fetus has a

moral stance from a biological perspective, but not a psychological one. The common view is that a fetus is not a 'person', and does not have independent rights. In addition, from a normative perspective, recognizing fetal rights is wrong for women, for the maternal-fetal relationship, and for the physician-patient relationship. Lastly, the term 'potential life' does not exist in a void; the state's interest in potential life is dependent upon the mother's willingness to have within her body such a potential.

5) The organ-donor model, which is reflected in the tissue gift laws, should not be applied to the case of a dead pregnant woman. However, this model teaches us that if a deceased did not ask that his or her body be used for any of the purposes mentioned in law, no other person is entitled to ask for it.

6) The gestational age of the fetus is an important factor, which has to be balanced with the pragmatic difficulties of maintaining a dead woman on life-support that include physical, financial, emotional and personal barricades.

7) Ascribing interests to brain-dead people is possible by subsuming the immediate aftermath of each dead person's life within the *overall* course of his or her existence through highlighting the ways in which the dead person still exists after his death. There are moral, psychological, religious, and metaphysical reasons for doing so, along with the profound value of the human body and the obligation to treat it humanely.

8) Obtaining the pregnant woman's consent is a precondition to any possible intervention with her body, including maintaining her on life-support. In the case of a brain-dead pregnant woman, an explicit consent is needed.

9) Life-saving treatment for dead pregnant women undermines the traditional physician-patient relationship, obliging physicians to withdraw their commitment to act in the best interest of their (one and only) patient, and instead become the fetus's practitioners.

FROM PRINCIPLES TO ACTIONS

Should physicians maintain a brain-dead pregnant woman on life-support for the delivery of her fetus? Applying the principles above leads to the following practical solution.

The first question is whether the woman had given explicit directions about what should be done in the case of maternal brain-death. If she had, physicians are obligated to follow her instructions, regardless of the gestational age of the fetus.

The second question is whether the woman had given explicit directions about what should be done in case of loss of competency (in general). If she had, physicians are obligated to follow her instructions if the fetus in its first or second trimester. No state interest in protecting potential life should apply before.

If there is no advance directive or durable power of attorney for health care decisions (specific for maternal death or general when the fetus is in its third trimester), directions must be sought from previously expressed statements of the deceased. Due to the undignified nature I see in the medical treatment proposed and the risks imposed on the fetus, the assessment by the surrogate as to what the deceased's wishes were, should be obtained through clear and convincing evidence.

If the woman's wishes cannot be obtained by a surrogate, maintaining the dead patient on life-support should be permitted only if the following three conditions are met:

1) The fetus is in its third trimester.
2) The medical treatment proposed guarantees in more than 75 per cent proof a successful outcome for the fetus (at least 75 per cent chance of survival). This proof should be obtained by at least two physicians. Every degree of proof below that would undermine Canada's unique approach to pregnant women and the protection of potential life.
3) The medical treatment will last 14 days or until a proof of 75 per cent that the fetus's chances to survive are above 85 per cent is reached – at least.

In order to avoid this difficult situation I would also recommend taking precautionary measures.

First, along with increasing the public awareness to advance directives in general, I would recommend inserting a question into the model of a living will form that inquires how the person wishes to be treated during pregnancy. This inquiry will prompt health care personnel, lawyers and the public to offer the woman an opportunity to address her wishes for the situation by writing the advance directive.

Second, medical and nursing schools should be dedicated to teaching students about advance directives and pregnancy provisions. Further education during school and in practice should be established by the health-care profession to keep health-care providers up to date on changes in advance directive laws and the specific provisions of the province in which they are practicing.

Third, the state should also play a role in educating attorneys and the public about advance directives and their legal effect in a multitude of circumstances, including pregnancy.

Fourth, as caring for the brain-dead pregnant woman creates a series of crises for the nurses (Diehl *et al.*, 1994),[5] it is important to train nurses in how to create meaning in the situation of maternal brain-death as a way to facilitate the special grieving process that is attached to the medical, legal and ethical dilemmas that arise here.

Finally, because all cases reported have resulted in premature delivery, families need to be counseled about the possible short and long-term complications the fetus may experience due to pre-term delivery.

If a human being has any just, prior claim to anything at all, it is a just, prior claim to his or her own body. The adoption of the brain-death standard was originally intended to avoid the prolongation of somatic life by facilitating the discontinuance of resuscitative apparatus (Jordan, 1988, p. 1163). A brain-dead body needs to be respected in a humane way. A woman's right to make decisions about her own body and reproductive choices should be substantially protected (Gertner, 1989). The tool of life-sustaining treatment threatens these elementary concepts.

As Judith Jarvis Thomson writes:

The mother and the unborn child are not like two tenants in a small house which has, by an unfortunate mistake, been rented to both: the mother owns the house.[6]

Let us all remember that it all starts (and ends) with (and in) the mother.

NOTES

1 Interesting to note that the title of this section is 'the salvation of the fetus'.
2 The Georgia Act stated that the directive 'shall have no force and effect during the course of pregnancy' – GA. CODE ANN. § 31–32–3 (Supp. 1990).
3 *Hecht v. Superior Court*, 1993; *Hart v. Shalala*, 1993; *R v. Human Fertilisation and Embryology Authority, ex parte Blood*, 1997); *Mrs U. v. Centre for Reproductive Medicine*, 2002); In Israel, in contrast to the legal view on posthumous reproduction by women, the *Rules Regarding Management of Sperm Banks and Guidelines for Artificial Insemination* 1992 provide in section 28 that a frozen sperm of a donor who died should be destroyed, unless the donor's wife asks, within a year from his death, to keep the sperm for further freezing. Up until now, the use of a frozen sperm after the death of the contributor, has also been approved by Israeli courts in two different cases: 1922/96, 1997 and 10440/99, 1999.
4 There are few methods to harvest the sperm. The 'easiest' method is by exposing the testicles of the deceased to electric pulses. The invasive procedures include taking samples of sperm by stabbing the testicles, producing sperm cells in the laboratory from a testicle tissue that was taken from the deceased, and the most invasive procedure is the cutting down of testicles and producing sperm cells in the laboratory.
5 Esther Santons reveals that when she and her colleagues were asked, if they would care again for a brain-dead woman, they all replied they would, but 'pray we'll never have to' (Santons, 1993, p. 48).
6 Thomson, 1999, p. 205.

Bibliography

LEGISLATION

Advance Directive Law, Minn. Stat. § 145C (1998).
Advance Health Care Directives Act, S.N.L. 1999, c. 22, s. 2.
Assisted Human Reproductive Act 2004, http://www.parl.gc.ca/PDF/37/3/parlbus/chambus/house/bills/government/C-6_3.pdf, accessed on 1st May 2004.
The *Anatomy and Pathology Act* 1953, s. 6 (Israel).
California Penal Code (West. Supp. 1986) § 187.
Canadian Charter of Rights and Freedoms, Part I of the Constitution Act, 1982, being schedule B to the Canada Act 1982 (U.K.), 1982, c. 11.
Canadian Criminal Code, R.S.C. 1985, c. C-46, s. 287.
Canadian Medical Association (1996), *Code of Ethics*, s. 12, http://www.cma.ca/cma/common/displayPage.do?pageId=/staticContent/HTML/N0/l2/where_we_stand/code.htmaccessed on 1 May, 2004.
Capacity and Guardianship Law, 1962 (Israel).
Child and Family Services Act, R.S.O. 1984, c. 55, s. 37.
Civil Code of Quebec, S.Q. 1991, c. 64, s. 11–25.
Civil Code, La. Civ. Code. Ann.Tit.1 § 25 (1990).
Code of Federal Regulations, 2002, Title 45, Part 46, Subpart B § 46.204(e), available at http://www.access.gpo.gov/nara/cfr/waisidx_02/45cfr46_02.html, accessed on 1 May, 2004.
Congenital Disabilities (Civil Liability) Act 1976, c. 28 § 1(1).
Consent to Treatment and Health Care Directives Act, R.S.P.E.I. 2000, c. C-17.2.
Criminal Code, Ga. Criminal Code § 26–1202 (1999).
Death with Dignity Act, Or. Rev. Stat. § 127.800 to .897 (1998).
Durable Power of Attorney for Health Care, Minn. Stat. § 145C (1998).
Enduring Power of Attorney Act, R.S.Y. 2002, c. 73.
Ga. Code Ann. § 31–32–3 (Supp. 1990).
Health Care Consent Act, S.O. 1996, c. 2, Schedule A.
Health Care (Consent) and Care Facility (Admission) Act, R.S.B.C 1996, c. 181.
Health Care Directives Act, C.C.S.M., 1998 c. H27.
Health Care Directive and Substitute Health Care Decision Makers Act, S.K.U. 1997, c. H-0.001.
Hospitals Act, R.S.N.S. 1989, c. 208.
The Human Fertilisation and Embryology Act 1990, (UK) 1990, c. 37, s. 28.
Human Tissue Act 1961 (U.K.), 1961, c. 54 s. 1–4.
Human Tissue Act, R.N.W.T. 1988, c. H-6 (Northwest territories).
Human Tissue Act, R.S.N. 1990, c. H-15 (Nunavut).

Human Tissue Act, R.S.S. 1978, c. H-15 (Saskatchewan).
Human Tissue Act, S.N.B. 1986, c. H-12 (New Brunswick).
Human Tissue Bill – Explanatory Notes, at § 4, available at www.publications. parliament.uk/pa/cm200304/cmbills/009/en/04009x--.htm, accessed on 10th April 2004 (UK).
Human Tissue Donation Act, R.S.P.E.I. 1988, c. H-12.1.
Human Tissue Gift Act, R.S.A. 2000, c. H-15 (Alberta).
Human Tissue Gift Act, R.S.B.C. 1996, c. 211 (British Columbia).
Human Tissue Gift Act, S.M. 1987–8, c. 39 (Manitoba).
Human Tissue Gift Act, R.S.Y. 1986, c. 89 (Yukon).
Human Tissue Gift Act, R.S.N.S. 1989, c. 215 (Nova Scotia).
Infirm Persons Act, R.S.N.B. 2000, c. I-8.
The Israeli Attorney General Guidelines no. 1.2202 (2003), *The Retrieval and Use of Sperm After Death*, available at www.justice.gov.il/ MOJHEB/YoezMespati/ Hanchayot/Hanchayot.htm, last visited on 1 May, 2004 (in Hebrew).
Medical Consent Act, R.S. 1989, c. 279.
Mental Health Act, R.S.O. 1980, c. 262, s. 10(1).
New Jersey statute annotated, 26–6A-5, Suppl 1994 (1987).
New York Compilation Codes Regulations, Rules 7 REGS, title 10, section 400.16 (d), (e)(3)(1992).
Ohio Rev. Ann. § 2133.01-.03 (Anderson Supp. 1992).
Oregon Review Statute (§ 127.00 to .660)(1990 & Supp. 1998).
Patient Self Determination Act. Omnibus Budget Reconciliation Act of 1990, Pub. L. No. 101–508, § 4751, 104 Stat. 1388–204 (1990).
Personal Directives Act, R.S.A. 2000, c. 6.
Processing and Distribution of Semen for Assisted Conception Regulations, SOR/96–254.
Public Health Act, R.S.A 2000, c. P-37, s. 29–36.
Regulations of the Health Security (In Vitro Fertilization) of 1981 (Israel).
Representation Agreement Act, R.S.B.C. 1996, c. 405.
Rules Regarding Management of Sperm Banks and Guidelines for Artificial Insemination of 1992 (Israel).
Substitute Decisions Act, S.O.1992, c. 30.
Trillium Gift of Life Network Act, R.S.O. 1990, c. H. 20.
Uniform Anatomical Gift Act, U.L.A. 40 1987, s. 3.
Uniform Brain Death Act, Uniform Laws Ann. 12:63 (West 1493; West Suppl 1997).
Uniform Determination of Death Act, 1980 available at http://www.law.upenn. edu/bll/ulc/fnact99/1980s/udda80.htm, accessed on 1 May 2004.
Uniform Determination of Death Bill, Senate File No. 209, S.J. 452 available at http://www.legis.state.ia.us/GA/78GA/Legislation/SF/00200/SF00209/Current. html, accessed on 17 August, 2003.
Uniform Rights of Terminally Ill Act of 1989, 6(c) (Supp. 1999).
U.S. Const. amend. XIII, §. 1.

JURISPRUDENCE

In re A (minor) [1993] 1 Med. L. Rev. 98.

In re A.C., 533 A. 2d 611 (D.C. 1987).

In re A.C., 539 A. 2d 203 (D.C. 1988).

In re A.C., 573 A. 2d 1235 (D.C. 1990).

A-G's Reference (No. 3 of 1994), [1997] 3 All E. R. 936.

Airedale N.H.S. Trust v. Bland, [1993] A.C. 789.

In re Baby Boy Doe 632 N.E.2d 326, 260 Ill App. 3d 392, 198 Ill Dec. 267, USLW 2632, Ill. App. 1 Dist., April 5, 1994.

Brooks v. Canada Safeway Ltd., [1989] 1 S.C.R. 1219.

Brotherton v. Cleveland 923 F.2d 477 (6ᵗʰ Cir. 1991).

C. v. S [1988] 1 Q.B. 135; *Re F (In Utero) (Wardship)*, [1988] 2 F.L.R. 307 (C.A.).

Canadian AIDS Society v. Ontario, [1995] 25 O.R. (3d) 388 (Gen. Div.).

Child and Family Services of Manitoba v. L. and H., [1997] 123 Man. R. (2d) 135 (C.A.).

Re Children's Aid Society for the District of Kenora and L.J., [1981] 134 D.L.R. (3d) 249 (Ont. Provc. Ct.).

Re Children's Aid Society of City of Belleville and T., [1978] 59 O.R. (2d) 204 (Prov. Ct.).

Ciarlariello v. Schacter, [1993] 2 S.C.R 119.

Couture-Jacquet v. Montreol Children's Hospital, [1986] 28 D.L.R. (4ᵗʰ) 22 (Que. C.A.).

Cruzan v. Director, Missouri Department of Health 497 U.S. 261 (1990).

Davis v. Davis 15 Family Law Reporter 1551 (1989); on appeal West Law 130807 (Tenn. App.) (1990).

Diamond v. Hirsch, [1989] M.J. No. 377 (QL) (Q.B.).

DiNino v. State 102 Wash. 2d 237, 684 P.2d 1297 (1984).

Dobson (Litigation Guardian of) v. Dobson, [1999] 2 S.C.R. 753 [1999] S.C.J. No. 41 (QL).

Doe v. Bolton 410 U.S. 179 (1973).

Re F (in utero), [1988] 2 All E.R. 193.

Ferguson v. City of Charleston, 121 S.Ct. 1281 (2001).

Gabrynowicz v. Heitkamp, 904 F.Supp. 1061 , D.N.D. (1995).

Georgia Lions Eye Bank, INC. et al. v. Lavant 335 S.E.2d 127, 255 Ga. 60, 54 A.L.R. 4th 1209 (1989).

Re German (The Supreme Court of Israel) Decided in March 13, 2002.

Griswold v. Connecticut 381 U.S. 479 (1965).

In re Guardianship of Browning 543 So. 2d 258 (Fla. Dist. Ct. App. 1989).

Hart v. Shalala, No. 94–3944 (E.D. La. Dec. 12, 1993).

Hecht v. Superior Court 20 Cal. Rptr 2d 275 (Ct. Appeal, 2ⁿᵈ District, 1993).

R. v. Human Fertilisation and Embryology Authority, ex parte Blood, [1997] 2 All E R 687.

Jefferson v. Griffin Spalding County Hospital 247 Ga. 86, 274 S.E.2d 457 (1981).

Lacy v. Cooper Hospital: University Medical Center, [1990] 745 F. Supp. 1029 (D.N.J.).

Lyon v. United States, 843 F. Supp. 531 (D. Minn. 1994).

Malette v. Shulman, [1990] 72 O.R. (2d) 417 (C.A).

Marshall v. Curry, [1933] 3 D.L.R. 260 (N.S.S.C.).

Re M.B. [1997] 8 Med. L.R. 217.

McFall v. Shimp 10 Pa. D. & C. 3d 90 (Allegheny Cnty., July 26, 1978).

M. (J.) v. Superintendent of Family and Child Services, [1982] 135 D.L.R. (3d) 330 (B.C.S.C.).

Mme Claire G v. CECOS Tribunal de Grande Instance de Toulouse (4 Ch. Cir) March 26, 1991.

Moore v. Regents of the University of California 51 Cal. 3d 120 (1990).

196/64 *The Attorney General v. Mordechai Bash* (The Supreme Court of Israel) 18 (4) 568 from 15 December 1964.

R. v. Morgentaler, [1988] 1 S.C.R. 30.

Murray v. McMurchy, [1949] 2 D.L.R. 442 (B.C.S.C.).

Nancy B. v. Hotel-Dieu de Quebec et al., [1992] 86 D.L.R. (4th) 385, [1992] R.L.Q. 361 (Sup.Ct.).

Newman v. Sathyavaglswaran, [2002] 287 F.3d 786 (9th Cir.).

O'Bonsawin v. Paradis, [1993] 15 C.C.L.T. (2d) 188 (Ont. Gen. Div.).

O'Brian v. Cunard Steamship Co., 28 N.E. 266 (1891).

Parpalaix v. CECOS Tribunal de Grande Instance de Creteil (1 Ch. Cir) August 1, 1984.

Paton v. British Pregnancy Advisory Service Trustees and Another, [1979] 1 Q.B. 276.

Paton v. Trustees of The British Pregnancy Advisory Service and Another, [1978] 2 All E. R. 987.

Paton v. UK, (1980) 3 E.H.R.R. 408.

Planned Parenthood v. Casey 505 U.S. 833 (1992).

Planned Parenthood of Central Missouri v. Danforth 428 U.S. 52 (1976).

Pratt v. Davis, [1995] 118 Ill. App.

In re Quinlan, 137 N.J. Super. 227, 237–45, 348 A. 2d 801, 807–11 (1975), modified, 70 N.J. 10 355 A.2d 647, cert. Denied, 429 U.S. 922 (1976).

Raleigh Fitkin-Paul Morgan Memorial Hospital v. Anderson 42 N.J. at 421, 422, 201 A. 2d 537, 538, cert. Denied, 377 U.S. 985 (1964).

Reynen v. Antonenko (1975), 30 C.R.N.S. 135 (Alta. T.D.).

Rodriguez v. British Columbia (Attorney General), [1993] 3 S.C.R. 519.

Roe v. Wade 410 U.S. 113 (1973).

In re S (Adult: refusal of medical treatment) [1992] 4 All E R 671.

Schloendorff v. New York Hospital, [1914] 211 N.Y. 125, 105 N.E.2d 92 (N.Y. Ct. App.).

Shimp v. McFall 10 Pa. D & C. 3d 90 (Allegheny County Ct. 1978).

State v. Powell, [1986] 490 So. 2d 1188 (Fla.).

R. v. Sullivan and Lemay, [1991] 1 S.C.R. 489.

Symes v. R., [1993] 4 S.C.R. 695.

In re T, C.A. [1992] 4 All E.R. 649.

Thornburgh v. American College of Obstetricians 476 U.S. 747 (1986).

T.M.A. 38/89 (The District Court of Jeruslaem), January, 18th 1989, published in Ygal Shifran (ed.), *A Question of Authority: Whether to Deliver a Fetus from the Body of a Deceased* (Jerusalem: Rabanut Harashit Le-Israel: 2001) 17–18 (Decision in Hebrew).

T.M.A.103/92 (The District Court of Jerusalem) February, 4th 1992 available at http://www.daat.ac.il/daat/kitveyet/assia/bazaq.htm, accessed on 26 April, 2004.

Tremblay v. Daigle, [1989] 62 D.L.R (4th) 634 (S.C.C.), 2 S.C.R. 530.

Mrs U. v. Centre for Reproductive Medicine [2002] EWCA Civ 565 CA.

University Health Services, Inc. v. Piazzi No. CV86-RCCV-464 Superior Court of Richmond Country, Georgia, August 4 1986, cited in Dyke, Molly C. (1990), 'A Matter of Life and Death: Pregnancy Clauses in Living Will Statutes', *Boston University Law Review*, 70, 867–86, p. 871.

Vacco v. Quill 521 U.S. 793 (1997).

Villeneuve v. Sisters of St. Joseph of Diocese of Salut Ste. Marie, [1971] 2 O.R. 593 (H.C.), revised [1972] 2 O.R. 119 (C.A.).

Washington v. Glucksberg 521 U.S. 702 (1997).

Watt v. Rama, [1972] V.R. 353.

Webster v. Reproductive Health Services 492 U.S. 490, 109 S.Ct. 3040 (1989).

Winnipeg Child and Family Services v. D.F.G., [1996] 138 D.L.R. (4th) 238 (Man. Q.B.), revd (1996), 138 D.L.R. (4th) 254 (C.A.), affd [1997] 3 S.C.R. 925.

10440/99 (The District Court of Tel-Aviv) November 25, 1999 (Decision in Hebrew).

1130/01 (The Family Court of Haifa) January 9, 2002 (Decision in Hebrew).

1922/96 (The District Court of Tel-Aviv) September 21, 1997 (Decision in Hebrew).

MONOGRAPHS, ARTICLES AND REPORTS

Ad Hoc Committee of the Harvard Medical School to Examine the Definition of Brain Death (1968), "A Definition of Irreversible Coma", *JAMA*, 205, 337–40.

Agich, George and Jones, Royce (1986), "Personal Identity and Brain Death: A Critical Response", *Philosophy and Public Affairs*, 15 (3), 267–74.

Allison, Dorothy (1994), *Skin*, Ithaca, NY: Firebrand Books.

American College of Obstetricians and Gynecologists (1999), *Patient Choice and the Maternal-Fetal Relationship: Committee opinion no. 214*, Washington, DC, Committee on Ethics.

American College of Obstetricians and Gynecologists (1987), *Patient Choice: Maternal-Fetal Conflict. Washington*, DC, Committee on Ethics.

Angell, Marcia (1993), "The Doctor As Double Agent", *Kennedy Institute of Ethics Journal*, 3 (3), 279–86.

Annas, George J. (1987), "Protecting the Liberty of Pregnant Patients", *New England Journal of Medicine*, 316 (19) 1213–14.

Anstotz, Christoph (1993), "Should A Brain-Dead Pregnant Woman Carry Her Child to Full Term? The Case of the 'Erlanfer Baby'", *Bioethics*, 7 (4), 340–50.

Antall, Kristin (1999), "Who Is My Mother?: Why States Should Ban Posthumous Reproduction By Women", *Health Matrix: Journal of Law-Medicine*, 9, 203–34.

Arras, D. John and Steinbock, Bonnie (eds) (2000), *Ethical Issues in Modern Medicine*, 5th edn, Mountain View, California: Mayfield Publication Co.

Arthur, Robert K. (1978), "Postmortem Cesarean Section", *American Journal of Obstetrics and Gynecology*, 132, 175–79.

Ascioti, Kathleen J. (1993), "Sheila's Death Created Many Rings of Life", *Nursing*, 3, 44–48.

Ayorinde, B.T., Scudamore, I. and Buggy, D.J. (2000), "Anaesthetic Management of a Pregnant Patient In a Persistent Vegetative State", 85 *British Journal of Anaesthesia*, 3, 479–81.

Aziza-Shuster, E. (1994), "A Child At All Cost: Posthumous Reproduction and the Meaning of Parenthood", *Human Reproduction*, 9 (11), 2182–5.

Beauchamp Tom L. and Walters LeRoy (eds) (1999), *Contemporary Issues in Bioethics*, 5th edn, Belmont, CA: Wadsworth Publishing Company.

Beauchamp Tom L. and Childress James F. (2001), *Principles of biomedical ethics*, 5th edn, New York: Oxford University Press.

Beaulieu, Marc-Andre, Seshia, Shashikant, Teitelbaum, Jeanne and Young, Bryan (1999), "Guidelines for the Diagnosis of Brain Death", *Canadian Journal of Neurological Sciences*, 26, 64–6.

Benton, Elizabeth Carlin (1990), "The Constitutionality of Pregnancy Clauses in Living Will Statutes", *Vanderbilt Law Review*, 43, 1821–37.

Benrubi, Guy I. (1999), "Discussion", *American Journal of Obstetrics and Gynecology*, 181 (2), 301–2.

Bernstein, I.M., Watson, M., Simmons, G.M., Catalano, P.M., Davis, G. and Collins, R. (1989), "Maternal Brain Death During Pregnancy and Prolonged Fetal Survival", *Obstetrics and Gynecology*, 74, 434–7.

Bishop, Walter G. (1978), "Postmortem Cesarean Section: Discussion", *American Journal of Obstetrics and Gynecology*, 132 (2), 177.

Blumer Barbara J. (1998), "Minnesota's New Health Care Directive", *Minnesota Medicine*, 81, 1, www.mnmed.org/publications/MnMed1998/September/blumer. cfm, accessed on 1st May, 2004.

Board of Trustees, American Medical Association (1990), "Legal Interventions During Pregnancy – Court-ordered Medical Treatments and Legal Penalties for Potentially Harmful Behavior By Pregnant Women", *Journal of the American Medical Association*, 264 (20), 2663–70.

Bourne, Richard W. (2003), "Abortion in 1938 and Today: *Plus Ca Change, Plus C'est La Meme Chose*", *Review of Law & Women Studies*, 12 (2), 225–75.

Brody, Baruch (1998), "Religion and Bioethics", in Khuse and Singer (eds), *A Companion to Bioethics*, Blackwell, p. 41.

Buchanan E. Allen and Brock W. Dan (eds) (1989), *Deciding for Others: The Ethics of Surrogate Decision Making*, Cambridge: Cambridge University Press.

Burch, Timothy J. (1995), "Incubator or Individual?: The Legal and Policy Deficiencies of Pregnancy Clauses in Living Will and Advance Health Care Directive Statutes", *Maryland Law Review*, 54, 528–70.

Callahan, Daniel (1994), "Bioethics: Private Choice and Common Good", *Hastings Center Report*, 24 (3), 28–31.

Canadian Congress Committee on Brain Death (1988), "Death and brain death: a new formulation for Canadian medicine", *Canadian Medical Association Journal*, 138, 405–6.

Canada, Department of Justice (1977), *Committee on the Operation of the Abortion Law, Report*, Ottawa, Canada: Minister of Supply and Services Canada.

Chervenak, Frank A. and McCullough, Laurence B. (1993), "Clinical Management of Brain Death During Pregnancy", *Journal of Clinical Ethics*, 4 (4), 349–50.

Code of Federal Regulations, 2002, Title 45, Part 46, Subpart B § 46.204(e), available at http://www.access.gpo.gov/nara/cfr/waisidx_02/45cfr46_02.html, accessed on 26th April, 2004.

Cohen Sherrill and Taub Nadine (eds) (1989), *Reproductive Laws for the 1990s*, Clifton, NJ: Humana Press.

David-Hillel, Ruben (2003), *Action and Its Explanation*, N.Y.: Oxford University Press.

Dickens, Bernard (1981), "Legal Aspects of Abortions", in Sachdev, Paul (ed.), *Abortion: Readings and Research*, Toronto, Canada: Butterworths, pp. 16–29.

Diehl, Carol, Haas, JoAnn and Schaefer, Karen Moore (1994), "The Brain-Dead Pregnant Woman: Finding Meaning to Help Cope", *Dimensions of Critical Care*, 13 (3), 133–41.

Dillon, William P. and Egan, Edmund A. (1981), "Aggressive Obstetric Management in Late Second-Trimester Deliveries", *American Journal of Obstetrics and Gynecology*, 58 (6), 685–90.

Dillon, William P., Lee, Richard V., Tronolone, Michael J., Buckwald, Sharon and Foote, Ronald J. (1982), "Life Support and Maternal Brain Death During Pregnancy", *Journal of the American Medical Association*, 248 (9), 1089–91.

Downie, J., Caulfield, T. and Flood, C. (eds) (2002), *Canadian Health Law and Policy*, 2nd edn, Toronto: Butterworths.

Dresser, Rebecca (1990), "Relitigating Life and Death", *Ohio Law Journal*, 51, 426–7.

Ducor, Philippe (1996), "The Legal Status of Human Materials", *Drake Law Review*, 44, 196–259.

Dworkin, Ronald (1993), *Life's Dominion. An Argument About Abortion, Euthanasia and Individual Freedom*, N.Y: Vintage Books.

Dyke, Molly C. (1990), "A Matter of Life and Death: Pregnancy Clauses in Living Will Statutes", *Boston University Law Review*, 70, 867–86.

Ethical Guidelines on Court-Authorised Obstetric Intervention: a Consideration of the Law and Ethics from 1996, available at http://www.rcog.org.uk/ guidelines. asp?PageID=109&GuidelineID=33, accessed on 26th April 2004.

Farley, Anthony (1997), "The Black Body As Fetish Object", *Oregon Law Review*, 76, 457–535.

Feinberg, Joel (1984), *Harm to Others*, N.Y.: Oxford University Press.

Feldman, Deborah M., Borgida, Adam F., Rodis, John F. and Campbell, Winston A. (2000), "Irreversible Maternal Brain Injury During Pregnancy: A Case Report and Review of the Literature", *Obstetrics and Gynecology Survey*, 55, 708–14.

Field, David R., Gates, Elena A., Creasy, Robert K., Jonsen, Albert R. and Laros, Russel K. (1988), "Maternal Brain Death During Pregnancy: Medical and ethical issues", *Journal of the American Medical Association*, 260, 816–22.

Final Report of the Royal Commission on New Reproductive Technologies (1994), *Proceed with Care* Vol. 2, Ottawa, Canada: Ministry of Supply and Services.

Fineman, Martha A. (2000), "Cracking the Foundational Myths: Independence, Autonomy, and Self-Sufficiency", *The Journal of Gender, Social Policy and the Law*, 8, 13–29.

Finnerty, James J., Chisholm, Christian A., Chapple, Helen, Login, Ivan S. and Pinkerton, Joan V. (1999), "Cerebral Arteriovenous Malformation in Pregnancy: Presentation and Neurologic, Obstetric, and Ethical Significance", *American Journal of Obstetrics and Gynecology*, 181 (2), 296–303.

Fleischman Alan R. (1989), "The Fetus is a Patient", in Sherrill Cohen and Nadine Taub (eds), *Reproductive Laws for the 1990s*, Clifton, NJ: Humana Press, pp. 249.

Fost, Norman (1994), "Case Study: The baby in the Body", *Hastings Center Report*, 24 (1), 31–2.

Fromm Erich (1963), *The Art of Loving*, Montreal: Bentam Books.

Gallagher, Janet (1989), "Fetus as Patient", in Sherrill Cohen and Nadine Taub (eds), *Reproductive Laws for the 1990s*, Clifton, NJ: Humana Press, p. 185.

Gatehouse, Jonathon, "Family Fights To Save Foetus", *National Post*, December 2, 1999.

Gelfand, Gregory (1987), "Living Will Statutes: The First Decade", *Wisconsin Law Review*, 1987, 737–822.

Gertner Nancy (1989), "Interference with Reproductive Choice", in Sherrill Cohen and Nadine Taub (eds), *Reproductive Laws for the 1990s*, Clifton, NJ: Humana Press, pp. 307.

Glover, Jacqeline J. (1993), "Incubators and Organ Donors", *Journal of Clinical Ethics*, 4 (4), 342–50.

Goodlin, Robert C. (1989), "Maternal Brain Death During Pregnancy – Letter to the Editor", *Journal of the American Medical Association*, 261 (12), 1728–9.

Goodwin, Brian (1994), *How the Leopard Changed Its Spots: The Evolution of Complexity*, Princeton, NJ: Princeton University Press.

Gowans, W. Christopher (1994), *Innocent Lost: An Examination of Inescapable Moral Wrongdoing*, New York: Oxford University Press.

Green, Michael B. and Wikler, Daniel (1980), "Brain Death and Personal Identity", *Philosophy and Public Affairs*, 9 (2), 105–33.

Halperin-Kadary Ruth (2002), "'To Leave Life Behind You': The Delivery of A Fetus from The Body of a Deceased – In Any Possible Case?", in Raphael Cohen-Almagor (ed.), *Dilemmas In Medical Ethics*, Jerusalem: Hakibutz Hameuhad, pp. 107–36 (Article in Hebrew).

Haycock, Christine E. (1984), "Emergency Care of the Pregnant Traumatized Patient", *Emergency Medicine Clinics of North America*, 2 (4), 843–51.

Heikkinen, J.E., Rinne, R.I., Alahuhta, S.M., Lumme, J.A., Koivisto, M.E., Kirkinen, P.P., Sotaniemi, K.A., Nuutinen, L.S. and Jarvinen, P.A. (1985), "Life Support For 10 Weeks With Successful Fetal Outcome After Maternal Brain Damage", *British Medical Journal*, 290, 1237–8.

Hill, Lyndon M., Parker, Daniel and Oneill, Brian P. (1985), "Management of Maternal Vegetative State During Pregnancy", *Mayo Clinic Proceedings*, 60, 469–72.

Hoagland, Sarah L. (1990), *Lesbian Ethics: Towards New* Value, Palo Alto, California: Institute of Lesbian Studies.

Hunter, Allen (1981), "In the Wings: New Right Ideology and Organization", *Radical America*, 15, 113.

Jerdee, Amy L. (2000), "Breaking through the Silence: Minnesota's Pregnancy Presumption and the Right to Refuse Medical Treatment", *Minnesota Law Review*, 84, 971–1006.

Johnson, Dawn (1992), "Shared Interests: Promoting Healthy Births without Sacrificing Women's Liberty", *Hastings Law Journal*, 43, 569–614.

Jones, Gareth D. (1995), "Making Human Life Captive to Biomedical Technology: Christianity and the Demise of Human Values", *LLU Center for Christian Bioethics Update*, 11 (4), available at http://www.llu.edu/llu/bioethics/llethup114a.htm, accessed on 26th April, 2004.

Jones, Gareth D. (2000), *Speaking For The Dead: Cadavers in Biology and Medicine*, Aldershot, UK: Dartmouth Publishing Company Ltd.

Jordan, James M. (1988), "Parents, Children and the Courts, Note", *Georgia Law Review*, 22, 1103–65.

Jost, Timothy Stoltzfus (2002), "Rights of Embryos and Foetus in Private Law", *American Journal of Comparative Law*, 50, 633–46.

Kant, Immanuel (1996), *The Metaphysics of Morals*, ed. and trans. Gregor, Mary, Cambridge: Cambridge University Press, pp. 76–77.

Kantor, Jay E. and Hoskins, Iffath Abbasi (1993), "Brain Death in Pregnant Women", *Journal of Clinical Ethics*, 4, 308–14.

Kittay, Eva F. (2001), "A Feminist Public Ethic of Care Meets The New Communitarian Family Policy", *Ethics*, 111, 523–47.

Kolder, V.E.B., Gallagher, J. and Parsons, M.T. (1987), "Court-ordered Obstetrical Interventions", *The New England Journal of Medicine*, 316, 1192–6.

Kramer, Matthew H. (2001), "Do Animals and Dead People Have Legal Rights?" *Canadian Journal of Law and Jurisprudence*, 14, 29–54.

Landau, Ruth (1999), "Planned Orphanhood", *Social Sciences and Medicine*, 49, 185–96.

Law Reform Commission of Canada (1992), *Medically Assisted Procreation Recommendations*, Ottawa, Canada: Ministry of Supply and Services.

Law Reform Commission of Canada (1983), *Report 20: Euthanasia, Aiding Suicide and Cessation of Treatment*, Ottawa, Canada: Minister of Supply and Services.

Law Reform Commission of Canada (1982), *Working Paper No. 28: Euthanasia, Aiding Suicide and Cessation of Treatment*, Ottawa, Canada: Minister of Supply and Services.

Lederman, Anne D. (1994), "A Womb of My Own: A Moral Evaluation of Ohio's Treatment of Pregnant Patients with Living Wills", *Case Western Reserve Law Review*, 45, 351–77.

Lemmens, Trudo and Dickens, Bernard (2001), "Canadian Law on Euthanasia: Contrasts and Comparisons", *European Journal of Health Law*, 8, 135–55.

Loewy, Erich H. (1987), "The Pregnant Brain Dead and the Fetus: Must We Always Try to Wrest Life from Death?", *American Journal of Obstetrics and Gynecology*, 157 (5), 1097–101.

Lomasky, Loren E. (1987), *Persons, Rights and the Moral Community*, N.Y.: Oxford University Press.

MacAvoy-Smitzer, Janice (1987), "Pregnancy Clauses in Living Will Statutes", *Columbia Law Review*, 87, 1280–1300.

MacIntyre, Alasdair (1984), *After Virtue*, South Bend, Ind.: University of Notre Dame Press.

Mahoney, Joan (1989), "Death with Dignity: Is There An Exception for Pregnant Women?", *University of Missouri-Kansas City Law Review*, 57, 221–31.

Manning, Ruth C. (1998), "A Care Approach", in Helga Kuhse and Peter Singer (eds), *A Companion to Bioethics*, Malden, Mass: Blackwell Publishers, p. 98.

Mappes, Thomas and DeGrazia, David (eds) (2001), *Biomedical Ethics*, 5th edn, Boston: McGraw-Hill.

Markwell, Hazel J. and Brown, Barry F (2001), "Bioethics for Clinicians: 27. Catholic bioethics", *Canadian Medical Association Journal*, 165 (2), 189–192.

Mattingly, Susan S. (1992), "The Maternal-Fetal Dyad: Exploring the Two-Patient Obstetric Model", *Hastings Center Report*, 22, 13–18.

May, William F. (1973), 'Attitudes toward the Newly Dead', *Hastings Center Studies*, 1 (1), 7–13.

McLean, Sheila A. M. (1999), "Creating Postmortem Pregnancies: A U.K. Perspective", *The Juridical Review*, 6, 323–42.

Meisel, Alan (1995), *The right to die*, vol. 2, 2nd edn, New York: Wiley Law Publications.

Molloy, William (1993), *Vital Choices: Life, Death and the Health Care Crisis*, Toronto, Canada: Penguin Books Canada Ltd., p. 218.

Mulholland, Kristin A. (1987), "A Time to Be Born and A Time to Die: A Pregnant Woman's Right to Die with Dignity", *Indiana Law Review*, 20, 859–78.

Murray, Thomas H. (1987), "Moral Obligation to the Not-Yet Born: The Fetus as Patient", *Clinics in Perinatology*, 14 (2), 329–43.

Mykitiuk, Roxanne and Wallrap, Albert (2002), "Regulating Reproductive Technologies in Canada", in Downie, J., Caulfield, T. and Flood, C. (eds), *Canadian Health Law and Policy*, 2nd edn, Toronto, Canada: Butterworths, pp. 367–431.

Nagel, Thomas (1979), "Death", in *Mortal Questions*, N.Y.: Cambridge University Press, pp. 1–10.

Nedelsky, Jennifer (1990), "Law, Boundaries, and the Bounded Self", Representations, 30, 162–89.

Nedelsky, Jennifer (1993), "Property in Potential Life? A Relational Approach to Choosing Legal Categories", *Canadian Journal of Law and Jurisprudence*, 6 (2), 343–65.

Nedelsky, Jennifer (1989), "Reconceiving Autonomy", *Yale Journal of Law and Feminism*, 1, 7–36.

Nedelsky, Jennifer (2002), "Relational Autonomy and the Trap of Social Determinism: Perspectives from Science And Theology", in *Feminist Theory: Challenges To Legal and Political Thought*, unpublished course materials, Faculty of Law, University of Toronto, pp. 40–58.

Nelson, Erin (2002), 'The Fundamentals of Consent', in Downie, J., Caulfield, T. and Flood, C. (eds), *Canadian Health Law and Policy*, 2nd edn, Toronto, Canada: Butterworths, pp. 111–28.

Nelson, Lawrence J. (1988), 'Compelled Medical Treatment of Pregnant Women: Life, Liberty, and Law in Conflict', *Journal of the American Medical Association*, 259 (7), 1060–66.

Nelson, Lindemann Hilde (1994), 'The Architect and the Bee: Some Reflections on Postmortem Pregnancy', *Bioethics*, 8 (3), 247–67.

Nelson, Lindemann James (1992), 'Making Peace in Gestational Conflicts', *Theoretical Medicine*, 13, 319–35.

Nelson, Lindemann Hilde and Nelson, Lindemann James (1995), *The Patient in the Family*, New York: Routledge.

Olick, Robert (2001), *Taking Advance Directives Seriously*, Washington, D.C.: Georgetown University Press.

Olick, Robert S. (1991), "Brain-Death, Religious Freedom, and Public Policy: New Jersey's Landmark Legislative Initiative", *Kennedy Institute of Ethics Journal*, 1 (4), 275–88.

Paige, Richard (2000), "Post-Mortem Pregnancies: A Legal Analysis", *Dispatches*, 9 (3), 2–5.

Peart, Nicola S., Campbell, Alastair V., Manara, Alex R., Renowden, Shelley A. and Stirrat, Gordon M. (2000), "Maintaining A Pregnancy Following Loss of Capacity", *Medical Law Review*, 8, 275–99.

Pellegrino, Edmund D. (1995), "Toward A Virtue-Based Normative Ethics for The Health Professions", *Kennedy Institute of Ethics Journal*, 5 (3), 253–77.

Pitcher, George (1984), "The Misfortunes of the Dead", *American Philosophical Quarterly*, 21 (2), 183–8.

Purdy, Laura M. (1990), "Are Pregnant Women Fetal Containers?", *Bioethics*, 4 (4), 273–91.

Randall, Melaine (1999), "Pregnant Embodiment and Women's Autonomy Rights in Law: An Analysis of the Language and Politics of Winnipeg Child and Family Services v. D.F.G.", *Saskatchewan Law Review*, 62, 515–42.

Report of The Committee of Inquiry into Human Fertilization and Embryology Cmnd. (1984), 9314/1984 ¶ 109.

Report of the Law Commission on Mental Incapacity (1995), London: H.M.S.O, § 5.25.

Report of the Special Senate Committee on Euthanasia and Assisted Suicide (1995), *Of Life and Death*, Ottawa, Canada: Minister of Supply and Services.

Robertson, John (1983), "Procreative Liberty and the Control of Conception, Pregnancy and Childbirth", *Virginia Law Review*, 69, 405–64.

Robertson, John (1984), "The Right to Procreate and *in-utero* Fetal Therapy", *Journal of Legal Medicine*, 3 (3), 333–66.

Robertson, John A. (1994), "Posthumous Reproduction", *Indiana Law Journal*, 69, 1027–65.

Robertson, John A. (1989), "Reconciling Offspring and Maternal Interests during Pregnancy", in Sherrill Cohen and Nadine Taub (eds), *Reproductive Laws for the 1990s*, Clifton, NJ: Humana Press, p. 259.

Rodgers, Sanda (2002), "The Legal Regulation of Women's Reproductive Capacity in Canada", in Downie, J., Caulfield, T. and Flood, C. (eds), *Canadian Health Law and Policy*, 2nd edn, Toronto, Canada: Butterworths, pp. 331–65.

Rothenberg, Karen H. (1996), "Feminism, Law and Bioethics", *Kennedy Institute of Ethics Journal*, 6 (1), 69–84.

Santos, Esther (1993), "Sheila's Death Created Many Rings of Life", *Nursing*, 3, 44–8.

Scales-Trent, Judy (1999), "Oppression, Lies, and the Dream of Autonomy", *William and Mary Law Review*, 40 (3), 857–68.

Scarre, Geoffrey (2003), "Archaeology and Respect for the Dead", (2003) *Journal of Applied Philosophy*, 20 (3), 237–49.

Schafer Daniel, (1998), "Ueber Leichenentbindungen am Ende des 20. Jahrhunderts: Historische Aspekte ethischen Handelns bei toten Schwangeren", *Ethik Med*, 10, 227–40 (Article in German).

Seymour, John (2000), *Childbirth and the Law*, N.Y: Oxford University Press.

Shanely, L. Mary (2001), *Making Babies, Making Families*, Boston: Beacon Press.

Sheikh, Asim A. and Cusack, Denis A. (2001), "Maternal Brain Death, Pregnancy and the Foetus: The Medico-Legal Implications", *Medico-Legal Journal of Ireland*, 7 (2), 75–85.

Shemie, Sam D., Christopher, Doig and Philip, Belitsky (2003), "Advancing Toward a Modern Death: the Path from Severe Brain Injury to Neurological Determination of Death", *Canadian Medical Association Journal*, 168 (8), 993–5.

Shrader, Douglas (1986), "On Dying More Than One Death", *Hastings Center Report*, 16 (1), 12–17.

Siegel, Reva (1996), "The Rule of Love", *Yale Law Journal*, 105, 2117–207.

Siegler, Mari and Wikler, Daniel (1982), "Brain Death and Live Birth", *The Journal of American Medical Association*, 248 (9), 1101–2.

Spike, Jeffery (1999), "Brain Death, Pregnancy, and Posthumous Motherhood", *Journal of Clinical Ethics*, 10 (1), 57–65.

Spike, Jeffery and Greenlaw, Jane (1995), "Ethics Consultation: Persistent Brain Death and Religion: Must a Person Believe in Death to Die?", *Journal of Law, Medicine and Ethics*, 23 (3), 291–4.

Taylor, Katherine A. (1997), "Compelling Pregnancy at Death's Door", *Columbia Journal of Gender and the Law*, 7 (1), 85–165.

Thomson, Judith Jarvis (1999), 'A Defense of Abortion', in Beauchamp, Tom L. and Walters, LeRoy (eds), *Contemporary Issues in Bioethics*, 5th edn, Belmont, C.A: Wadsworth Publishing Company, p. 202.

Veatch, Robert (1982), 'Maternal Brain-Death: An Ethicist's Thoughts', *The Journal of American Medical Association*, 248 (9), 1102–3.

Vives, A., Carmona, F., Zabala, E., Fernandez, C., Cararach, V. and Iglesias, X. (1996), "Maternal Brain Death During Pregnancy", *International. Journal of Gynecology and Obstetrics*, 52, 67–9.

Warren, Mary Anne (1984), "On the Moral and Legal Status of Abortion" in Feinberg, Joel (ed.), *The Problem of Abortion*, 2nd edn, Belmont, CA: Wadsworth, p. 102.

Wear, Stephen, Dillon, William P. and Lee, Richard V. (1989), "Maternal Brain Death during Pregnancy: Letter to the Editor", *The Journal of American Medical Association*, 261 (12), 1728–9.

Weisbrad, A.J. (1995), "A Model Integrated Advance Directive for Health Care", *Bioethics Bull*, 4, 2–12.
Wijdicks, Eelco (2002), "Brain Death World Wild: Accepted Fact But No Global Consensus in Diagnostic Criteria", *Neurology*, 58 (1), 20–25.
Wilcox, Samantha A. (2003), 'Presumed Consent Organ Donation in Pennsylvania: One Small Step for Pennsylvania, One Giant Leap for Organ Donation', *Dickinson Law Review*, 107, 935–51.
Wilkinson, T.M. (2002), "Last Rights: the Ethics of Research on the Dead", *Journal of Applied Philosophy*, 19 (1), 31–41.
Willett, Cynthia (2001), *The Soul of Justice: Social Bonds and Racial Hubris*, Ithaca and London: Cornell University Press.
Young, Iris M. (1990), "Pregnant Embodiment: Subjectivity and Alienation", in Young, Iris M. (ed.), *Throwing Like a Girl and Other Essays in Feminist Philosophy and Social* Theory, Bloomington: Indiana University Press, p. 160.

WEBSITES

http://www.butterworthsireland.ie/newsdirect/archive/2001/june/foetus15, accessed on 17th March 2003.
http://images.maariv.co.il/channels/1/ART/477/314.httml, accessed on 15th May 2003.
http://www.mnmed.org/publications/MnMed1998/September/blumer.cfm, accessed on 17th March, 2003.
http://www.news.bbc.co.uk/1/hi/world/europe/2737015.stm, accessed on 20th March, 2003.
www.utoronto.ca/jcb/main.html, accessed on 1 May, 2004.
http://www.ynet.co.il/articles/1,7340, accessed on 13 May 2003.

Index